Speaking the Truth in Love

to Mormons

MARK J. CARES

Second edition revised and expanded

WELS OUTREACH®
RESOURCES

Milwaukee, Wisconsin

ISBN 1-893702-06-5
© 1998 WELS Outreach Resources
2929 Mayfair Rd.
Milwaukee, WI 53222
Published 1998
Printed in the United States of America

TABLE OF
CONTENTS

FOREWORD

Since writing this book five years ago, some things have changed in Mormonism while others have stayed the same. The changes have been mostly cosmetic. The Mormon church is working on numerous fronts in an effort to be accepted as Christian. They have changed their logo to make Jesus Christ more prominent in their church name. They have started offering free Bibles rather than the Book of Mormon in some of their ads. President Gordon B. Hinckley has downplayed and has, at times, even appeared to deny classic Mormon teachings. Mormon authors, like Stephen E. Robinson, have written books that use Christian terminology and thus sound more Christian, but always with the disclaimer that they are not speaking for the church, but only for themselves.

As a result, more and more Christians either don't know what to make of Mormonism or even end up defending it. As I write this preface, former President Jimmy Carter is in the news rebuking the Southern Baptist Convention for saying that Mormons are not Christian. His comments represent the feelings of many Christians today.

Regarding Mormons as Christians is nothing short of tragic. That view dramatically increases the danger of more Christians joining the Mormon church. It also puts the damper on efforts to reach Mormons with the message of forgiveness through Christ. Why witness to them, if they are already Christian?

In spite of some cosmetic changes, the Mormon church remains non-Christian, that is, if we define Christians in the biblical sense as people who trust that God forgives them solely because of what Jesus has done for them. Mormonism doesn't lead people to such belief. Rather it continues to condition God's forgiveness on what people do.

> "Repentance means not only to convict yourselves of the horror of sin, but to confess it, abandon it, and restore to all who have been damaged to the total extent possible; then spend the balance of your lives trying to live the commandments of the Lord so he can eventually pardon you and cleanse you." (Spencer W. Kimball, quoted in *Gospel Principles*, p. 126)

1

When it comes to any of its basic teachings, Mormonism hasn't changed. About the time former President Carter was defending them, the November 1997 issue of the LDS magazine, *Ensign*, came out. This issue contains the talks given by the General Authorities at the October 1997 general conference. These talks are so official that they are considered equivalent to Scripture. The following quotes from that issue illustrate that nothing of substance has changed in their teachings.

They still teach complete obedience to the living prophet.

> There must be listening ears and obedience to the living prophet of the Church. President Marion G. Romney stated it well: "It is an easy thing to believe in the dead prophets, but it is a greater thing to believe in the living prophets." (President James E. Faust, p. 54)

They still speak very highly of Joseph Smith.

> I am also grateful for Joseph Smith, who never shrank from his calling as the prophet of the Restoration and all that it entailed. John Taylor wrote, "Joseph Smith, the Prophet and Seer of the Lord, has done more, save Jesus only, for the salvation of men in this world, than any other man that ever lived in it" (D&C 135:3). (J. Kent Jolley, p. 80)

They still urge people to strive for perfection. "Mercy is at least a beginning synonym for the perfection God has and for which all of us must strive." (Jeffery R. Holland, p. 66)

They still talk about redeeming the dead.

> "Missionary work is not limited to proclaiming the gospel to . . . people now living on the earth. [It] is also continuing beyond the veil among [those] who have died either without hearing the gospel or without accepting it while they lived on the earth. Our great part . . . is to perform on this earth the ordinances required for those who accept the gospel over there . . . I hope to see us dissolve the artificial boundary line . . . between missionary work and temple and genealogical work, because it is the same redemptive work!" (Spencer W. Kimball, quoted by Richard G. Scott, p. 36)

They still talk about our meriting eternal life.

2

Thus, brothers and sisters, along with the great and free gift of the universal and personal resurrection there is also the personal possibility of meriting eternal life. (Neal A. Maxwell, p. 23)

I wish to state unequivocally that the commandments of God must be kept to receive the blessings and promises of the Savior. The Ten Commandments are still a vital thread in the fabric of the gospel of Christ... (President James E. Faust, p.53)

They still talk about people becoming gods.

"Peter and John had little secular learning, being termed ignorant . . . Their righteous lives opened the door to godhood for them and creation of worlds with eternal increase." (Spencer W. Kimball, quoted by L. Tom Perry, p. 60)

The Mormon church does not teach Christian doctrine! The Mormon people are not Christian! Therefore they still desperately need to hear the wonderful and liberating message of free and full forgiveness through the merits of Jesus Christ.

But because they are becoming less and less open about their teachings, this is becoming increasingly difficult to do. Therefore I feel that it is becoming more and more important for the Christian witness to be familiar with LDS official resources. I still recommend obtaining their basic manual, *Gospel Principles*, even though, over the years, they have weakened many of its strongest statements. In spite of those changes, it still clearly illustrates the non-Christian nature of Mormonism. In addition, I think it's becoming even more important for the committed witness to subscribe to *Ensign*, their monthly magazine (1-800-453-3860 ext. 2947). This will not only provide you with the two all-important conference issues (May & November), but the other issues will help you keep the pulse of Mormonism.

Being familiar with these resources and *quoting* them as you witness, you will be able to deflect many of the misleading or confusing statements made by Mormons. Even if they quote a popular Mormon author like Stephen Robinson, you can respond by asking: "Who is the greater authority - Robinson or a General Authority? Or whose book is more authoritative - Robinson's or an official manual (or conference talk)?"

I feel I need to sound a word of caution here. Since an increasing number of Mormons are citing some of the confusing and misleading statements made by some of their popular authors, it is easy to conclude that they themselves are being deliberately deceptive. At times, such a conclusion is warranted. But many times the Mormons themselves are in a state of confusion. They too are struggling to understand some of these words and concepts.

But one thing always comes through loud and clear. All Mormons think they have to become perfect and work themselves back into Heavenly Father's presence. Mormonism hasn't given them the peace and joy of knowing Jesus was perfect for them. They still have to be told about the Savior who has done everything for them. We still need to tell them that!

It is my prayer this book continues to serve as an aid for Christians striving to witness to Mormons. In this second edition, I have updated some of the quotations to help you stay current as you witness. People have told me they find the Dictionary of Mormonese especially helpful. Therefore I have added a few more words and have expanded some explanations. The meat of the book, however, remains relatively unchanged. The experiences of the last five years have only reinforced for me that the approach to witnessing it proposes forcefully conveys God's truth to Mormons.

Finally, I would like to thank all the people at WELS Outreach Resources for their help and encouragement with this second edition. I especially extend my thanks to Mr. John Barber for his expertise, encouragement, and help.

Mark J. Cares
December, 1997

PREFACE

"Another book on Mormonism? Hasn't everything been covered already?" Even a brief visit to a Christian bookstore demonstrates that Mormonism has become a popular field of investigation. Books abound on the subject. Why, then, this book?

In this book I have attempted to take a markedly different approach from the others. Two major elements differentiate it. First, I have limited myself to investigating current LDS literature. (LDS is a common abbreviation in Mormonism. It stands for Latter-day Saints and is derived from the church's official name: The Church of Jesus Christ of Latter-day Saints.) I worked mainly with current church manuals instead of the historical documents of Mormonism. Second, I am proposing a method of witnessing to Mormons different from methods commonly used. What follows elaborates these two points.

Most strategies for witnessing to Mormons revolve around one of two topics: the history of Mormonism or the nature of God. The proponents of the first method thoroughly examine LDS history, especially its historical documents. Such an examination reveals numerous contradictions. A witness will then point these out, in the hope that they will shatter a Mormon's faith in Mormonism. Numerous books do an excellent job of unearthing these contradictions. The work of Jerald and Sandra Tanner, *Mormonism — Shadow or Reality?*, is especially recommended.

This approach, however, has some drawbacks. First, people must become thorough students of LDS history, if not experts in it, before they feel comfortable talking seriously with Mormons. Second, and more serious, too often this approach virtually ignores the gospel. The discussion can easily turn into a debate on Mormon history rather than being a witness to Jesus' saving work. And the less gospel, the more inclined Mormons will be to interpret our efforts as a "search and destroy" mission rather than that rescue mission we intend it to be.

The other popular method of witnessing to Mormons focuses the discussion on the conflict between the biblical teaching of one God and the LDS teaching of a plurality of gods. Central to this method are Bible passages, especially from Isaiah, that refer to God's nature. Again, many books detail this approach.

This method is attractive because a person doesn't have to become an expert in Mormonism to use it. But here again the gospel too often comes in a poor second, as the discussion frequently turns into nothing more than a debate on God's nature. Far too often, proponents of both this and the history-centered approach rely on human reason rather than on the power of the gospel to bring Mormons to faith in Jesus.

The approach I am proposing makes the gospel of Jesus' saving work the center of discussion. The Bible clearly teaches that people do not have the ability in and of themselves to make rational decisions to accept Christ. "The man without the Spirit does not accept the things that come from the Spirit of God, for they are foolishness to him, and he cannot understand them, because they are spiritually discerned" (1 Corinthians 2:14).

As that passage intimates, saving faith is entirely the work of the Holy Spirit. Other passages reveal that he creates faith by means of the gospel. "I am not ashamed of the gospel, because it is the power of God for the salvation of everyone who believes" (Romans 1:16). These truths thus dictate that God's gospel, not man's reason, play the dominant role in any attempt to bring people to faith.

By concentrating on the gospel's positive message, we hope also to convey the message that we are trying to help Mormons rather than attack them. I say "hope" because many Mormons feel persecuted even before we talk to them. Many will have difficulty believing that we are concerned about them. Therefore, we need to stress what Jesus has already done for them that relieves the pressure of their trying to do everything for themselves. We have to depend on the gospel itself to help us gain their confidence.

They desperately need to hear what Jesus has done for them. They need to hear this because they are not Christians, even though they claim that name. According to the Bible, Christians are persons who trust that they have eternal life, not because of anything they have done or have to do, but solely because of the merits of Jesus Christ. Christians believe the following:

However, to the man who does not work but trusts God who justifies the wicked, his faith is credited as righteousness. (Romans 4:5)

For it is by grace you have been saved, through faith — and this not from yourself, it is the gift of God — not by works, so that no one can boast. (Ephesians 2:8,9)

Because Mormons don't believe this, they are not Christians. That is the truth we need to speak to them. To do that lovingly, however, we need to understand them. For this reason, the first half of this book contains an in-depth look at current LDS teachings and practices. There it will be demonstrated that Mormonism is more than a religion — it is also a culture and way of life. It is my hope that this comprehensive examination will not only reveal the vast differences between Mormonism and Christianity, but also illustrate the pressures many Mormons live under. As you read these chapters, try to imagine what it is like being a Mormon. As you walk through these pages, walk a mile in a Mormon's shoes.

A word of caution is in place here. You might become dismayed by the complexity of some of these chapters. Especially the first few chapters, with their many quotations, are not light reading. But these quotations are essential. Many Mormons are unclear about their church's official teaching on many topics. These quotes, therefore, will not only acquaint you with LDS teaching, they can also serve you well in proving to your LDS friend that what you are saying about Mormonism is true. The more you talk with Mormons, the more occasions you will find to cite these references to them.

In order to fulfill that purpose, the references need to be authoritative. They are. The majority of quotations are taken from *official* and *current* LDS manuals and publications. Any publication bearing the copyright of the "Corporation of the President of The Church of Jesus Christ of Latter-day Saints" can be considered official. Since Mormon doctrine changes, I have found it more effective to quote such sources than historical LDS writings, with which many Mormons are not familiar.

Some readers might be surprised at the lack of quotations from the Book of Mormon, Doctrine and Covenants, and The Pearl of Great Price. Although Mormons regard these as scripture, many seldom read them. Most are more familiar with the various church manuals, their hymnbook, and the monthly *Ensign* magazine. Those are the sources that will help you identify with the average Mormon.

One of the more critical aspects of talking effectively with Mormons is knowing their terminology. Frequently they define words differently than most others do. It is vital to recognize this. Otherwise you will not only find yourself talking past them, but may also unjustly charge them with deception. What may appear deceptive is often miscommunication. Frequently Mormons have no concept whatsoever of what Christians believe. Often they are just as surprised at our definition of a word as we are at their definition. The appended dictionary of "Mormonese" contains definitions for many of their commonly used terms.

Making a sincere effort to understand Mormons accomplishes two things: it gives us confidence to speak to them, and it increases our compassion for them. Nevertheless, being confident and compassionate doesn't help our LDS friends unless we act. Helping you act is the purpose of the second half of the book. There I will present the details of a gospel-centered witness to Mormons.

I would like to explain my use of the name "Mormon." Some well-meaning Christians have characterized it as a slur against the members of The Church of Jesus Christ of Latter-day Saints. (Note the hyphen in Latter-day. Using that hyphen properly will establish your credibility with some Mormons.) It is not a slur, however, as their own writings demonstrate:

> "While there can be no disgrace nor condemnation in being called 'Mormons,' and the Church, the 'Mormon Church,' the fact remains, and this we should all emphasize, that we belong to The Church of Jesus Christ of Latter-day Saints, the name the Lord has given by which we are to be known and called." (Joseph Fielding Smith, quoted in the *Book of Mormon Manual*, p. 126)

Another of their apostles, Bruce R. McConkie, wrote: "The nickname 'Mormon' is in no sense offensive to members of The Church of Jesus Christ of Latter-day Saints" (*Mormon Doctrine*, p. 512). This becomes quite evident to anyone who has lived for any length of time among large LDS population. Mormon is a name they themselves commonly use. Think, for example, of the *Mormon* Tabernacle Choir.

Incidently, Mormon is the name of a prophet in the Book of Mormon.

Finally, many people, too numerous to mention by name, have encouraged and helped me in the writing of this book. Special thanks go to the members of Messiah Lutheran Church of Nampa, Idaho, for their support of this project. I would also like to thank WELS Kingdom Workers for helping our congregation support an additional pastor for three years, enabling me to work on an outreach to Mormons. Rev. Bob Hartman, the administrator for the WELS Commission of Evangelism, gave much sound advice and formulated many of the discussion questions. Special thanks are also due to Rev. Gary Baumler and the staff of Northwestern Publishing House for their encouragement and help. And I would particularly like to acknowledge the support of my wife, Bonnie, and my children. They were always understanding, helpful, and encouraging.

It is my prayer that the Lord will use this book to encourage many Christians to reach out to Mormons with the wonderful message of Jesus who saved them, not by his example, but by his substitution. May God move us to tell the Mormons of the eternal life Jesus has already earned for all people through his perfect obedience and substitutionary death. May he help us to illustrate to them how Jesus' glorious resurrection proves he not only conquered death for us but also earned eternal life for us. May those truths always occupy center stage in our witnessing efforts.

INTRODUCTION

What are your feelings about Mormons? What kind of emotions do they evoke in you? Is compassion one of them?

Many times compassion is not the predominant Christian reaction. Often anger dominates as Christians see how Mormons twist Scripture and devalue Christ. Other times ridicule takes the forefront as Christians encounter some of Mormonism's more exotic beliefs. Still other reactions that come to mind are apathy, puzzlement, fear, and rejection. But compassion does *not* often come to mind—for Mormons don't look as if they are hurting.

But they are. Ephesians 2:12 tells us that people who are without Christ are without hope. Isaiah 57:20,21 tells us that "there is no peace . . . for the wicked." This refers to *all* unbelievers, since unbelief is the greatest of all wickedness. Romans 2:14,15 reminds us that their consciences accuse them. No hope, no peace, accusing consciences— that is a small slice of how the Bible pictures the state of all unbelievers, including Mormons.

Nevertheless, we have difficulty applying this to Mormons since they appear so happy and successful. Even when their unhappiness does surface, it is still difficult for us to be compassionate. Even then they don't act or look like victims.

In reality, however, large numbers of Mormons are hurting: people who are victims; people who are not intentionally deceptive but sincerely deceive; who are not arrogantly self-righteous but incredibly unhappy; who need not only our compassion, but most importantly our Savior. May we be led both to be compassionate to them and to reach out compassionately to them with the saving message of the true gospel.

PART I

KNOW
MORMONS

CHAPTER ONE:
KNOW THEIR
GOAL

To witness *compassionately* to Mormons, we need to know them. Otherwise, we will run roughshod over them.

We begin, then, by trying to understand the ultimate goal Mormonism offers people. In some respects, that's like trying to catch a greased pig. It is easy to see, but it is difficult to keep firmly in hand. Quite simply, the goal Mormonism seductively holds out is godhood.

Godhood: Their Ultimate Goal

Because they don't often talk about it, the fact that godhood is the Mormons' goal can easily slip from view. Instead they talk about exaltation, or gaining eternal life, or having an eternal family. But all these expressions are synonymous. Each refers to becoming a god!

EXALTATION	⎤	BECOMING
GAINING ETERNAL LIFE	⎬►	A
HAVING AN ETERNAL FAMILY	⎦	GOD

Complicating matters even further, Mormons assign unique definitions to each of these phrases. Therefore, not only do we have to remember that each one describes godhood, but we also have to be aware of *their* definition for each expression. As we will see, this causes problems not only for non-Mormons, but also, at times, for Mormons themselves.

The foundational passage for their doctrine of godhood is Doctrine and Covenants (D&C) 132:19,20. It describes the final destiny of faithful Mormons:

They shall pass by the angels, and the gods, which are set

13

there, to their *exaltation* and glory in all things, as hath been sealed upon their heads, which glory shall be a fulness and a continuation of the seeds forever and ever.

Then shall they be gods, because they have no end; therefore shall they be from everlasting to everlasting because they continue; then shall they be above all, because all things are subject unto them. *Then shall they be gods*, because they have all power, and the angels are subject unto them. (emphasis added)

Not only does this passage say that faithful Mormons will become gods, it also describes that goal as exaltation. Exaltation, then, is synonymous with becoming a god, as their manuals clearly state.

Those who receive exaltation in the celestial kingdom through faith in Jesus Christ will receive special blessings . . . They will become gods. (*Gospel Principles*, p. 302)

Exaltation means godhood, creatorship. (Spencer W. Kimball quoted in *Ensign*, August 1996, p. 15)

Exaltation is one of the basic terms of Mormonism. Mormons talk about exaltation much like Christians talk about salvation. If we want to get to the heart of the matter with a Mormon, we need to talk about how they think they will be exalted, not how they think they are saved.

Still, in spite of the above quotes, some Mormons claim that the goal of attaining godhood is rarely taught today. They give the impression that this teaching lies in Mormonism's distant past. That this is not an obscure teaching within modern-day Mormonism, however, is clearly seen from a look at their current manuals, general conference addresses, and Ensign articles:

"Brethren, 225,000 of you are here tonight. I suppose 225,000 of you may become gods. There seems to be plenty of space out there in the universe." (Spencer W. Kimball, quoted in the *D&C Student Manual*, p. 358)

He that overcomes shall retain his name in the book of life, reach godhood, and be with Jesus as he is with the

Father. (Heading for Revelation chapter three in the LDS edition of the Bible)

On the other hand, the whole design of the gospel is to lead us onward and upward to greater achievement, even eventually, to godhood. This great possibility was enunciated by the Prophet Joseph Smith in the King Follet sermon . . . and emphasized by President Lorenzo Snow. It is a grand and incomparable concept: *As God now is, man may become*! (Gordon B. Hinckley, *Ensign*, November 1994, p. 48)

He is preparing you to be a god. (Elder Richard G. Scott, *Ensign*, November 1995, p. 18)

We know that many of the ancient Saints were successful in their quest for eternity. Abraham, Isaac, and Jacob, for example, "have entered into their exaltation, according to the promises, and sit upon thrones, and are not angels but are gods," (D&C 132:37). Are those same promises given to Abraham, Sarah, and their posterity in force today? Yes -- and they apply to us! (Andrew Skinner, *Ensign*, March 1997, p.22)

In spite of all such evidence, there appears to be a movement within Mormonism that downplays the attaining of godhood. Although all we can do is speculate about the reason for this, it appears they are doing it because this teaching reveals just how different Mormonism is from Christianity. That causes them problems because they consider themselves Christians and are aggressively contending that they are Christians.

Latter-day Saints are Christians because they emphatically believe in Christ, use His name in their official church title and believe in the Bible and the Book of Mormon, which testify repeatedly of the reality of Christ and the truth of His teachings. (Schraffs, *The Truth About the Godmakers*, p. 71)

Mormonism is Christianity; Christianity is Mormonism;

they are one and the same, and they are not to be distinguished from each other in the minutest detail. (McConkie, *Mormon Doctrine*, p. 513)

The teaching of becoming gods naturally makes it difficult for them to convince people they are Christian. It has become a serious obstacle even to some Mormons, especially the prospective or new members. Apparently for this reason, they have toned down this teaching.

Although downplayed, obtaining godhood has not become an antiquated, dusty doctrine of Mormonism. Still today, one of the first things Mormon children learn is the couplet:

As man now is, God once was;
As God now is, man may be.
(The Life and Teachings of Jesus
& His Apostles, p. 59)

On the other hand, there is some truth in the following statement made by an LDS author:

Not too often did I even find the idea of becoming gods and goddesses mentioned in Church lessons or talks by general authorities. I sometimes find members even saying they don't desire that kind of responsibility. I seldom find a Mormon who has an "ambition" to reach this goal. A more typical attitude is that "it is considered a challenging possibility and it would maybe be an honor to qualify, but I'll just do the best I can here and now and strive to be a good parent, citizen and Church member. Whatever rewards and leadership responsibilities come my way in the eternities I'll worry about later." This seems to be closer to the way Mormons look at possible godhood . . . Latter-day Saints are much more likely to find joy in the thought of having an eternal family and that a beautiful relationship between husband and wife and parents, grandparents, children and grandchildren can continue forever. That is where real joy comes in this life and in the eternities. (Schraffs' *The Truth About the Godmakers*, pp. 92f.)

I personally have seen evidence of this downplaying of godhood among Mormons. For example, one LDS woman expressed genuine surprise as we discussed the possibility of attaining godhood. She emphatically said that this was not taught her. Only after I showed her some clear statements affirming it in *Gospel Principles*, did she begin to realize that her church indeed taught so. Her unfamiliarity with this teaching surprised me since she was very active as a Mormon.

How can her surprise be explained? One explanation is that she knew this teaching but didn't want to admit it to me. In other words, she was being deliberately deceptive. That explanation, I felt, applied to her husband, who had remained silent during this part of the conversation. After I pointed out those statements in *Gospel Principles*, he readily admitted that this was LDS teaching. But I don't think his wife was being deliberately deceptive. Her surprise was too genuine.

Rather, I feel that this is an example of the problems Mormon terminology causes even for Mormons. Because the emphasis today is on attaining eternal life and especially on having eternal families, I think this woman did not fully understand the statements she had encountered concerning godhood. Instead of being deceptive, I feel, she herself was deceived. She said she was taught that she could become *like* God, in the sense of becoming perfect, but she did not think she could become a god.

Even though some Mormons no longer emphasize or even fully comprehend the idea of attaining godhood, we should not think Mormonism's goal has changed. *What has changed is not their goal but rather their description of that goal.* We see, for example, that attaining eternal life and having eternal families are the exclusive property of God-according to the LDS view of God. In other words, to have eternal life and an eternal family a person has to become a god.

Consider their description of eternal life. Unlike the Christian definition, Mormons do not equate eternal life with going to heaven. They equate it with exaltation or becoming a god.

> "Our whole purpose in life should be to do those things which will enable us to gain eternal life, and eternal life is the name of the kind of life possessed by the Father and the Son; it is exaltation in the eternal realms." (Joseph Fielding Smith, quoted in *The Life and Teachings of Jesus & His Apostles*, p. 327)

17

Exaltation means the same thing as eternal life. (*Learn of Me*, p. 72)

As these quotations illustrate, eternal life in Mormonese does not mean living eternally *with* God, but rather living eternally *as* god. McConkie simply declares: "Those who gain eternal life become gods!" (quoted in *The Life and Teachings of Jesus & His Apostles*, p. 453). As we will see in the next chapter, Mormonism teaches that almost all people, to some degree or other, will live with God for all eternity. To them, however, that is not eternal life. According to Mormonism, eternal life is nothing less than becoming a god.

If this is not complicated enough, we still need to come to grips with their teaching concerning the eternal family. That's what is in the spotlight today. That's what they are highlighting in their advertising. But they do not mention that only gods can have eternal families.

"Marriage and the family unit are the central part of the plan of progression and exaltation. All things center in and around the family unit in the eternal perspective. *Exaltation consists in the continuation of the family unit in eternity. Those for whom the family unit continues have eternal life*; all others have a lesser degree of salvation in the mansions that are prepared." (McConkie, quoted in *The Life and Teachings of Jesus & His Apostles*, p. 130, emphasis added)

Such statements help us see why Mormons value the family so highly. Because of this emphasis on the family, Mormons can easily give the impression that family is more important than God. And for many Mormons, family has taken the place of God.

But there's a second aspect to the eternal family that catches us completely unaware. Having an eternal family also means a person will be able to procreate spirit children for all eternity! This ability to procreate spirit children is what is meant by "a continuation of the seeds forever and ever" in D&C 132:19, cited at the beginning of this chapter.

This idea of procreating spirit children is so foreign that it needs further explanation. This unique teaching is rooted in their unique concept of God. The Mormon god is very human. In fact, he was once a man who progressed to godhood. Remember that couplet? "As man now is, God once was; As God now is, man may be." Other statements expand on this.

"God Himself was once as we are now, and is an exalted man . . . We have imagined and supposed that God was God from all eternity. I will refute that idea . . . God himself, the Father of us all, dwelt on earth, the same as Jesus Christ himself did, and I will show it from the Bible." (Joseph Smith, quoted in *The Life and Teachings of Jesus & His Apostles*, p. 325)

"Remember that God, our heavenly Father, was perhaps once a child, and mortal like we ourselves, and rose step by step in the scale of progress, in the school of advancement: has moved forward and overcome, until He has arrived at the point where He now is." (Orson Hyde, quoted in *Achieving A Celestial Marriage*, p 129)

These quotations refer to the LDS belief that to become a god, Heavenly Father had to do the same work and follow the same plan that Mormons believe they are presently following to become gods. In addition, they claim that many other gods of many other worlds did the same thing.

"*You have got to learn how to be Gods yourselves*, and to be kings and priests to God, the same as all Gods have done before you, namely by going from one small degree to another, and from a small capacity to a great one; from grace to grace." (Joseph Smith, quoted in *The Life and Teachings of Jesus & His Apostles*, p. 24, emphasis added)

A question Mormons can't answer is where the first god originated. If all gods were humans who progressed to godhood, where did it all start? The two most common answers I have received were that this has not been revealed to them or that they have never thought about it.

Not only was God, as Mormons speak of him, once a man, but as God he keeps his human characteristics! As Joseph Smith stated above, the LDS god is an exalted man.

"I say, if you were to see him today, you would see him like a man in form . . ." [*Teachings of the Prophet Joseph Smith*, p. 345]. God is a glorified and perfected man, a personage of flesh and bones. (*Gospel Principles*, p. 9)

That quotation mentions one of the major tenets of Mormonism, namely, that God has a body of flesh and bones. They have gone so far as to make this a touchstone of faith. When Mormons talk about knowing his character and attributes, they are referring to the belief that he has a body of flesh and bones. They feel that all who don't believe God has a body don't truly know God. It is not surprising, therefore, that they ridicule the belief that God is a spirit .

> Soon pagan beliefs dominate the thinking of those called "Christians." . . . Members of this church believed that God was a being without from or substance. (*Gospel Principles*, p. 105)

The Mormon god is so human that he is even married. According to Mormonism, we have a heavenly mother:

> Our Heavenly Father and mother live in an exalted state because they achieved a celestial marriage. (*Achieving A Celestial Marriage*, p. 1)

> For as we have a Father in heaven, so also we have a Mother there, a glorified, exalted, ennobled Mother. (*Achieving A Celestial Marriage*, p. 129)

Although this heavenly mother is occasionally mentioned, she is never stressed.

What is stressed is this idea of celestial marriage. Building on that belief, Mormons maintain that God's greatest glory is procreating spirit children for all eternity. Human beings are some of those spirit children. In the next chapter we will be looking at the implications they draw from that, as we take an in-depth look at their progression to godhood.

The point we need to see here is that when people attain godhood, they do the same thing as the gods before them. They create new worlds and procreate spirit children to populate those new worlds.

> As we achieve a like marriage we shall become as they are and begin the creation of worlds for our own spirit

children. (*Achieving A Celestial Marriage*, p. 1)

" We shall stand in our relationship to them as God our Eternal Father does to us, and thereby this is the most glorious and wonderful privilege that ever will come to any of the sons and daughters of God." (Melvin J. Ballard, quoted in *D&C Student Manual,* p.359)

Their spirit children will then have a chance to attain godhood and procreate their own spirit children. Mormons contend that this cycle of spirit children attaining godhood and procreating more spirit children has been going on from eternity and will continue for all eternity.

"To become like him we must have all the powers of godhood; thus a man and his wife when glorified will have spirit children who eventually will go on an earth like this one we are on and pass through the same kind of experiences, being subject to mortal conditions, and if faithful, then, they also will receive the fulness of exaltation and partake of the same blessings. There is no end to this development; it will go on forever. *We will become gods and have jurisdiction over worlds, and these worlds will be peopled by our own offspring.* We will have an endless eternity for this." (Joseph Smith, quoted in *Achieving A Celestial Marriage*, p. 132)

How these spirit children are procreated is never addressed. I make that point because sometimes non-Mormons mockingly speak about LDS women being eternally pregnant. But I have never heard Mormons describe it in that way. To them, procreating spirit children is the essence of eternal glory, not eternal drudgery. As D&C 132:19 states: "which *glory* shall be a fulness and a continuation of the seeds forever and ever" (emphasis added).

This procreating of spirit children is also called "having eternal increase" or "gaining eternal lives." (Gaining eternal *life* = godhood; gaining eternal *lives* = procreating spirit children.)

" Those who gain eternal life (exaltation) also gain *eternal lives*, meaning that in the resurrection they have *eternal 'increase,' 'a continuation of the seeds,' 'a continuation of the lives.'* Their spirit progeny will ' continue as innumerable as the stars; or, if you were to count the sand upon the seashore ye could not number them.'" (Bruce R. McConkie, quoted in *Achieving A Celestial Marriage*, p.136)

Where has this all taken us? We have gone full circle and are right back at the beginning. *I repeat: today's emphasis on the eternal family does not mark a changing of goals within Mormonism but just a different description of that goal.* Whether one talks about exaltation or having an eternal family or obtaining eternal life, the ultimate goal is the same: it is to become a god.

By now you probably feel as you have been wrestling with a greased pig. That's how I felt as I tried to sort out all this. I struggled with this so much that I made an appointment with a member of the local LDS leadership to make sure my conclusions were correct.

I did so because I was discovering that even many Mormons weren't making this connection between becoming a god and having an eternal family. Many feel they will have an eternal family, but few claim they will become a god. Once they think it through, they realize they can't have one without the other. It seems, however, that they don't often think about it. Even that LDS leader had to give it some thought and told me I was right.

In summary, it is evident that a Mormon's ultimate goal, whether it is described as exaltation or eternal life or having an eternal family, is the same goal it has always been, namely, becoming a god.

Perfection: Their Intermediate Goal

It is common to set intermediate goals to measure progress toward an ultimate goal. That is also the case with Mormonism. All its intermediate goals can be gathered under the one broad umbrella of perfection. *Mormonism has an obsession with perfection.* "To perfect the saints" is one of the main missions of the LDS church.

Unlike the unclarity that surrounds its ultimate goal, there is not much confusion here. The Bible passage cited most often in Mormonism is Matthew 5:48: "Be ye therefore perfect, even as your Father which is in heaven is perfect." (Mormons use the King James Version exclusively.) References to perfection are liberally sprinkled throughout LDS literature. I have asked many Mormons and ex-Mormons what

Mormonism's greatest emphasis is, and almost unanimously and without hesitation, they have singled out perfection.

Therefore, we should thoroughly understand this emphasis. In fact, perfection serves as the focal point for the witnessing method that will be presented in Part Two. If you choose to use that method, you need to be well acquainted with LDS beliefs concerning perfection. The following chapters will examine individual components of LDS perfection. Here I will only illustrate the prominent place perfection holds in ever Mormon's life.

To do that, I have chosen to cite numerous quotations. They will give you some flavor of how Mormons speak about perfection. As you read these statements, imagine the pressures and burdens they place on people. Imagine trying to live up to the standards they set out.

Perfection is a word that causes different reactions from many people. Some people say, "Perfection? Why that is impossible!" Others say, "Perfection! I get discouraged just thinking about it!"

Yet, would the Lord give us a commandment that was impossible for us to keep? And when he gives a commandment, doesn't he, as Nephi said, prepare a way for us to accomplish what he commands? (*Life and Teachings of Jesus & His Apostles,* p. 57)

Our goal as children of God has been clearly stated. Jesus said: "Be ye therefore perfect, even as your Father which is in heaven is perfect." (*Achieving A Celestial Marriage,* p. 27)

Do you think the Lord will excuse you if you do not try to be as perfect in this world as it is possible to be? Elder Joseph Fielding Smith has said this: "Here we lay the foundation . . . It is our duty to be better today than we were yesterday, and better tomorrow than we are today. Why? Because we are on that road . . . to perfection, and that can only come through obedience and the desire in our hearts to overcome the world." (*Life and Teachings of Jesus & His Apostles,* p. 292)

"Progress toward eternal life is a matter of achieving perfection. Living all the commandments guarantees total forgiveness of sins and assures one of exaltation through that perfection which comes by complying with the formula the Lord gave us. In his Sermon on the Mount he made the command to all men: 'Be ye therefore perfect, even as you Father which is in heaven is perfect' (Matt. 5:48). Being perfect means to triumph over sin. This is a mandate from the Lord. He is just and wise and kind. He would never require anything from his children which was not for their benefit and which was not attainable. Perfection therefore is an achievable goal." (Spencer W. Kimball, quoted in *Life and Teachings of Jesus & His Apostles,* p. 386)

The words of the Savior in his Sermon on the Mount, "Be ye therefore perfect, even as your Father which is in heaven is perfect," have served as a text for many a sermon. We have been informed that his meaning is that we, in this life, should try to perform every duty and keep every law and thus endeavor to be perfect in our sphere as the Father is in his. This is all good and true, but does it go far enough? (Joseph Fielding Smith, *The Way to Perfection,* p. 7)

Now one might wonder how they can seriously talk about perfection when sin is so evident in everybody's life. One answer is that they substantially weaken the concept of sin, a subject that will be explored in a subsequent chapter. Another answer is that, although the Bible says "*be* perfect," and many times they urge each other to be perfect, they explain that as *becoming* perfect. They teach that people are to *progress* towards perfection.

That progression is not limited to this lifetime either. It reaches far into eternity. A few years back, I asked a guide at Temple Square in Salt Lake City how long it would take him to attain godhood. His answer: "A thousand eternities." (The plural eternities is one that occurs frequently in Mormonism, I have never found a good explanation of it. When I have asked Mormons about it, they said they have never thought about it. They are surprised that I am puzzled by it since they have grown up using it.) In this he was faithfully echoing the teachings of his church.

Along with exaltation, this principle of eternal progression is foundational.

Worthiness is a process, and perfection is an eternal trek . . . If I understand the teachings of the prophets of this dispensation correctly, we will not become perfect in this life, though we can make significant strides toward that goal.

Elder Joseph Fielding Smith offers this counsel: "Salvation does not come all at once, we are commanded to be perfect even as our Father in heaven is perfect. It will take us ages to accomplish this end, for there will be greater progress beyond the grave . . . I believe the Lord meant just what he said: that we should be perfect as our Father in heaven is perfect. That will not come all at once, but line upon line, and precept upon precept, example upon example, and even then not as long as we live in this mortal life, for we will have to go even beyond the grave before we reach that perfection and shall be like God." (Elder Marvin J. Ashton, *Ensign* May 1989, pp. 20,21)

We can become perfect, or near perfect, in many different parts of our life. We can work step-by-step and achieve success by degrees along the road to exaltation. (*Latter-day Saint Woman B*, p. 278)

The Prophet Joseph Smith taught: "When you climb up a ladder, you must begin at the bottom, and ascend step by step, until you arrive at the top; and so it is with the principles of the Gospel—you must begin with the first, and go on until you learn all the principles of exaltation. But it will be a great while after you have passed through the veil (died) before you will have learned them. It is not all to be comprehended in this world; it will be a great work to learn our salvation and exaltation beyond the grave." (*Gospel Principles*, p. 305)

In the next chapter we will examine the steps involved in this eternal progression to godhood.

Key Concepts

Exaltation: Mormonism's ultimate goal. It includes becoming a god and having an eternal family.

Eternal life: Not living with God but living as God; synonymous with exaltation.

Eternal family: The continuation of the family unit in eternity and the ability to procreate spirit children for all eternity. Only those who attain godhood will have eternal families.

God: An exalted man who is married and is procreating spirit children.

Perfection: The intermediate goal constantly set before Mormons that enables them to attain godhood.

Eternal progression: The idea that persons, throughout all eternity, progress towards godhood.

CHAPTER TWO: KNOW THEIR PLAN- CHRONOLOGICALLY

Mormonism glorifies mankind. We saw that in the last chapter when it stated that humans could become gods. We see that in this chapter in their plan of salvation. In contrast to the biblical plan of salvation, which centers on Christ's efforts for us, the Mormon plan of salvation concentrates on human effort. By means of this work oriented plan, Mormons feel they can eventually become perfect and achieve exaltation. This man-centered plan serves as their gospel.

> But the Lord, through his grace, appeared to man, gave him the gospel or eternal plan whereby he might rise above the carnal and selfish things of life and obtain spiritual perfection. But he must rise by his own efforts and he must walk by faith. (*The Life and Teachings of Jesus & His Apostles*, p. 351)

> The plan of salvation, or code of laws, which is known as the gospel of Jesus Christ . . . (*Sharing the Gospel*, p. 70)

> . . . Mormonism so-called-which actually is the gospel of Christ, restored anew in this day . . . (*Sharing the Gospel*, p. 176)

These statements give us some interesting insights into how Mormons use the word "gospel." Not only do they equate it with their plan of salvation, they also define it as a "code of laws." They further identify it with the specific laws of Mormonism. Thus Mormonism's gospel is not good news. Instead of relieving the pressure on them, it intensifies that pressure, by giving them more laws.

> The Ten Commandments are still a vital thread in the
> fabric of the gospel of Christ, but with His coming came
> new light and life which brings a fuller measure of joy and
> happiness. *Jesus introduced a higher and more difficult*
> *standard of human conduct.* It is simpler as well as more
> difficult because it focuses on internal rather than
> external requirements: do unto others as you would have
> them do unto you. Love your neighbor as yourself . . . *This*
> *was the essence of the new gospel.* (President James E.
> Faust, *Ensign*, November 1997, p. 53, emphasis added)

How much more attractive is the good news of the Bible!
Contrary to Mormonism, the Bible clearly says: "no one will be declared
righteous in his sight by observing the law; rather, through the law we
become conscious of sin" (Romans 3:20). But what we could not do,
Jesus did for us. "God made him who had no sin to be sin for us, so that
in him we might become the righteousness of God" (2 Corinthians 5:21).
Instead of giving us a plan of salvation that we have to carry out to save
ourselves, God gave us salvation itself. "For it is by grace you have been
saved, through faith—and this not from yourselves, it is the gift of God—
not by works, so that no one can boast" (Ephesians 2:8,9).

In spite of their work-intensive gospel, Mormons still sincerely
speak of God's love for them. They see his love in the fact that he gave
them this plan!

> Great beyond comprehension is the love of God. He is our
> loving Eternal Father. Out of His love for us, He has given
> an eternal plan which, when followed, leads to exaltation
> in His kingdom. (Gordon B. Hinckley, *Ensign*, May 1989,
> p. 66)

The only alternative Mormons see is to have no plan and,
therefore, have no chance. Christians, who are accustomed to seeing
God's love in his gift of salvation itself, aren't impressed by such a plan.
Many Mormons, however, are. We need to remember this if we truly want
to understand them. Otherwise we will be prone to charge them with
deception or insincerity whenever they talk about God's love for them.

28

CHRISTIANITY	MORMONISM
God gives us *salvation* that is based on Jesus' perfection for us.	God gives us a *plan of salvation* that demands perfection from us.

Just how demanding their gospel is will be abundantly illustrated in the following pages.

Agency

The bedrock on which their plan of salvation rests is their teaching concerning human agency. *Gospel Principles* defines agency as "The right to choose between good and evil" (p. 18). Mormons not only believe that agency is every person's birthright, but also that everyone, from birth, is inclined to choose good.

> "It is critically important that you understand that you already know right from wrong, that you're innately, inherently, and intuitively good." (Boyd K. Packer, quoted in *Duties and Blessings of the Priesthood*, Part B, p. 186).

This same manual illustrates how important agency is to Mormons:

> Next to the bestowal of life itself, the right to direct our lives is God's greatest gift to man. Freedom of choice is more to be treasured than any possession earth can give. It is inherent in the spirit of man. It is a divine gift to every normal being . . . Without this divine power to choose, humanity cannot progress. (p.245)

From these statements we cull the following points concerning the LDS teaching of agency:

1. People are born "inherently good."
2. People have the freedom (agency) to make the right decisions.
3. People progress by the wise use of their agency.

Each of these points, however, stands in direct opposition to the Bible. God's Word clearly states that no one, by nature, has the capacity

29

either to make good decisions or to do good deeds.

> There is no one righteous, not even one; there is no one who understands, no one who seeks God. All have turned away, they have together become worthless; there is no one who does good, not even one. (Romans 3:10-12)

> The Lord . . . said in his heart: "Never again will I curse the ground because of man, even though every inclination of his heart is evil from childhood." (Genesis 8:21)

It is difficult to grasp just how fully this idea of agency permeates Mormon life. As I was browsing in an LDS bookstore one day, I happened to overhear a conversation between three LDS women. (I didn't mean to listen, but they were talking quite loudly!) They were discussing the difficulty one of their daughters was having deciding whether to marry a certain young man. Repeatedly they said such things as: "Tell her to exercise her agency." "To make decisions like this is why Heavenly Father gave her agency in the first place!"

Referring to a person's agency in such everyday contexts is not unusual. Consider this advice to fathers:

> Work within the framework of a person's free agency. . . After encouraging our children to share their feelings and views—which they need to express and which we need to hear—we have a sacred responsibility to help our children use their agency wisely and learn to follow the Lord's direction. (*Lay Hold Upon the Word of God*, pp. 18,19)

Nothing is more important to Mormons for achieving exaltation than the proper exercise of their agency. To see that, we must study in detail the LDS plan of salvation. Mormons believe mankind progresses through three distinct stages. Human history, according to Mormonism, begins before birth in *premortality*. It continues through *mortality*, ending up in *postmortality*. As we will see, Mormonism has developed numerous exotic beliefs for each stage. The diagram on the next page gives an overview of this plan of salvation.

Before looking at the particulars, it will be wise to recall a point made in the last chapter, namely, Mormonism teaches that this progression from premortality to postmortality is not unique to mankind. It says that Heavenly Father had to take the same journey, as did all the other gods. In addition, other spirit children of other gods are presently making this journey on other worlds. Finally, the future spirit children of those presently progressing to godhood will also need to take this journey. According to Mormonism, what is happening on earth is just one small slice of a never-ending, ever-expanding cycle of countless spiritual children progressing to godhood.

Premortality

A Mormon's journey to godhood begins in premortality. Mormonism teaches that all people existed as spirit children of God before being born into this world. They call this state preexistence, premortality, or our first estate. Some Mormons expressed surprise when told that Christians didn't believe this. They thought all "Christians" believed it.

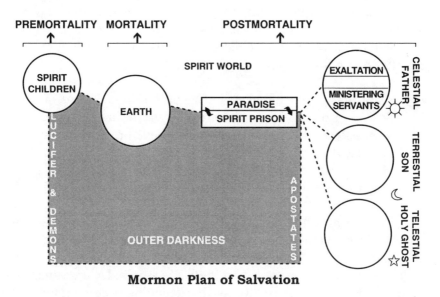

Mormon Plan of Salvation

This illustrates one reason many Mormons think they are Christians. They don't know what Christians believe and thus don't realize that Christianity and Mormonism are vastly different.

At times, a person studying Mormonism comes across an aspect of their belief that is filled with obscure statements and explanations so intricate that they confuse even Mormons. Preexistence is one such area. It is a subject that raises more questions than answers. Most Mormons, however, don't concern themselves with such questions. Most limit their interest in premortality to two main subjects.

Spirit Children

One teaching that all Mormons are familiar with is the belief that Heavenly Father spiritually begot everybody in preexistence.

> Man, as a spirit, was begotten and born of heavenly parents, and reared to maturity in the eternal mansion of the Father, prior to coming upon the earth in a temporal [physical] body. (*Gospel Principles*, p. 11)

Because they believe they are God's literal children, the favorite LDS term for God is Heavenly Father. This is also how they explain away the many biblical references to one God. Although they believe in a plurality of gods, they say there is only one god *for this world*, namely Heavenly Father. Although there are many other gods, none of them is their god—because none of those gods spiritually begot them.

A manual for teaching children gives us some information about the nature of spirit children.

> What are we like as spirits? (We do not have bodies of flesh and bones, but our spirit bodies are in the same form as the physical bodies we will have on earth.) As spirits, what can we do? (As spirits, we are able to move about, talk, listen, think, learn, make choices, and prepare for earthly life.) (*Walk In His Ways A*, p. 22)

Not only are all humans Heavenly Father's spirit children, so also are all angels and demons, even Jesus and Lucifer. All—angels, demons, humans, Jesus, the devil—are spirit brothers and sisters. This belief that Jesus and Lucifer are spirit brothers has received a large amount of negative publicity. As repulsive as that teaching is to Christians, we need to realize that Mormons have a difficult time understanding why this bothers us. To them, being spirit brothers is equivalent to being fellow creatures of God. They can talk about Jesus and Lucifer being spirit brothers just as dispassionately as we can state that humans and angels (including the demons who fell) are fellow creatures of God.

Of greater importance to Mormons is their teaching that being

God's spirit children means that mankind possesses his divine nature. This, they believe, gives every human being the potential to be divine.

> "Man can transform himself and he must. Man has in himself the seeds of godhood, which can germinate and grow and develop. As the acorn becomes the oak, the mortal man becomes a god. It is within his power to lift himself by his very bootstraps from the plane on which he finds himself to the plane on which he should be. It may be a long, hard lift with many obstacles, but it is a real possibility." (Spencer W. Kimball, quoted in *Doctrines of the Gospel*, p. 52)

> MEN ARE GODS IN EMBRYO
> Man is the child of God, formed in the divine image and endowed with divine attributes, and even as the infant son of our earthly father and mother is capable in due time of becoming a man, so the undeveloped offspring of celestial parentage is capable, by experience through ages of aeons, of evolving into a God. *[Improvement Era*, Nov. 1909, p. 81] (*Achieving A Celestial Marriage*, p. 130)

Therefore, one reason Mormons value this teaching of the preexistence is that it explains why they can become gods. As God's literal children they have the potential to become like him. This "divine heritage" is something that is often held up as an encouragement for them to realize their "own celestial potential."

Preexistence Worthiness

To confirm their divine potential is not the only reason Mormons refer to their preexistence. They also look to it as proof that they have already exercised their agency wisely. LDS preexistence is not a shadowy world where spirit children wait in a coma-like state to be born on earth. A previous quote talked about these spirit children being "reared to maturity." In line with that, Mormons believe that the premortal world is a place of great activity and achievement.

> "During the ages in which we dwelt in the premortal state we not only developed our various characteristics and

showed our worthiness and ability, or lack of it, but we were also where such progress could be observed. It is reasonable to believe that there was a Church organization there . . . Priesthood, without any question, had been conferred and the leaders were chosen to officiate. Ordinances pertaining to that pre-existence were required and the love of God prevailed. Under such conditions it was natural for our Father to discern and choose those who were most worthy and evaluate the talents of each individual. He knew not only what each of us could do, but also what each of us would do." (Joseph Fielding Smith, quoted in *The Life and Teachings of Jesus & His Apostles*, p. 350)

Note especially how they believe that spirit children begin progression towards godhood already in premortality. Mormons teach that the very fact that a person is born on this earth is proof that he or she, as a spirit child, had used his or her agency wisely. They say it proves that he or she had not followed Lucifer; for all who did became demons.

Because we are here on earth and have mortal bodies we know that we chose to follow Jesus Christ and our Heavenly Father . . . In our pre-mortal life, we chose the right. We must continue to choose the right here on earth. (*Gospel Principles*, p. 19)

Mormons believe we rejected Satan in preexistence by not joining his rebellion in heaven. But they have a unique view of that rebellion. They believe that, in the preexistent world, Heavenly Father called a Grand Council to present his plan of salvation to all his spirit children. He needed somebody to come to the earth that would be created and show people how to return to him. Jesus and Lucifer both volunteered. But they proposed different ways of doing this. Lucifer wanted to do everything for mankind. Jesus, on the other hand, said mankind had to prove their worthiness for exaltation through the wise use of their agency. Heavenly Father chose Jesus. Lucifer became angry and rebelled, with the result that he and his followers were cast out of heaven. Jesus' followers remained in heaven as spirit children. Eventually they all will come to earth to continue their progression. Therefore the very

34

fact of our being on earth is proof to a Mormon that we have already used our agency wisely in the premortal world.

This preexistent use of agency is something Mormons frequently refer to in order to encourage people to continue on the right course. (See quotes above.) In line with this, they like to refer to each other as "choice spirits." Consider, for example, the following unpublished letter written by a father to his adult daughter.

Dear _____,

When we think about life, it brings to mind some very profound thoughts. Did you ever entertain the thought, "What if there was no beginning?" This is a very negative thought which subdues the spirit and brings out the notion, eat, drink, and be merry, for tomorrow we die. This is one of the ways the adversary has of deceiving us.

Rather than think negative think positive. In the beginning we existed. We existed thousands and thousands of ages as an intelligent spirit before we took on this mortal state. Life is eternal. We have always existed. We will exist forever. Life is everlasting. Compare it to a ring on your finger. There is no beginning and no end.

Throughout the eternities we gain knowledge and progress by learning and obeying correct principles [sic]. Our sojourn in this corporal state as compared to the eternities is but a blink of the eye.

_____, you and your family are choice spirits and you chose to come here and receive a body. We had to receive a body of flesh and bones, for the body and spirit, when separated, cannot have a fullness of joy. We progressed and gained knowledge in the spirit world. We gain knowledge and progress in this sphere of action, and we will regain our previous knowledge when we leave this mortal state and go to paradise.

Some Mormons take preexistence worthiness a step further.

Some cite it as the reason that people are born into a particular family. I have had them point specifically to it as the reason why they were born into an LDS family. One manual explains Romans 9:11 in a similar way: "This election to a chosen lineage is based on preexistent worthiness and is made 'according to the foreknowledge of God.' " (*The Life and Teachings of Jesus & His Apostles*, p. 332).

To summarize, preexistence is important to Mormons for two reasons:

1. On the basis of their being the spirit children of God, they find an explanation of why they can attain godhood. As God's children, they are "gods in embryo" with the potential to attain godhood.

2. On the basis of their preexistent worthiness, they believe they have already made good progress toward exaltation. This, then, encourages them to continue on that path during their days of mortality.

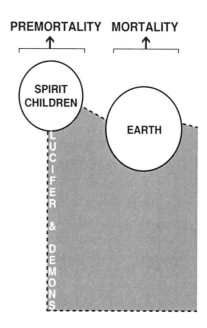

Mortality

Mormons believe this mortal life is the time of greatest opportunity to work the plan of salvation and progress to exaltation. Their reason for thinking this surprises most Christians. It isn't that they feel this life offers them their only chance. Mormonism teaches that people will have the opportunity to progress even after they die, as we will see later in this chapter. This lifetime affords them the greatest opportunity to progress simply because here they have a body and thus can be tested.

Why are you here on planet earth?

One of the most important reasons is to receive a mortal body. Another is to be tested—to experience mortality—to determine what you will do with life's challenging opportunities. (Russell M. Nelson, *Ensign*, Nov. 1990, p. 74)

As Nelson's words indicate, Mormons believe there is a close connection between being tested and having a body. They feel that to be tested thoroughly, a person needs to face physical temptations.

Clearly it is difficult to repent in the spirit world of sins involving physical habits and actions. There one has spirit and mind but not the physical power to overcome a physical habit. He can desire to change his life, but how can he overcome the lusts of the flesh unless he has flesh to control and transform? How can he overcome the tobacco or the drink habit in the spirit world where there is no liquor nor tobacco and no flesh to crave it? Similarly with other sins involving lack of control over the body. (Spencer W. Kimball, *The Miracle of Forgiveness*, p. 168)

Some might think that this time of testing wouldn't be genuine because, as spirit children, they had already learned the truth. But Mormonism teaches that all memory of preexistence is removed when people become mortal.

The point to remember is that Mormons believe a person must face physical temptations to become a god. It is this belief that lies behind Mormonism's emphasis on large families. By providing bodies for spirit children, a couple helps those spirit children progress to godhood.

Knowing that the primary work of God is "to bring to pass the immortality and eternal life of man" (Moses 1:39) and knowing that without a physical body man could not have a fullness of joy (see D&C 93:33-35) and knowing that coming to earth to prove oneself is a prcrequisite to eternal progression (see Abraham 3:25), one could safely say that bringing children into the world is one of the high priorities in the Lord's plan. (*Old Testament: Genesis-2*

Samuel, Student Manual, p. 31)

We see the importance they attach to the body also in their interpretation of demon possession. They believe the worst punishment God inflicted on the devil and his demons was denying them the possibility of their ever obtaining a body. "To be denied the privilege of mortal bodies forever is the greatest curse of all" (Joseph Fielding Smith, *The Way to Perfection*, p. 234). Nothing is more disastrous because this effectively stops progression to godhood, since a person must overcome physical temptations to become a god. As an extension of this thought, Mormons see in demon possession the desperate attempt of demons to obtain bodies.

> "The devil has no body, and herein is his punishment. He is pleased when he can obtain the tabernacle of man, and when cast out by the Savior he asked to go into the herd of swine, showing that he would prefer a swine's body to having none. (Joseph Smith, quoted in *Doctrine and Covenants Student Manual*, p. 358)

> Those so rejected are denied, eternally, the right to have bodies of their own. In this dejection and damnable state they seek to house themselves unlawfully in the bodies of mortal men. (*The Life and Teachings of Jesus & His Apostles*, p. 44)

I have described their beliefs concerning the body in some detail because it is such a foreign thought to Christians, yet such an important doctrine to Mormons.

> No other people on earth understand the sacred nature and purpose of our physical bodies as do Latter-day Saints . . . We knew that by gaining physical bodies to house our spirits , we would have the opportunity to become more like our Father. (*Come Unto Me*, p. 143)

> Joseph Smith simply said: "The great principle of happiness consists in having a body" (quoted in *Doctrine and Covenants Student Manual*, p. 221). Without a proper understanding of the body's significance in

Mormonism, it is difficult to understand the pressure many Mormons feel to do all they can in this life to become perfect. We might conclude that they would feel no urgency to work at perfection now since they have all eternity to do that. But, for many Mormons, working at becoming perfect is the overriding purpose of their lives.

First Principles and Ordinances

This striving for perfection formally starts with their acceptance of the first principles and ordinances of the gospel. Mormonism's fourth Article of Faith identifies these for us:

> We believe that the first principles and ordinances of the Gospel are: first, Faith in the Lord Jesus Christ; second, Repentance; third, Baptism by immersion for the remission of sins; fourth, Laying on of hands for the gift of the Holy Ghost.

They call faith and repentance the first principles while labeling baptism and the laying on of hands as the first ordinances. We will withhold our examination of faith and repentance until the next chapter when we study the theological aspects of their plan. A discussion of the first ordinances fits in here, however, as they signal a person's formal acceptance of Mormonism.

Baptism especially signifies that.

> Baptism is the formally appointed means and ordinance which the Lord has provided so that man can signify his personal acceptance of all of the terms and conditions of the eternal gospel covenant. Thus in baptism . . . man covenants to abide by all of the laws and requirements of the whole gospel. (McConkie, *Mormon Doctrine*, p. 70)

Note how depressing their doctrine of baptism is. Instead of relieving them of their burden of sin, it places a heavy burden on them. Instead of emphasizing God's forgiveness, it stresses man's obligations.

Children are baptized at the age of eight; adult converts are encouraged to be baptized as quickly as possible. One of the first goals

Mormon missionaries attempt to achieve is to have interested people "commit themselves to be baptized on a specific date" (*Uniform System For Teaching the Gospel*, p. 2-1). To be valid, a baptism must be by immersion and must be performed by a member of the LDS priesthood. The closest relative holding the priesthood usually performs the baptism. If there is no such relative, one of the missionaries will do the baptizing.

Many Christians are surprised to learn that Mormons baptize in the name of the Father, and of the Son and of the Holy Ghost. (See D&C 20:73.) But right terminology alone does not make for a valid Christian baptism. The baptism administered by the LDS church is not a Christian baptism because the LDS church is not a Christian church. Their denial of God's gift of salvation through Jesus Christ makes their baptism nothing but an empty ritual.

Immediately following baptism, a person is confirmed by receiving the laying on of hands for the gift of the Holy Ghost. This is important for two reasons: 1) it gives the right to have the Holy Ghost as a constant companion; 2) it allows the person to receive inspiration and guidance from the Holy Ghost.

> While the Holy Ghost may inspire all mankind, the gift carries the right to have it as a "constant companion". It is "by the power of the Holy Ghost [that you] may know the truth of all things." (Boyd K. Packer, *Ensign*, Nov. 1994, p.59)

In chapter four we will see the huge role this plays in every Mormon's life. Now, however, we continue our journey through LDS mortality.

Worthiness

Being worthy and being perfect are the two main thoughts of day-to-day Mormonism. They are closely connected and, at times, used interchangeably. Probably the best way to distinguish them is to say that being worthy is the way to becoming perfect. Every day Mormons are faced with the challenge of being worthy. They must prove themselves worthy not only of eternal rewards but also of temporal blessings. To advance within the church, to enter the temple, to do almost anything, they must be worthy as the following quotes illustrate:

Here on earth we are often judged as to our worthiness to receive opportunities within the kingdom of God. At the time we are baptized we are judged worthy to receive this ordinance. (*Gospel Principles*, p. 294)

Men, young and old are baptized into the Church, and when they are judged worthy, they are ordained to the priesthood. (*Gospel Principles*, p. 85)

Before we can go to the temple, we must be active, worthy members of the Church for at least one year. (*Gospel Principles*, p. 244)

In official Declaration 2, accepted by the Church on September 30, 1978, we are reminded that certain privileges have worthiness as a prerequisite. In this official declaration, the word worthy or worthiness is used six times. This leaves little doubt as to the importance of being worthy if specific blessings are to be available to us. (Elder Marvin S. Ashton, *Ensign*, May 1989, p.22)

The idea of worthiness is one that is never far from their thoughts.

The key to being worthy is being a good person. *Mormonism is a religion of outward morality.* Laws, laws, and more laws is what Mormonism is all about. In stark contrast to Christianity's emphasis on God's grace, Mormonism glorifies law.

Laws provide the way for the Saint to grow, progress, and obtain happiness . . . Although God's laws are exact and immovable, they are revealed and given to mankind for one specific purpose—to bring to pass their ultimate joy . . . The Doctrine and Covenants teaches that all blessings are predicted upon laws and that if one desires a particular blessing, one must abide by the law that guarantees that blessing . . . God has said that no one can come unto him except by his laws. *Doctrine and Covenants Student Manual*, pp. 392,394)

Every law is meant to lift and inspire, reconcile and perfect. (*Old Testament Manual I*, p. 159)

In line with this, their literature deals almost exclusively with how to be a better person. Article after article and lesson after lesson exhort them to be good. But rarely are Heavenly Father or Jesus presented as sources of help, much less of forgiveness. Heavenly Father gave the plan; Jesus showed them how to work the plan; now it is up to them to carry it out. At best, Jesus and the Father are pictured as being on the sidelines cheering them on.

> Knowing that becoming perfect through Christ is eventually possible and that the Savior is "pulling for us" is a compelling thought. (*Ensign*, Feb. 1991, p.11)

The constant repetition of "Be good," "Be worthy," "Be perfect" are like drops of water ceaselessly dripping on them. It is slowly but surely wearing many Mormons out.

It would take another book to address individually the varied laws Mormons are to keep in order to be worthy. But arguably the most important one to the average Mormon is the Word of Wisdom.

The Word of Wisdom

The Word of Wisdom is the well-known prohibition against drinking coffee contained in D&C 89. More specifically, it prohibits the use of liquor, tobacco, and hot drinks. Over the years, Mormons have hotly debated this section, especially its prohibition against the use of hot drinks. "Hot drinks" is officially interpreted as tea and coffee. But does it also ban iced tea, cola drinks, or anything with caffeine in it? These are important questions to Mormons because the Word of Wisdom is so important to them.

Mormons have no uniform practice in these areas. Some drink iced tea while others don't. Some refrain from drinking caffeinated soft drinks.

> Although soft drinks are not mentioned specifically in the Word of Wisdom, an official statement by the Church's leaders reads: "With reference to cola drinks, the Church has never officially taken a position on this matter, but the leaders of the Church have advised, and we do now specifically advise, against the use of any drink containing harmful habit-forming drugs under circum-

stances that would result in acquiring the habit. Any beverage that contains ingredients harmful to the body should be avoided." (*Doctrine and Covenants Student Manual*, p. 209)

A survey cited by Spencer W. Kimball reveals the prominent place the Word of Wisdom occupies.

> When seminary teachers asked students to place certain commandments of the Lord in the order of their importance, the Word of Wisdom placed first and chastity fifth. (*The Miracle of Forgiveness*, p. 64f.)

(An LDS seminary is not a school which trains clergy. Seminary refers to classes on Mormonism offered daily to high school students.)

So many Mormons focus so much attention on the Word of Wisdom that we find this disclaimer in the manual, *Life and Teachings of Jesus & His Apostles*: "It should be understood that the Word of Wisdom is not the gospel, and the gospel is not the Word of Wisdom" (p.364).

In spite of such disclaimers, it is quite easy to see why Mormons place so much emphasis on the Word of Wisdom. They do because their church does. It is taught prospective members before they join the church. It is one of the most frequently mentioned topics at their semiannual general conferences. Keeping it is one of the basic requirements for being worthy to enter the temple. Obviously, keeping the Word of Wisdom is one of the most important things Mormons can do.

> The Word of Wisdom put restrictions on members of the Church. To this day those regulations apply to every member and to everyone who seeks to join the Church. They are so compelling that no one is to be baptized into the Church without first agreeing to live by them. No one will be called to teach or to lead unless they accept them. When you want to go to the temple, you will be asked if you keep the Word of Wisdom. If you do not, you cannot go to the house of the Lord until you are fully worthy. (Boyd K. Packer, *Ensign*, May 1996, p.17)

"For observing the Word of Wisdom the reward is life, not

43

only prolonged mortal life but life eternal." (Spencer W. Kimball, quoted in *Gospel Principles*, p. 195)

Before proceeding, I would like to point out that there is no proof for the commonly made charge that the LDS Church at one time owned or still owns The Coca-Cola Company. This accusation is often made in an attempt to demonstrate hypocrisy on their part (i.e., the LDS church makes money selling Coke even though they can't drink it). Heinerman and Shupe, in their well-researched book, *The Mormon Corporate Empire*, find no proof for this charge. When Christians make this charge, all they are doing is damaging their own credibility and making the task of reaching out to Mormons even more difficult.

Temple Ordinances and Temple Work

Besides obeying the various laws of Mormonism, Mormons need to be actively participating in temple work to further their progression. Nothing stands more prominently along the road to godhood than the temple. In fact, the road to exaltation passes right through it. It is impossible for a Mormon to gain exaltation outside of it.

> It is a wonderful thing to come into the Church, but you cannot receive an exaltation until you have made covenants in the house of the Lord and received the keys and authorities that are there bestowed and which cannot be given in any other place on the earth today. (Joseph F. Smith, quoted in *Endowed From On High*, p. 26)

> The temple is the key to salvation. (Elder Lance B. Wickham, *Ensign*, Nov. 1994, p. 83)

The temple occupies the same place in Mormonism that Christ's cross occupies in Christianity. They even are to have pictures of it displayed prominently in their homes.

But many Mormons never see the inside of a temple much less participate in its work. Only those who are worthy can enter. The only time non-Mormons or nonworthy Mormons can enter it is before it is dedicated. Then, for a limited time, it is open to the public for guided tours. During such times no temple work is done. After its dedication, it is closed to all but temple-worthy Mormons.

Persons must be members of the church for at least a year before they can even consider going to the temple. Then they need to be interviewed by their bishop and a member of their stake presidency. This interview is to ascertain their worthiness to go to the temple. They are questioned about their moral life and their keeping of the Word of Wisdom. In recent years there has also been an emphasis on determining whether divorced men have remained current in family support payments. Other questions revolve around tithing and respect for church authorities. LDS apostle Russell M. Nelson described how important these interviews are.

> Interviews, as for temple recommends, with your bishop and members of your stake presidency are precious experiences. And, in a way, they could be considered meaningful "dress rehearsals" for that grand colloquy when you will stand before the Great Judge. (*Ensign*, Nov. 1990, p. 75)

Try to imagine the stress such an interview causes a person, especially one who is painfully aware of his or her sinfulness.

If found worthy, persons are issued a temple recommend. This is a small card, resembling an ID card, that verifies the person's worthiness to enter the temple. Each time a person goes to the temple it is checked at the door. This recommend is valid for one year, after which the person must be interviewed again.

Only about 25% to 30% of Mormons are temple worthy. One reason for this low percentage is geographical. Some who live a great distance from a temple don't bother going through the process of remaining temple-worthy. That is one reason why the LDS church is building more and more temples. But the main reason why so few are temple-worthy is simply that many do not make the grade.

Before going any further, it might be well to clarify that the local LDS chapels are not temples. At the end of 1997 there were 50 temples worldwide with working plans for an additional seventeen. A stated goal of LDS leadership is to build more temples so that members do not have to travel so far to do their temple work.

Another common misconception is that Mormons conduct worship services in the temple. The temple is used solely to administer certain rituals and ordinances. It is divided into many rooms so numerous ordinances can be performed simultaneously. In keeping with the importance they attach to these ordinances, these rooms are very ornate.

Because they regard the temple as sacred, Mormons say that many details concerning the work that takes place there cannot be discussed out side the temple. Consider, for example, these instructions to teachers who are preparing members for their first visit to the temple.

> To many members of the Church, the temple is a very mysterious place . . . A discussion of the temple must be handled with utmost propriety and care. Much of what is done in the temple cannot be talked about outside the temple. Our guide as to what we can say outside the temple is governed by what has been said by apostles and prophets in printed sermons and discourses. Questions about the temple that are not answered by these public statements should be responded to by saying, "You will learn the answer to that question as you serve in the temple." It is therefore recommended that the teacher stay very close to the format of this lesson and avoid other areas that may only tend to confuse the participants. (*Temple Preparation Seminar Discussions*, p. 78)

Temple Mormons take such instructions so seriously that most will not even discuss their temple experiences with their spouses. This often causes them stress as they have no one with whom to share their questions and doubts concerning the various temple ordinances.

There are three main ordinances performed in the temple: endowments, marriages, and baptisms. Another rite, similar to marriage, is the sealing of children to their parents. This is performed only when the children were born before the parents were married in the temple. Joseph Smith supposedly received instructions concerning these ordinances by direct revelation. (See D&C 127, 128, 132.) Before looking at each one individually, it is important to realize that they all can also be performed vicariously for the dead. In the case of baptisms *performed in the temple*, all are performed for the dead. (The living are baptized in their local chapels.)

As we will see in a few pages, the belief that even the dead have a chance to accept Mormonism hinges on this vicarious temple work. The point to see now is that doing this work also helps the living person doing the work progress towards exaltation.

> But greater than all this, so far as our individual responsibilities are concerned, the greatest is to become saviors, in our lesser degree which is assigned us, for the dead who have died without a knowledge of the Gospel. . . . Said Joseph Smith: "Those saints who neglect it, in behalf of their deceased relatives, do it at the peril of their own salvation." (Joseph Fielding Smith, *The Way to Perfection*, p. 153)

> As the Prophet Joseph Smith said, "The greatest responsibility in this world that God has laid upon us is to seek after our dead." (James E. Faust, *Ensign*, May 1997, p. 20)

> As surely as Christ offered Himself a vicarious sacrifice for all mankind, so we can engage in vicarious service in behalf of some of mankind, thus affording them the opportunity to move forward on the road of immortality and eternal life. Great is the work of love which goes on in these holy houses. Legion are the men and women who, with total unselfishness, labor day and night in this work which speaks of divinity. (Gordon B. Hinckley, *Ensign*, May 1989, p. 66)

Note how they describe this work as one "which speaks of divinity" and a work that allows people "to become saviors." Note also how people neglect it "at the peril of their own salvation." Such statements explain why one of my LDS acquaintances gets up as early as 3:00 A.M. each week to do this work, while others drive long distances each month to participate. Such statements also reveal why "redeeming the dead" is one of the three main missions of the LDS church. (The other two are "perfecting the saints" and "proclaiming the gospel.")

Baptism for the Dead

As was already mentioned, the only baptisms performed in the temple are those for the dead. As we will see later in this chapter, Mormons contend that the spirits of the dead can accept Mormonism in the spirit world. But such spirits have a problem. Since they have no bodies, they can't be baptized. But baptism is essential to their progression. The LDS solution is for the living to be baptized for them.

> Many times the questions arise: "What about my loved ones who have passed away? How can they enjoy these same blessings? These are very real concerns. All must be baptized in order to enter the celestial kingdom [see John 3:5] not only the living, but also those who have died. How can persons who have passed away be baptized? Only with our help. We must be baptized for them. (*From You to Your Ancestors*, p. 1)

In this connection the LDS church gets a lot of mileage out of 1 Corinthians 15:29. "Else what shall they do which are baptized for the dead, if the dead rise not at all? Why are they then baptized for the dead?" (KJV) Admittedly, this is a difficult passage to interpret. Someone has counted over three hundred different interpretations of it.

Instead of "for the dead," Luther translated "over the dead." He went on to say that people were baptized as they stood over the grave of a loved one. This would dramatically demonstrate their hope that they would be reunited with this loved one at the resurrection. Others have interpreted it to mean that at the time of baptism, a person was given the name of a departed loved one. For example, a grandson might receive the name John in memory of his grandfather by the same name. But these are only possible interpretations. We do not definitely know what Paul was referring to in this verse.

One thing that is clear, however, is that the LDS idea of being baptized for the dead for their salvation is ruled out by the *rest of Scripture*. This lifetime, and only this lifetime, is when people can come to faith. "Man is destined to die once, and after that to face judgement" (Hebrews 9:27). "When a wicked man dies, his hope perishes" (Proverbs 11:7).

Their belief that they can help their ancestors in this way is the reason Mormons are so committed to developing genealogies. They are urged to trace their ancestry back at least four generations.

> Every family in the Church has been asked to submit family group sheets on the first four generations of their ancestry. This assignment is given not just as a recommendation but as a *priesthood obligation*. (*Doctrine and Covenants Student Manual*, p. 448, emphasis added)

Some also donate up to twenty hours a week working at

extraction centers. At these centers, names and other pertinent data are extracted from centuries-old records. When I was shown around one such center, the people were working with seventeenth century Lutheran church records from Germany.

The practice of baptizing for the dead also serves the practical purpose of introducing their youth to temple work, since it is the only temple ordinance the youth can participate in. Many wards organize regular temple trips for their youth groups. On such trips, each youth is baptized for at least one dead individual. Not only does this get them accustomed to going to the temple, but it also increases their curiosity about it since the rest of the temple is off limits to them. Of course, youths need to be temple-worthy to participate in these temple trips.

Endowment Ceremony

A person's formal introduction to the temple is the endowment ceremony. The earliest that persons can receive their endowment is in their late teens. The two most common times they receive their endowments are in preparation for their mission or at their temple marriage.

This ordinance receives its name from the belief that it endows people with power and protection.

> If we realize what we are doing, then the endowment will be a protection to us all our lives—a protection which a man who does not go to the temple does not have. (*Temples of The Church of Jesus Christ of Latter-day Saints*, p. 14)

Although these rituals are not to be discussed outside the temple, various Mormons have tape-recorded especially the endowment ceremony. Transcripts of these recordings have been published, so we do have an accurate record of what it entails.

The ceremony begins with temple workers ceremonially washing and anointing various parts of the participant's body. This is to symbolize a person's total dedication to the Lord. The participant then receives sacred undergarments which are to be worn for the rest of his or her life.

Church members who have been clothed with the

garment in the temple have made a covenant to wear it throughout their lives. This has been interpreted to mean that it is worn as underclothing both day and night. . . The fundamental principle ought to be to wear the garment and not to find occasions to remove it . . . When the garment must be removed, . . . it should be restored as soon as possible. (Statement of the First Presidency, quoted in *Endowed From On High*, p. 26)

Some ex-Mormons claim that many Mormons feel that these temple garments offer the wearer supernatural protection. The following quotes seem to lend credence to such claims.

For many Church members the garment has formed a barrier of protection when the wearer has been faced with temptation. (Boyd K. Packer, quoted in *Endowed From On High*, p. 24)

Parents who faithfully wear the sacred temple garment teach the principle of modesty to their children. With the new emphasis on fitness and exercise has come the temptation to wear sporting outfits for unnecessarily long periods of time, without wearing the temple garment. When we fail to honor our own commitments to be modest, *we weaken the Lord's promises of protection*, the blessings of the law of chastity, and the ability to teach our children modest behavior. (*Remember Me*, pp. 176f., emphasis added)

Since practicing temple Mormons cannot speak about the affairs of the temple, it is difficult to say how widespread such a feeling is. The one thing that is evident is that most temple Mormons take seriously the command to wear these garments at all times.

As part of these preparatory rites, the participant receives a new name, which he or she is not to reveal to anyone. This new name, Mormons believe, will be one of the things that will enable the person to enter the celestial kingdom.

A person goes through the endowment ceremony only once for himself or herself. But many have received endowments hundreds of times vicariously for the dead. According to Mormonism, being baptized for the dead allows the spirits of the dead to enter paradise, while being endowed for them aids them in their progression to godhood. People receiving the endowment vicariously do not receive the ceremonial washing and anointing. They do, however, receive new names for their respective persons since having a new name is essential for exaltation.

At this point in the ceremony everyone is ushered into a room where they view a presentation of the LDS view of creation, the Fall, and the subsequent history of the world.

> This course of instruction includes a recital of the most prominent events of the creative period, the condition of our first parents in the Garden of Eden, their disobedience and consequent expulsion from that blissful abode, their condition in the lone and dreary world when doomed to live by labor and sweat, the plan of redemption by which the great transgression may be atoned, the period of the great apostasy, the restoration of the Gospel with all its ancient powers and privileges, the absolute and indispensable condition of personal purity and devotion to the right in present life, and a strict compliance with Gospel requirements. (*Temples of The Church of Jesus Christ of Latter-day Saints,* p. 14)

During the course of this presentation the participant learns various handshakes that will

> "enable you to walk back to the presence of the Father, passing the angels who stand as sentinels, being enabled to give them the key words, the signs and tokens, pertaining to the holy Priesthood, and gain your eternal exaltation in spite of earth and hell." (Brigham Young, quoted in *Temples of The Church of Jesus Christ of Latter-day Saints,* p. 14)

At the end of the presentation the participants go to one end of the room where a veil hangs representing death. On the other side of the veil is the celestial room representing the celestial kingdom. To enter it, the participants must pass a temple worker who represents Heavenly Father. He is standing on the other side of the veil in the celestial room. In order to pass him, they must give him the correct handshakes through holes cut in the veil. In this way, they act out what they think will one day actually happen, as the above quotation indicates.

This ritual illustrates one of the reasons why the road to godhood runs directly through the temple. Mormons believe that a person must know these signs and tokens to be exalted, and the only place they can be learned is in the temple.

This endowment ceremony has received much negative publicity over the years. Since its institution in 1842 it portrayed Christian ministers as pawns of Satan. It also contained numerous bloody oaths. In the spring of 1990, the LDS church removed these and other objectionable features. They took that action even though they teach that this ceremony was given by divine revelation.

Eternal Marriage

The third main temple ordinance is eternal marriage. It is also called celestial marriage or being sealed. Mormonism teaches that marriages performed in the temple are for time *and eternity*. All others, even those performed in their meetinghouses, are only for time. Being married *for eternity* is all-important.

> Our exaltation depends on marriage . . . Heavenly Father has given us the law of eternal marriage so that we can become like him. (*Gospel Principles*, pp. 241f.)

> Celestial or eternal marriage is the gate to exaltation. To fill the full measure of his creation and obtain eternal life a man must enter into this order of matrimony and keep all of the covenants and obligations that go with it. (*The Life and Teachings of Jesus & His Apostles*, p. 130)

Once we remember that exaltation equals godhood, and that the essence of godhood is procreating spirit children, it doesn't surprise us to see such strong statements concerning eternal marriage. This also means that every person needs a spouse in order to be exalted. There are no exceptions.

> No man can be saved and exalted in the kingdom of God without the woman, and no woman can reach the perfection and exaltation in the kingdom of God alone.

> (*The Life and Teachings of Jesus & His Apostles*, p. 291)
> "No one! It matters not how righteous they may have
> been, how intelligent or how well trained they are. No one
> will enter this highest glory unless he enters into this
> covenant, and this means the new and everlasting
> covenant of marriage." (Spencer W. Kimball, quoted in
> *Doctrine and Covenants Student Manual*, p. 326)

Because eternal marriage is essential for exaltation, many LDS couples who were not initially married in the temple are married there sometime subsequent. That is, IF they become temple-worthy.

Because eternal marriage is so important, it too is performed vicariously for the dead. For example, a couple might go to the temple to be married for their deceased grandparents. By doing this, they would insure that nothing would hinder their grandparents' progression to exaltation. If, for some reason, their grandparents' spirits had not accepted Mormonism, no harm is done and the living couple still gets credit for their efforts.

Faithful Mormons, for whom it is not possible to be married eternally in this life, are also comforted with the possibility of a vicarious temple marriage.

> "To you women, we can only say we have no control over
> the heartbeats or the affections of men, but pray that you
> may find fulfillment. And in the meantime, we promise
> you that insofar as eternity is concerned, no soul will be
> deprived of rich and high and eternal blessings for
> anything which that person could not help, that the Lord
> never fails in his promises, and that every righteous
> person will receive eventually all to which the person is
> entitled and which he or she has not forfeited through
> any fault of his or her own." (Spencer W. Kimball, quoted
> in *Doctrine and Covenants Student Manual*, p. 328)

This comfort is directed mainly at single women. Men are told that they have the opportunity and *responsibility* to marry a worthy woman. This then becomes an additional source of pressure for some LDS men.

> "I want the young men of Zion to realize that this

institution of marriage is not a man-made institution. It is of God; it is honorable and no man who is of marriageable age is living his religion who remains single." (Joseph Fielding Smith, quoted in *Achieving A Celestial Marriage*, p. 181)

"Every person should *want* to be married. There are some who might not be able to. But every person should want to be married because this is what God in heaven planned for us." (Spencer W. Kimball, quoted in *Doctrines of the Gospel*, p. 75)

In summary, the temple stands squarely in the middle of the road to exaltation for two reasons:

1. It is the only place where Mormons can receive their endowments and be married for all eternity—both of which are essential to exaltation.

2. It is the only place where they can do vicarious work for the dead, which is one of the greatest works they can do to further their own progression.

Postmortality

Postmortality is the third main division in the LDS plan of salvation. At death, Mormons claim that the spirit enters the spirit world, which consists of two parts: paradise and spirit prison. The spirits of Mormons go to paradise while non-Mormons' spirits go to spirit prison. Since Mormonism is so work-oriented, it doesn't surprise us to hear that the spirits in paradise continue to work on their progression towards godhood.

All spirits are in adult form . . . spirits may progress from one level to another as they learn gospel principles and live in accordance with them . . . The Church is organized in the spirit world, with each prophet standing at the head of his own generation. (*Gospel Principles*, pp. 290f.)

One major activity of the LDS spirits is to engage in mission work among the spirits in spirit prison. Joseph F. Smith, the sixth president of the church, received a revelation in 1918 (D&C 138) that explained how Jesus supposedly organized this work when he descended into hell. Because of this missionary activity nearly everybody will have the chance to accept Mormonism.

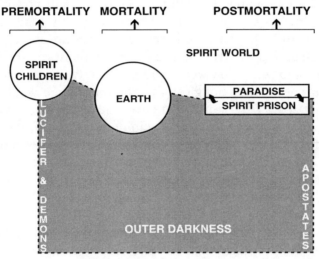

In the spirit prison are the spirits of those who have not yet received the gospel of Jesus Christ. These spirits have agency and may be enticed by both good and evil. If they accept the gospel and the ordinances performed for them in the temples, they may prepare themselves to leave the spirit prison and dwell in paradise. (*Gospel Principles*, p. 292.)

When a spirit accepts Mormonism, he enters paradise, that is, if someone has been baptized for him. If that hasn't happened, the spirit must wait until it does. Naturally, therefore, Mormons feel heavy pressure to do their genealogy and temple work.

Can you imagine the frustration you would feel if you had fully embraced the gospel in the spirit world but could not enter paradise because you had to wait until some of your descendants were motivated to do the ordinance work? Imagine your own great-grandfather and great-grandmother who desire to unite their family but are helpless to do so because the saving ordinances have not been performed and they lack the power of the priesthood. (*Doctrine and Covenants Student Manual*, p. 446)

Bob, your ancestors who died without a knowledge of the gospel are probably being taught the truth right now in the spirit world. Many of them are probably just as anxious to be baptized and receive the blessings of the Church as you were two years ago. But without you they will have to wait. How would you have felt two years ago if your parents had not given their permission for you to be baptized? What would you have said if they had told you not to bother them about joining the Church, that maybe someday they'd get around to giving you permission? You are in that same position as far as your ancestors are concerned. They are waiting for you. (*The Life and Teachings of Jesus & His Apostles*, pp. 418f.)

Once he enters paradise, the spirit can begin working on his own progression. But he might not be able to progress all the way to exaltation. Only those who never had the opportunity in this life to accept Mormonism have the possibility of progressing that far.

"If the person had every opportunity to receive these blessings in person and refused, or through procrastination and lack of faith did not receive them, then he is not entitled to them, and it is doubtful if the work for him will be valid if done within one week or 1,000 years." (Joseph Fielding Smith, quoted in *Doctrine and Covenants Student Manual*, p. 360).

Elder Bruce R. McConkie taught the foolishness of believing that a person can reject the gospel in this life, accept it in the next, and still inherit celestial glory. "There are those who believe that the doctrine of salvation for the dead offers men a second chance of salvation . . . There is no such thing as a second chance to gain salvation." (*Doctrine and Covenants Student Manual*, pp. 164f.)

This, then, offers no relief for Mormons. They can't wait until the spirit world to receive vicariously their endowments and temple marriage. When it comes to their being exalted, it is now or never.

The Three Kingdoms

All this activity in the spirit world will continue unabated until Judgment Day. Numerous exotic beliefs concerning Judgment Day have sprung up in the fertile soil of Mormonism. We will examine a handful of them in chapter five when we look at Mormon mythology. The one

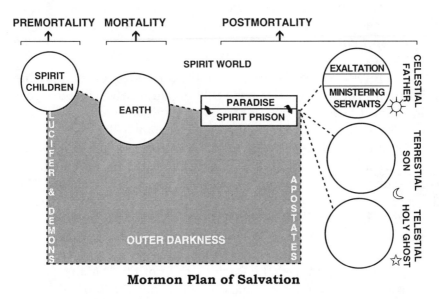

Mormon Plan of Salvation

point pertinent here is that they believe everyone will be raised from the dead. They deny, however, that all will be raised by Jesus. Rather they picture the resurrection as a progression of people calling other people out of the grave.

> As one cannot baptize himself, nor can he baptize others until he himself is baptized and ordained and given the authority, even so one cannot resurrect himself, but will be called forth by someone in authority. Men will be given the authority to perform this ordinance after they are resurrected, and then can resurrect others. (*Ensign*, April 1991, p. 11)

The most familiar aspect of this teaching is that husbands are to resurrect their wives. We can only begin to imagine the leverage this gives many LDS husbands and the accompanying stress this places on many of their wives.

At the end of the world, Christ will assign everybody to one of four places: the celestial kingdom, the terrestrial kingdom, the telestial kingdom, or outer darkness. Once a person is assigned to one of the kingdoms, he cannot progress to a different one. A person's worthiness determines his final destination.

> There are three degrees of glory in the heavens and men will be rewarded according to their actions on earth. (*Gospel Principles*, p. 113)

The three degrees of glory refer to the three kingdoms. Note that they all are part of heaven. Mormons believe that nearly everybody goes to some part of heaven. Only the "sons of perdition" are sent to outer darkness which is the LDS equivalent to an *eternal* hell.

Only apostasy (i.e., leaving the LDS church) qualifies a person as a son of perdition. What is unclear is whether *all* apostates qualify. Talking about outer darkness, Joseph Smith made this comment: "This is the case with many apostates of The Church of Jesus Christ of Latter-day Saints" (quoted in *Doctrine and Covenants Student Manual*, p. 358). McConkie expands on this:

> Among other things, this statement from the Prophet, explodes forever the mythical fantasy that the sons of perdition are so few they can be numbered on the fingers of the hand. (*Mormon Doctrine*, p. 817)

The mythical fantasy he refers to seems to be one believed by most Mormons. Any number have told me that, besides the devil and the demons, hardly anybody will be in outer darkness. One LDS leader went so far as to say that he feels nobody has qualified as a son of perdition in the whole history of the church. It appears that the average Mormon believes that everybody will end up in one of the three kingdoms of heaven.

In keeping with the basic humanity of their god, life in these kingdoms has a remarkably earthy look to it.

"A Saint who is one in deed and in truth, does not look for an immaterial heaven, but he expects a heaven with lands, houses, cities, vegetation, rivers, and animals; with thrones, temples, palaces, kings, princes, priests, and angels; with food, raiment, musical instruments, etc., all of which are material. Indeed, the Saints' heaven is a redeemed, glorified, celestial, material creation, inhabited by glorified material beings, male and female, organized into families, embracing all the relationships of husbands and wives, parents and children, where sorrow, crying, pain, and death will be known no more. Or to speak still more definitely, this earth, when glorified, is the Saints' eternal heaven. On it they expect to live, with body, parts, and holy passions; on it they expect to move and have their being; to eat, drink, converse, worship, sing, play on musical instruments, engage in joyful, innocent, social amusements, visit neighboring towns and neighboring worlds." (Orson Pratt, quoted in *Sharing the Gospel*, p.57)

The Celestial Kingdom

The above description applies especially to the highest kingdom, the celestial kingdom, which is often symbolized with a picture of the sun. Only faithful Mormons and children who die before the age of eight will inherit this kingdom.

Of the total number of people who come to earth, those who earn celestial glory may be a relatively small percentage, but in numbers there will be millions who inherit the glory of the sun. In addition to those who qualify for this kingdom by virtue of their faithfulness in this life or in the spirit world, there will be the millions of children who died before they reached the age of accountability. (*Doctrine and Covenants Student Manual*, p. 358)

Although all these will reside with Heavenly Father, not all will be exalted. Within the celestial kingdom are three different levels, only the highest of which constitutes exaltation. Only the people who progress to this highest level will attain godhood, have eternal families, create their own worlds, and produce eternal increase.

In contrast, the lowest level of the celestial kingdom is reserved for faithful Mormons who were not married for eternity in the temple. That fact alone stopped their progression short of exaltation. Such faithful Mormons reside in the presence of the Heavenly Father, but only as "ministering servants" (D&C 132:16-17). They inherit the "eternal deaths," the LDS expression for remaining single for all eternity.

> "The opposite of eternal lives is *eternal deaths*. Those who come up separately and singly in the resurrection and who therefore do not have spirit children eternally are said to inherit 'the deaths.'" (Bruce R. McConkie, quoted in *Achieving A Celestial Marriage*, p. 136)

This condition of singleness spells terrible loneliness. "How lonely and barren will be the so-called single blessedness throughout eternity!" (*Temples of The Church of Jesus Christ of Latter-day Saints*, p. 19) Although they are in the highest kingdom of heaven, they will not be very happy!

Here we do well to address the LDS concept of damnation, since inheriting the "eternal deaths" is one form of damnation. Everyone, except those who progress to godhood, experience some kind of damnation. In Mormonese, damnation is anything that stops a person's progression to godhood. Mormons speak of damnation in the same way we speak of a dam damming up a stream.

> President Kimball stressed forcefully how the Saints should view this commandment, for those who reject this covenant are truly damned, or stopped, in their eternal progression because they do not inherit the blessings of eternal increase. (*Doctrine and Covenants Student Manual*, p. 328)

> Damnation is the opposite of salvation, and exists in varying degrees. All who do not obtain the fulness of celestial exaltation *will to some degree be limited in their progress and privileges*, and hence be damned to that extent. (*Bible Dictionary* in LDS Bible, p.652, emphasis added)

There is one more level in the celestial kingdom, the middle level. Not much can be said about it because not much has been written about it. Not much has been written, as one LDS leader told me, because God has not revealed anything about that level except that it exists.

The Terrestrial Kingdom

The middle kingdom in LDS heaven is the terrestrial kingdom, symbolized by a moon. This is where moral non-Mormons and less than "valiant" Mormons go. Its lesser glory is evident by two things. The first is that this kingdom will be visited by Jesus but not by Heavenly Father. Secondly, everybody in this kingdom "will live separately and singly forever and ever" (Gospel Principles, p. 298).

The Telestial Kingdom

The lowest kingdom is the telestial kingdom. Here is where the great majority of people end up. Even though this is the lowest kingdom, it still has tremendous glory, being symbolized by a star.

> "The book (Doctrine and Covenants) explains clearly that the lowest glory to which man is assigned is so glorious as to be beyond the understanding of man. It is a doctrine fundamental in Mormonism that the meanest sinner, in the final judgment, will receive a glory which is beyond human understanding, which is so great that we are unable to describe it adequately." (John A. Widtsoe, quoted in *Doctrine and Covenants Student Manual*, p. 166)

One woman confided in me that, because of such statements, she, as a child, wasn't that concerned about following all the laws of Mormonism. She had been taught that the slums of heaven (the telestial kingdom) were much better than this life. If that was the case, she reasoned, why work so hard?

I thought that I would find more Mormons thinking along those lines. But that hasn't been the case. Most to whom I have spoken have been striving for the celestial kingdom. The only ones who weren't were "jack Mormons," that is, Mormons in name only. "Exaltation or bust" appears to be the motto of many.

One reason many Mormons might not be satisfied with the telestial kingdom is that people suffer hell before they enter it.

> Also in the spirit prison are those who rejected the gospel
> after it was preached to them on earth or in the spirit
> prison. These spirits suffer in a condition known as hell
> ... After suffering in full for their sins, they will be allowed
> to inherit the lowest degree of glory, which is the telestial
> kingdom. The hell in the spirit world will not continue
> forever. Even the spirits who have committed the
> greatest sins will have suffered sufficiently by the end of
> the Millennium (see Acts 2:25-27). They will then be
> resurrected. (*Gospel Principles*, pp. 292f.)

What constitutes hell is never explained. This quote makes clear, however, that Mormons don't believe that hell lasts forever. It lasts only for the millennium. (We will look at the LDS concept of the millennium in chapter five.)

Surprisingly then, they still talk about an eternal hell and eternal punishment. By that, however, they mean the punishment administered by an eternal god, not a punishment that lasts for all eternity. We speak of blessings that come from God as divine blessings; they speak of punishment that comes from God as eternal punishment.

> Eternal punishment is, thus, the kind of punishment
> imposed by God who is eternal, and those subject to it
> may suffer therefrom [sic] for either a short or a long
> period. After their buffetings and trials cause them to
> repent, they are freed from this type of eternal
> damnation. (McConkie, *Mormon Doctrine*, p. 236)

In addition to the hell a person experiences before entering the telestial kingdom, they also talk about the hell a person experiences in the telestial kingdom.

> "Of course, those who enter the telestial kingdom, and
> those who enter the terrestrial kingdom will have the
> eternal punishment which will come to them in knowing
> that they might, if they had kept the commandments of
> the Lord, have returned to his presence as his sons and

his daughters. This will be a torment to them, and in that sense it will be hell." (Joseph Fielding Smith, quoted in *The Life and Teachings of Jesus & His Apostles*, p. 66)

I have not figured out how they reconcile this torment with the great glory they say people will also experience in the telestial kingdom. But Mormons have commonly expressed both ideas to me and seem surprised that I see them as contradictory.

Conclusion

This journey from Mormon premortality to postmortality has been a long one. But it was a necessary one to take if we want to witness to Mormons in a loving manner. Essential to a loving witness is meeting people where they are, not where we are. This chapter has told you where Mormons are.

Key Concepts

Agency: The LDS belief that persons have the innate free will to choose the right.

Spirit Children: Mormons teach that everyone was procreated by Heavenly Father in preexistence.

Gospel: Mormonism, the LDS plan of salvation.

Preexistence: The LDS belief that all people existed as spirit children of God before they were born on this earth.

Worthiness: A key word in the daily practice of Mormonism. Mormons become worthy by obeying LDS laws and authorities.

Temple work: "Sacred" work done by worthy Mormons inside the temple. Most often refers to their work for the dead.

Vicarious work: Temple work done for the dead.

Endowment: The temple ceremony that serves as their formal introduction to the temple. During this ceremony they receive their sacred undergarments, their new name, and learn the secret handshakes that are essential for exaltation.

Baptism for the dead: Mormons believe that the living can be baptized for the dead. This can be done only in the temple.

Eternal marriage: Being married in the temple. Also called celestial marriage or sealing, it is essential for exaltation.

Spirit world: The place where spirits go after death. LDS spirits go to paradise; the spirits of non-Mormons go to spirit prison. LDS spirits do missionary work among those in spirit prison.

The three kingdoms of LDS heaven: celestial, terrestrial, telestial.

Damnation: Being stopped in your progression to godhood. It does not mean going to hell.

Hell: (1) The temporary punishment some suffer in spirit prison.

(2) The regret people in the telestial kingdom will experience.

CHAPTER THREE: KNOW THEIR PLAN- THEOLOGICALLY

After taking that trip from LDS premortality to postmortality, a Christian's mind swarms with questions. How do Mormons view sin? What role does Jesus play in Mormonism? How do they define grace, justification, salvation, and similar words? Let's address such questions by looking at the theological aspects of their plan of salvation.

Adam's Fall

We begin with their view of Adam's fall. The Book of Mormon states:

> And now, behold, if Adam had not transgressed he would not have fallen, but he would have remained in the garden of Eden. And all things which were created must have remained in the same state in which they were after they were created; and they must have remained forever, and had no end.
> And they would have had no children; wherefore they would have remained in a state of innocence, *having no joy*, for they knew no misery; doing no good, for they knew no sin.

> But behold, all things have been done in the wisdom of him who knoweth all things.

> *Adam fell that men might be: and men are, that they might have joy.* (2Nephi 2:22-25, emphasis added)

Another LDS scripture, the Pearl of Great Price, says:

> And in that day Adam blessed God and was filled, and began to prophesy concerning all the families of the earth, saying: *Blessed be the name of God, for because of my transgressions my eyes are opened, and in this life I shall have joy, and again in the flesh I shall see God.*

> And Eve, his wife, heard all these things and was glad, saying: Were it not for our transgression we never should have known good and evil, and the joy of our redemption, and the eternal life which God giveth unto all the obedient. (Moses 5:10,11, emphasis added)

Note that both passages state that the Fall resulted in mankind receiving joy. But in the biblical presentation of Adam's fall (Genesis 3), we see nothing but negative consequences. All other biblical references to the Fall are consistent with that.

How, then can Mormons view it positively? The reasoning they employ to reach that conclusion is very confusing to Christians. It hinges on the importance Mormonism attaches to bearing children. Note how both the above passages link procreation with the Fall. Mormons go so far as to equate mortality with the ability to have children.

> Created in the image of God and not yet mortal, they could not grow old and die. And they would have had no children nor experience the trials of life . . . The creation of Adam and Eve was a *paradisiacal creation,* one that required a significant change before they could fulfill the commandment to have children and thus provide earthly bodies for premortal spirit sons and daughters of God . . . The Fall of Adam (and Eve) constituted the *mortal creation* and brought about the required changes in their bodies, including the circulation of blood and other modifications as well. They were now able to have children. (Russell M. Nelson, *Ensign*, Nov. 1996, p. 33)

All dictionaries agree that the word mortal deals with dying, not with bringing new life into the world. In the sense of dying, Adam's fall did make man mortal. "Therefore, just as sin entered the world through one man, and death through sin, and in this way death came to all men . . ." (Romans 5:12). Death, not the capacity to have children, is the result of Adam's fall.

Mormons would agree that the Fall introduced death into the world, but that is not what they emphasize. They stress that becoming mortal *included* the capacity to have children. That view, however, finds no support in dictionaries or the Bible. No dictionaries hint at it; the Bible excludes it. From the moment they were created, Adam and Eve were designated as "man and woman" and "male and female." Together they were called "man" in the sense of "human." *Before they fell,* God told them to be fruitful and multiply. These facts demonstrate that God *created* them capable of bearing children.

In spite of that, Mormons cling to their unique definition of mortality. It allows them to overlook the Fall's negative aspects and view it in a positive way. As we have already seen, the procreating of children, both physically and spiritually, lies at the very heart of Mormonism. Anything, therefore, that aids mankind in fulfilling that function is essentially good.

Consequently Mormons *commend* rather than *condemn* Adam and Eve. They contend that Adam and Eve wisely used their agency to obey God's command to be fruitful and multiply.

> Adam found himself in a position that made it impossible for him to obey both of the specific commandments given by the Lord. He and his wife had been commanded to multiply and replenish the earth. Adam had not yet fallen to the state of mortality, but Eve already had; and in such dissimilar constitutions the two could not remain together, and therefore could not fulfill the divine requirement as to procreation. On the other hand, Adam would be disobeying another commandment by yielding to Eve's request. He deliberately and wisely decided to stand by the first and greater commandment and, therefore, with understanding of the nature of his act, he also partook of the fruit that grew on the tree of knowledge. (Talmage, *The Articles of Faith,* p. 65)

Some people believe that Adam and Eve committed a serious sin when they ate of the tree of knowledge of good and evil. However, latter-day scriptures help us understand that their fall was a necessary step in the plan of life and *a great blessing to all of us.* Because of the fall, we are blessed with physical bodies, the right to choose between good and evil, and the opportunity to gain eternal life. (*Gospel Principles*, p. 33, emphasis added)

"I do not look upon Adam's action as a sin. I think it was a deliberate act of free agency. He chose to do that which had to be done to further the purposes of God. The consequences of his act made necessary the atonement of the Redeemer." (Marion G. Rommey, quoted in *Sharing the Gospel*, p. 69)

As these statements demonstrate, Mormons go so far as to say that Adam and Eve did not sin and that the Fall was a necessary part of God's plan of salvation. "Adam and Eve didn't catch heaven by surprise. The Fall and Redemption had always been part of the plan" (*Ensign*, Jan. 1990, p. 22). True, Adam's fall did not catch God by surprise, since he is all-knowing. But his foreknowledge of an event doesn't mean he planned it. "When tempted, no one should say, 'God is tempting me.' For God cannot be tempted by evil, *nor does he tempt anyone*" (James 1:13, emphasis added). Mormons, however, believe that God specifically chose Adam and Eve for this difficult task of falling.

Adam and Eve were chosen to be the first people to live on the earth [see Moses 1:34]. Their part in the Father's plan was to bring mortality into the world. . . Adam and Eve were among our Father's noblest children. (*Gospel Principles*, p. 31)

In light of such statements, we see that it is not an exaggeration to characterize the LDS teaching of Adam's fall as "a fall upward."

To summarize, Mormons use the following line of reasoning to come to their conclusion that the Fall was a blessing:
1. The Fall made man mortal.
2. One major characteristic of being mortal is the capacity to

have children.

3. God's spirit children need bodies of progress, therefore, it is essential that mankind has the capacity to have children.

4. Adam's fall, by giving mankind this capacity, was a blessing.

Totally ignored is the biblical view (Romans 5:12) that the Fall constitutes the greatest tragedy in human history.

Sin

Seeing how Mormons deal with Adam's sin prepares us for how they handle sin in general. In a word, they downplay it. The word "sin" doesn't surface much in their literature or conversations. Instead they talk about mistakes, blunders, bad judgment calls, inadequacies, bad habits, imperfections and the like.

> Jesus knew the destructive influence of bad habits when he said: ". . . if thy eye offend the, pluck it out, if thy right hand offend thee, cut it off" [sic, Matthew 5:29,30]. (*Latter-day Trumpet*, Jan. 1988, "Today I Begin A New Life")

> Adam's and Eve's transgression was not really a wrongful act of "sin" as we usually use the term . . . Like Adam and Eve we make many judgment-call choices that inflict pain . . . Think of unkind words and forgotten promises among family members. Such incidents can lead to ugly consequences, but not all of them are the result of conscious sin.(*Ensign*, April 1990, p. 9)

> The Savior's atonement is thus portrayed as the healing power not only for sin, but also for carelessness, inadequacy, and all mortal bitterness. The Atonement is not just for sinners. (*Ensign*, April 1990, p. 7)

Mortal bitterness is not considered sinful; unkind words are nothing but bad judgment calls. Matthew 5:29,30 applies to bad habits. Even a transgression is not a sin.

Their interpretation of certain Bible stories also reveals this downplaying of sin. Not only Adam has his sin explained away. In

Numbers 20 we read that God did not allow Moses to enter the Promised Land because Moses had disobeyed him. Following is Mormonism's explanation of this incident.

> Did Moses really sin against the Lord? . . . Was this one error enough to cancel out years of great faith, obedience, and devotion?

> At least two other Old Testament passages indicate that Moses did sin in striking the rock at Meribah [see Numbers 27:12-14; Deuteronomy 32:51-52]. Other passages, however, help to clarify the matter. Deuteronomy 3:26 and 4:21 indicate that the Lord told Moses that the reason he could not enter the promised land was that the Lord was angry with him "*for your sakes.*" This statement could imply that there were reasons other than the error of Moses for the prohibition. Two other facts strengthen this supposition. First, both Moses and the higher priesthood were taken from Israel *because of the people's unworthiness, not Moses'* [see D&C 84:23-25]. Second, Moses was translated when his mortal ministry was finished [see Alma 45:19]. In other words, Moses was privileged to enter a land of promise far greater than the land of Canaan. He had finished his calling in mortality, and a new leader was to take Israel into the promised land. And , Moses was translated— hardly a punishment for sinning against God. (*Old Testament Manual Religion* 301, p. 208)

Note how the seriousness of sin is neutralized by this explanation. Moses's sin becomes Moses's error. Instead of being punished, he is rewarded. We are left with the impression that God was well-pleased with Moses, rather than angry.

Similarly, the Mormons excuse Peter's denial of Jesus.

> "Remember that Peter never denied the divinity of Christ. He only denied his association or acquaintance with the Christ, which is quite a different matter. . ."

"Is it possible that there might have been some other reason for Peter's triple denial? Could he have felt that circumstances justified expediency? When he bore a strong testimony in Caesarea Philippi, he had been told that 'they should tell no man that he was Jesus the Christ.' " (Spencer W. Kimball, quoted in *The Life and Teachings of Jesus & His Apostles*, p. 489)

After reading such interpretations, we are not surprised to see Mormons applying the same reasoning to themselves. They severely restrict what constitutes a sin. First, they say people have to know what they are doing before they can sin.

Knowledge of good and evil is an essential element in the commission of sin, and our first parents did not have this knowledge until after they had partaken of the fruit of the tree of knowledge of good and evil. (*Mormon Doctrine*, p. 804)

"Sin is the transgression of divine law, as made known through the conscience or by revelation. A man sins when he violates his conscience, going contrary to light and knowledge—not the light and knowledge that has come to his neighbor, but that which has come to himself. He sins when he does the opposite of what he knows to be right. Up to that point he only blunders. One may suffer painful consequences for only blundering, but he cannot commit sin unless he knows better than to do the thing in which the sin consists. One must have a conscience before he can violate it." (Whitney, quoted in *The Life and Teachings of Jesus & His Apostles*, p. 410)

Combining statements like these with their belief that people are born innately good leads to the Mormons' conviction that children are innocent until they reach accountability at the age of eight.

The Bible, however, teaches that all people, regardless of age, are by nature thoroughly sinful. In the last chapter, we already looked at God's blanket condemnation of mankind found in Romans 3:10-12. There no one is exempt. Ephesians 2;3 says, "We were by nature objects of wrath." We are by nature so sinful that "all of us have become like one who is unclean, and all our righteous acts are like filthy rags" (Isaiah 64:6). David's confession applies to us all: "Surely I was sinful at birth, sinful from the time my mother conceived me" (Psalm 51:5).

Furthermore, the Bible does not make awareness of wrongdoing a condition to determine sinfulness. Paul confesses about himself:

> Even though I was once a blasphemer and a persecutor and a violent man, I was shown mercy because *I acted in ignorance* and unbelief . . . Here is a trustworthy saying that deserves full acceptance: Christ Jesus came into the world to save *sinners—of whom I am the worst.* (1 Timothy 1:13,15, emphasis added)

Paul was shown mercy, but his sin was not excused away. Clearly, sin is sin regardless of a person's awareness of it. That is why David prays: "Who can discern his errors? Forgive my hidden faults" (Psalm 19:12).

Mormonism minimizes sinfulness in more ways than the test of awareness. It also waters down the sinfulness of thoughts and desires.

> It is not that our desires are necessarily evil in and of themselves, but it is our responsibility to bridle our own passions lest they devolve to lusts which will invariably lead to sin. (*The Life and Teachings of Jesus & His Apostles*, p. 411)

We overstate the matter if we say that Mormons never believe a person's thoughts are sinful. For them to consider it a sin, however, a thought needs to consume a person. As we saw above, moral bitterness, even unkind words, are not considered sinful.

One of their apostles, James E. Talmage, offers an interesting insight into their view of sin:

> Sin is any condition, whether omission of things required or in commission of acts forbidden, that tends to prevent or hinder the development of the human soul. (*The Articles of Faith*, p. 57)

Note how he does not mention sin angering or even displeasing God. In fact, none of the above passages mention that. To a Mormon, sin is evil because of what it does to them, not because of what it does to God. Even when it comes to sin, we see how entirely man-centered Mormonism is.

By now you might be wondering what is sinful in their sight. Although there are more than five, I like to talk about the five major sins of Mormonism. Murder and apostasy head the list. In regard to murder, we read: "Thou shalt not kill; and he that kills shall not have forgiveness in this world, nor in the world to come" (D&C 42:18). In line with that is this comment on Acts 2:29-34:

> A murderer, for instance, one that sheds innocent blood, cannot have forgiveness. David sought repentance at the hand of God carefully with tears, for the murder of Uriah; but he could only get it through hell: he got a promise that his soul should not be left in hell. (*The Life and Teachings of Jesus & His Apostles*, p. 244)

McConkie explains:

> "No *murderer* hath eternal life abiding in him" [1 John 3:15]. He cannot join the Church by baptism; he is outside the pail of redeeming grace . . . Murderers are forgiven eventually but only in the sense that all sins are forgiven except the sin against the Holy Ghost; they are not forgiven in the sense that celestial salvation is made available to them. (*Mormon Doctrine*, p. 520)

What McConkie is referring to when he says murderers will be forgiven eventually is the LDS belief that they will end up in the telestial kingdom. One thing that helps a murderer atone for his sin is by having his own blood shed. For that reason Utah still gives murderers the option of being executed by firing squad.

Apostates, however, are even worse off. Apostasy is the worst sin Mormons can commit. They identify it with the sin against the Holy Ghost. It is the only thing that qualifies a person as a son of perdition. But as we saw in the last chapter, much confusion exists in this area. The church officially includes many apostates in this group while the average Mormon doesn't. Whether or not they think an apostate becomes a son of perdition, however, all would agree that apostasy is the worst sin of all.

> But whoso breaketh this covenant after he hath received it, and altogether turneth therefrom, shall not have forgiveness of sins in this world nor in the worlds to come. (D&C 84:41)

This is one reason why it is often hard for people to leave the LDS church. It is extremely difficult for them not to see themselves as apostates. And when they think of themselves in that way, often a tinge of doubt persists that, by leaving, they have become sons of perdition.

Sexual immorality trails closely behind murder and apostasy in seriousness.

> Unchastity is next to murder in seriousness. (*Gospel Principles*, p. 251)

> Loss of virtue is too great a price to pay even for the preservation of one's life—better dead clean, than alive unclean. Many is the faithful Latter-day Saint parent who has sent a son or a daughter on a mission or otherwise out into the world with the direction: "I would rather have you come back in a pine box with your virtue than return alive without it." (McConkie, *Mormon Doctrine*, p. 124)

In spite of such strong statements, many Mormons regard the breaking of the Word of Wisdom as a more serious sin than sexual impurity. Think back to that survey of LDS high school students mentioned in the last chapter. They rated the breaking of the Word of Wisdom as the worst sin while ranking chastity fifth. The same point is stressed in a hypothetical conversation between a Mormon bishop and a young woman who had engaged in premarital sex.

> In deep meditation a bishop sat across his office desk listening to a seventeen-year-old girl explain how she "just couldn't see that the natural feelings God gave me could be so wrong." . . .

> "Have you any problem with the Word of Wisdom? Do you smoke or drink?"

Her response was immediate. "Oh no, Bishop, I wouldn't do that! That's against our religion. . . ."

"Don't you see? In your own mind, you have placed your sinful behavior below that of breaking the Word of Wisdom." (*Achieving a Celestial Marriage*, p. 20)

The fifth major sin is the refusal to bear children. "It is contradictory to this covenant to prevent the birth of children if the parents are in good health." (Elder J. Ballard Washburn, *Ensign*, May 1995, p. 12) A few years ago the condemnation was even stronger. For example, the 1979 edition of Gospel Principles said: "Bearing children is one of the greatest of all blessings. To refuse to do so is a serious sin." (p. 229) The 1995 edition drops the second sentence. But many Mormons still take this very seriously. One LDS woman told her doctor after being warned about the dangers of having any more children: "It would be an honor to die in childbearing."

For the same reason abortion is a grave sin.

One of the most evil myths of our day is that a woman who has joined hands with God in creation can destroy that creation because she claims the right to control her own body. Since the life within her is not her own, how can she justify its termination and deflect that life from an earth which it may never inherit. (*Achieving A Celestial Marriage*, p. 144)

Apostasy, murder, sexual immorality, breaking the Word of Wisdom, and refusing to bear children (including abortion) are the five major sins of Mormonism. Mormons who are obedient in these areas often feel quite good about themselves. Such Mormons view the attainment of perfection as a heavy but manageable burden. Occasionally they chafe under it, but in the whole, they are content to live with it. They don't think they're perfect, but neither do they consider themselves as being in any major trouble. Some have even given me the impression that they would not describe themselves as sinners.

But not all are like that. Nearly as many are miserable because of Mormonism. For example, one man gets up in the middle of the night to sneak a cup of coffee because he is afraid of even his family finding out.

Another Mormon has doubts about Mormonism but is terrified to voice them out of fear of being labeled an apostate. An LDS couple resents having so many children but continues to have more because they don't want to sin. In such cases, we don't see self-righteous Mormons; we see stressed-out ones. We see people who need to hear about Jesus' love and forgiveness.

Atonement and Salvation

Unfortunately, that is not what they will hear from their church. With such a diluted view of sin, it is not surprising to see Mormonism diminishing the role Jesus played in salvation. Mormons, however, would deny that vehemently. They would point to the fact that they are members of the Church of *Jesus Christ* of Latter-day Saints. They would talk about how they revere Jesus; how they, more that many churches, proclaim his divinity; how their lives are dedicated to glorifying him. In all this they would be completely sincere.

In spite of that, the judgment stands that Mormonism minimizes Jesus. Especially revealing is their view of Christ's atonement:

> The atonement of Jesus Christ redeems all mankind from the fall of Adam and causes all to be answerable for their own manner of life. (*LDS Bible Dictionary*, p. 617)

> He was to be born into mortality to suffer, to bleed, and to die.

> Why? That each of us might ultimately be one (atoned) with God after our mortal experience, that we might be able to live with Him once again, as we did as spirit beings before our birth. His atonement would allow our resurrection from the dead. (Russell M. Nelson, *Ensign*, Aug. 1991, p. 7)

> In some magnificent way, which we do not understand, Jesus of Nazareth, thought by many only to be the carpenter's son, opened the door of immortality for all to walk through. He paid the price for us to rise from the grave. Through His own willful sacrifice—the infinite and eternal atonement—we all shall live again. (*Church*

News, March 18, 1989, p. 16)

As these statements reveal, Mormons apply Jesus' atonement mainly to Adam's fall. They believe his suffering wiped out its effect, namely, permanent *physical death.* Because of Jesus' atonement, all people will be resurrected.

Being resurrected is extremely important to Mormons. It is so important because having a body is so important. Especially noteworthy is their belief that without resurrected bodies they could not become gods because they could not propagate spirit children. In fact, the Book of Mormon takes it one step further. It states that without the resurrection everyone would have become devils.

> O the wisdom of God, his mercy and grace! For behold, if the flesh should rise no more our spirits must become subject to that angel who fell from before the presence of the Eternal God, and became the devil, to rise no more.

> And our spirits must have become like unto him, and we become devils, angels to a devil, to be shut out from the presence of our God, and to remain with the father of lies, in misery, like unto himself. (2 Nephi 9:8-9)

Seeing how Mormons limit Jesus' atonement to his conquering physical death for us is a key insight into understanding Mormonism. According to Mormonism, the *main role Jesus played in the plan of salvation was making it possible for all to be resurrected.* Once we grasp that, much of what they say about Jesus falls into place. But because Jesus' role is never stated in exactly this way, not everybody agrees with this assessment. Its correctness, however, can easily be demonstrated.

One proof of its validity is that when they talk about what Jesus has done for them, they usually talk about his atonement. Or they speak about redemption which, in Mormonese, is synonymous with atonement. Both describe Jesus' conquering physical death. Rarely do they talk about being justified or reconciled. They seldom mention grace. Their stress on the atonement, especially when that is contrasted with their neglect of terms such as grace, supports the validity of the above observation.

One interesting sidelight to this discussion of the atonement is how Mormonism emphasizes Jesus' sufferings in the Garden of

Gethsemane over his crucifixion.

> Where and under what circumstances was the atoning
> sacrifice of the Son of God made? Was it on the Cross of
> Calvary or in the Garden of Gethsemane? It is the Cross
> of Christ that most Christians look to when centering
> their attention upon the infinite and eternal atonement.
> And certainly the sacrifice of our Lord was completed
> when he was lifted up by men; also, that part of his life
> and suffering is more dramatic and, perhaps, more soul
> stirring. But in reality the pain and suffering, the
> triumph and grandeur, of the atonement took place
> primarily in Gethsemane . . . Many have been crucified
> and the torment and pain is extreme. But only one, and
> he the Man who had God as his Father, has bowed
> beneath the burden of grief and sorrow that lay upon him
> in that awful night. (*The Life and Teachings of Jesus &
> His Apostles*, p. 172)

This is one reason why LDS meetinghouses never contain crosses. Neither do Mormons wear crosses as jewelry or display them in their homes. They regard them as objects of death rather than as symbols of Christ's victory. It borders on understatement to say that crosses evoke strong negative emotions in them.

They also misunderstand the Christian's use of crosses. Some Mormons feel that Christians use them as good luck charms, similar to a rabbit's foot. Others think that Christians worship the cross. "Latter-day Saints respect the cross, but choose not to make it an object of veneration." (Scharffs, *The Truth About the Godmakers*, p. 18).

Their different feelings about the cross seem somehow to mirror their interpretation of Jesus' role. The LDS definition of salvation also supports the observation that his main role in their plan of salvation was making it possible for all to be resurrected.

> Unconditional or general salvation, that which comes by
> grace alone without obedience to gospel law, consists in
> the mere fact of being resurrected. (McConkie, *Mormon
> Doctrine*, p. 669)

> SALVATION: Inseparable connection of body and spirit

brought about through the Savior's atonement and resurrection; eternal life. (*Gospel Principles*, p. 380)

Note how both these definitions stress our resurrection. It is true that the definition in *Gospel Principles* mentions eternal life. It is also true that McConkie goes on to equate *conditional* salvation with going to the celestial kingdom. To the average Mormon, however, salvation equals resurrection.

It seems that whenever the subject of being saved by grace surfaces, many Latter-day Saints become defensive and eagerly move to one of two conclusions: (1) the word salvation refers only to resurrection, to deliverance from the grave; or (2) exaltation or eternal life is something which must be wholly merited or *earned*. (Millet, *By Grace Are We Saved*, vii)

My own experiences have confirmed this. When I first started witnessing to Mormons, I often became frustrated because they always agreed that they were saved freely through the work of Jesus. I knew enough to know that they didn't mean what I meant by that. Only after I discovered that they considered salvation equivalent to resurrection did I make progress talking with them. Those experiences convinced me that most Mormons do not think of anything but resurrection when they hear the word salvation.

Knowing this has not only improved my witness to them but also my attitude towards them. Previous to knowing this, I would conclude that they were being deliberately deceptive when they would agree with me. I assumed they knew what I meant but didn't want to admit that they believed differently. Although I feel that occasionally this is still the case, I am now convinced that many don't know that Christians equate salvation with eternal life. And why should they? That's not what they're taught. Consider the following excerpt from a book for young children.

Jesus was the first to be resurrected and because of him, all the people on the earth will someday be resurrected. That is why we call him "the Savior." He saved the world from death. He is the resurrection and the life. (Joyce B. Maughan, *Talks for Tots*, p. 113)

Here we see no mention of heaven or eternal life. Neither does it talk about salvation from sin. They believe Jesus saved them only from physical death. This illustrates how desperately Mormons need someone to tell them all that Jesus has done for them.

Jesus as Creditor

The best single source I have found that demonstrates this need is a parable from *Gospel Principles*. It casts Heavenly Father in the role of man's creditor and Jesus as the mediator. It is lengthy, but it is well worth quoting in full.

> Elder Boyd K. Packer of the Council of the twelve gave the following illustration to show how Christ's atonement makes it possible to be saved from sin *if* we do our part. Let me tell you a story—a parable.
>
> There once was a man who wanted something very much. It seemed more important than anything else in his life. In order for him to have his desire, he incurred a great debt.
>
> He had been warned about going into that much debt, and particularly about his creditor. But it seemed so important for him to do what he wanted to and to have what he wanted right now. He was sure he could pay for it later.
>
> So he signed a contract. He would pay it off sometime along the way. He didn't worry too much about it, for the due day seemed such a long time away. He had what he wanted now, and that was what seemed important.
>
> The creditor was always somewhere in the back of his mind, and he made token payments now and again, thinking somehow that the day of reckoning really would never come.
>
> But as it always does, the day came, and the contract fell due. The debt had not been fully paid. His creditor

appeared and demanded payment in full.

Only then did he realize that his creditor not only had the power to repossess all that he owned, but the power to cast him into prison as well.

"I cannot pay you, for I have not the power to do so," he confessed.

"Then," said the creditor, "we will exercise the contract, take your possessions and you shall go to prison. You agreed to that. It was your choice. You signed the contract, and now it must be enforced."

"Can you not extend the time or forgive the debt?" The debtor begged. "Arrange some way for me to keep what I have and not go to prison. Surely you believe in mercy? Will you not show mercy?"

The creditor replied, "Mercy is always so one-sided. It would serve only you. If I show mercy to you, it will leave me unpaid. It is justice I demand. Do you believe in justice?"

"I believed in justice when I signed the contract," the debtor said. "It was on my side then, for I thought it would protect me. I did not need mercy then, nor think I should need it ever. Justice, I thought, would serve both of us equally as well."

"It is justice that demands that you pay the contract or suffer the penalty," the creditor replied. "That is the law. You have agreed to it and that is the way it must be. Mercy cannot rob justice."

There they were. One meting out justice, the other pleading for mercy. Neither could prevail except at the expense of the other.

"If you do not forgive the debt there will be no mercy," the debtor pleaded.

"If I do, there will be no justice," was the reply.

Both laws, it seemed, could not be served. They are two eternal ideals that appear to contradict one another. Is there no way for justice to be fully served, and mercy also?

There is a way! The law of justice can be fully satisfied and mercy can be fully extended—but it takes someone else. And so it happened this time.

The debtor had a friend. He came to help. He knew the debtor well. He knew him to be shortsighted. He thought him foolish to have gotten himself into such a predicament. Nevertheless, he wanted to help because he loved him. He stepped between them, faced the creditor, and made this offer.

"I will pay the debt if you will free the debtor from his contract so that he may keep his possessions and not go to prison."

As the creditor was pondering the offer, the mediator added, "You demanded justice. Though he cannot pay you, I will do so. You will have been justly dealt with and can ask no more. It would not be just."

And so the creditor agreed.

The mediator turned then to the debtor. "If I pay your debt, will you accept me as your creditor?"

"Oh yes, yes," cried the debtor. "You saved me from prison and show mercy to me."

"Then," said the benefactor, "you will pay the debt to me and I will set the terms. It will not be easy, but it will be possible. I will provide a way. You need not go to prison."

And so it was that the creditor was paid in full. He had

been justly dealt with. No contract had been broken.

The debtor, in turn, had been extended mercy. Both laws stood fulfilled. Because there was a mediator, justice had claimed its full share, and mercy was satisfied. (pp.75-77)

A number of things in this parable deserve our study. One such thing is its portrayal of God the Father. We, however, want to concentrate on how it explains Jesus' work on our behalf. I call your attention especially to the following paragraphs.

The mediator turned then to the debtor. "If I pay your debt, will you accept me as your creditor?"

"Oh yes, yes," cried the debtor. "You saved me from prison and show mercy to me."

"Then," said the benefactor, "you will pay the debt to me and I will set the terms. It will not be easy, but it will be possible. I will provide a way. You need not go to prison."

According to this, what Jesus did for us was assume our loan, refinance it, and spread out the payments! Jesus our mediator becomes Jesus our *creditor*! We now owe him, but because he conquered death for us, we now have all eternity to pay him back. Still, pay him back we must.

Mormons consider this a great act of love on Jesus' part. Without his assuming the role of creditor, they believe they wouldn't have any chance of being exalted. Therefore, they can, with all sincerity, call him their Savior.

This parable is not an isolated example of how Mormonism pictures Jesus' work. The following illustration is similar:

"So, the effect of Adam's transgression was to place all of us in the pit with him. Then the Savior comes along, not subject to that pit, and lowers the ladder. He comes down into the pit and makes it possible for us to use the ladder to escape." (Joseph Smith, quoted in *Sharing the Gospel*,

p. 71)

The Bible, however, doesn't say God just made it possible for us to escape from the pit. It tells us that he took us out of the pit.

> For he has rescued us from the dominion of darkness and brought us into the kingdom of the Son he loves, in whom we have redemption, the forgiveness of sins. (Colossians 1:13,14)

It does not say either that Jesus refinanced our loan. It joyfully proclaims that he paid it in full and tore up the note.

> He forgave us all our sins, having canceled the written code, with its regulations, that was against us and that stood opposed to us; he took it away, nailing it to the cross. (Colossians 2:13,14)

Jesus as Example

We now have seen two ways Mormons believe Jesus has helped them: (1) he paid for their sin, but they must pay him back; and (2) he overcame death for them (atonement), thus buying more time for them to pay their debt.

The third way they feel Jesus has helped them is by being their example.

> The Sermon on the Mount is the Lord's blueprint for perfection. Of this sermon Elder Harold B. Lee said:

> "Christ came not only into the world to make an atonement for the sins of mankind but to set an example before the world of the standard of perfection of God's law and of obedience to the Father. In his Sermon on the Mount the Master has given us somewhat of a revelation of his own character, which was perfect, or what might be said to be 'an autobiography, every syllable of which he had written down in deeds,' and in so doing has given us a blueprint for our own lives." (*The Life and Teachings of Jesus & His Apostles*, p. 57)

"But notwithstanding all this, he (Jesus) kept the law of God, ans remained without sin, showing thereby that it is in the power of man to keep the law and remain also without sin; and also, that by him a righteous judgment might come upon all flesh, and that all who walk not in the law of God may justly be condemned by the law, and have no excuse for their sins." (Joseph Smith, quoted in *Mormon Doctrine*, p. 320)

Or, consider the following excerpt from a children's Christmas poem. Observe especially the reason for the angels' joyful song.

> God sent us this loving baby
> From his home in heaven above.
> Christ came down to show all people
> How to help and how to love.
>
> This is why the angels bright
> Sang for joy that Christmas night.
> (Maughan, *Talks for Tots*, p. 120)

Put yourself in a Mormon's place. Picture yourself receiving such instruction from little on up. Imagine having Jesus presented mainly as an example for you to follow. Envision yourself trying to walk in his footsteps as you are told that it is entirely possible. That's not a pretty picture. But that is the picture of a Mormon's life.

The Divinity of Jesus

In spite of all this evidence to the contrary, Mormons still object vehemently to any suggestion that they have minimized Jesus in any way. The main reason they do that is simply that they have never seen the true Jesus. In addition, they often defend themselves by pointing to church statements affirming his deity. They point out that they teach that Jesus is Jehovah. (They identify the Father with Elohim.) In fact, stating that Jesus is divine is a main part of their testimony.

> The third message is the testimony of our Lord and Savior. We declare to the world that Jesus is the Christ. We abhor the doctrine that He is a myth or a creation of

conspiring men in the world. We denounce the idea that He was just a great teacher. We testify of the divinity of Jesus of Nazareth, that He is the Son of God, the Savior of the world. (Elder L. Tom Perry, *Ensign*, May 1989, p. 14)

Such statements, no matter how good they sound, do not mean that Mormons consider Jesus as being equal with the Father. According to the Bible, however, seeing Jesus as the Father's equal is essential.

Moreover, the Father judges no one, but has entrusted all judgment to the Son, that all may honor the Son *just as* they honor the Father. He who does not honor the Son does not honor the Father, who sent him. (John 5:22,23, emphasis added)

Mormons don't honor Jesus *just as* they do the Father. They teach that he was the Father's first spirit child who had already progressed to godhood in preexistence.

The first spirit born to our heavenly parents was Jesus Christ [see D&C 93:21]. (*Gospel Principles*, p. 11)

He was the birthright son, and he retained that birthright by his strict obedience. Through the aeons and ages of premortality, he advanced and progressed until, as Abraham described, he stood as one "like unto God" [Abr. 3:24]. "Our Savior was a God before he was born into this world," wrote President Joseph Fielding Smith, "and he brought with him that same status when he came here. He was as much a God when he was born into the world as he was before" [Doctrine of Salvation 1:39]. In that premortal estate, Jesus was, under the Father, the Creator and Redeemer of the Father's worlds. (*The Life and Teachings of Jesus & His Apostles*, p. 15)

It is interesting that Mormons believe Jesus attained godhood *before* he came to earth and received a body. This contradicts the statement cited in the last chapter which declares that an essential part of progressing to godhood is the attaining of a physical body. I have asked

86

numerous Mormons to explain this contradiction. Their answer has always been the same: "I have never thought about that." That sounds evasive, but for many of them, it is the truth. They truly never have thought about it.

The same problem exists with the Holy Ghost. They believe the Holy Ghost is a god although he doesn't have a physical body. They refer to him as a "personage of spirit."

In keeping with these beliefs, they reject the teaching of the Trinity. To support their rejection, they uniquely interpret the biblical passages which state there is only one God. They say such passages mean there is only one god *for this world*, namely, the Father. Furthermore they interpret the passages that talk about the unity of the Father and Son as referring only to a unity of purpose. Many Christians don't realize that Mormons reject the Trinity since they do talk about the *godhead* of Father, Son, and Holy Ghost. Their first Article of Faith says: "We believe in God, the Eternal Father, and in His Son, Jesus Christ, and in the Holy Ghost." But the fact that their godhead is vastly different from the historic Christian belief of the Trinity is apparent from statements like the following:

> And virtually all the millions of apostate Christendom have abased themselves before the mythical throne of a mythical Christ whom they vainly suppose to be a spirit essence who is incorporeal, uncreated, immaterial, and three-in-one with the Father and the Holy Spirit. (McConkie, *Mormon Doctrine*, p. 269)

The Incarnation

Not only do they consider Jesus the Father's literal spirit child, they also think he is the Father's literal physical child. They describe his conception as a physical act between Heavenly Father and Mary. That is why they can call Jesus the only-begotten Son of God. They believe he is the Father's only *physical* child.

> She [was] . . . about to give birth to a half-Deity. No other man in the history of this world of ours has ever had such an ancestry—God the Father on the one hand and May the Virgin on the other . . . He lived in a lowly home, the only man born to this earth half Divine and half-mortal.

(The Life and Teachings of Jesus & His Apostles, p. 10)

God was the Father of his fleshly tabernacle, and Mary—a mortal woman and a virgin—was His mother. He is therefore, the only person born who rightfully deserved the title "the Only Begotten Son of God." (Ezra Taft Benson, *Ensign*, April 1991, p. 2)

"We believe that he came into the world, born of Mary, literally and actually, as we are born of our mothers: that he came into the world, born of God the Eternal Father, the Almighty Elohim, literally and actually, as we are born of our earthly fathers." (McConkie, quoted in *Sharing the Gospel Manual*, p. 74)

This teaching has received abundant negative publicity over the years. In fairness, however, it needs to be pointed out that this coincides with everything Mormons believe. Many of them do not find this literal union between Mary and Heavenly Father a strange or repulsive idea. The exception would be new members who had been raised in a Christian setting. Many of them are shocked when they are told this particular teaching.

Jesus and Man in Partnership

As has been amply demonstrated, Jesus' role in the LDS plan of salvation can best be summed up as that of a big brother or a strong partner. He had his part; we have our part. This idea of partnership, especially its stress on man's responsibility, permeates LDS literature.

When he became our Savior, he did his part to help us return to our heavenly home. It is now up to each of us to do our part and become worthy of exaltation. (*Gospel Principles*, p. 19)

An outstanding doctrine of the Church is that each individual carries the responsibility to work out his own salvation, and salvation is a process of gradual development. (*The Life and Teachings of Jesus & His Apostles*, p. 361)

These blessings are not free gifts. Except for the free gift of immortality . . . all rewards gained in the eternal worlds must be earned. That perfection sought by the saints is both temporal and spiritual and comes only as a result of full obedience. (McConkie, *Mormon Doctrine*, p. 641)

Even small children are told this.

The Lord has told us how we may get to heaven. We must obey all the commandments of God. We can be sure that only those who live the commandments of God will ever see heaven.

["Heaven" in this story refers to exaltation in the kingdom of God, which is the goal of Latter-day Saints.] (Maughan, *Talks for Tots*, p. 85)

After reading statement after statement sounding this same theme, one begins to wonder if there is a partnership at all, or if man has to do everything. Hugh W. Pinnock clearly left that impression at a general conference when he stated: "Each of us must stand before our Redeemer *alone* and account for what we have done" (*Ensign*, May 1989, p. 10, emphasis in the original). That impression is strengthened as we now look at the Mormons' view of forgiveness, grace, and related topics.

Grace

Grace, according to the Bible, is God's love that is not conditioned on anything we do. Entirely exclusive of who we are and of what we do, God loves us. We do not merit or deserve it. God loves the unlovable. Grace is God's unconditional, undeserved, unfathomable love for sinful mankind. Solely because of grace are we saved. "For it is by grace you have been saved, through faith—and this not from yourselves, it is the gift of God—not by works, so that no one can boast" (Ephesians 2:8,9).

In sharp contrast stands this passage from the Book of Mormon: "for we know that it is by grace that we are saved, after all we can do" (2 Nephi 25:23). This is one of a handful of passages from the Book of Mormon that many Mormons know by memory. They especially stress the last phrase, "after all we can do." Typical is an article in the April 1990 *Ensign.* Although the subject of the article is Jesus' atonement, the author refers to the phrase "after all we can do" no fewer that eight times. For example, he writes:

> Our reluctance to stress the doctrine of grace is understandable. Nephi wrote, "For we know that it is by grace that we are saved, *after all we can do*" [2 Ne. 25:23; italics added]. A constant public emphasis on grace might encourage some people to ignore the crucial "all we can do" in that two-part process. (p. 8)

As the author states, Mormons are reluctant to talk about grace—so much so that most Mormons feel quite lost talking about it. A promotional blurb on the jacket of an LDS book states:

> What is the grace of God, and what is its significance for Latter-day Saints? This book examines that crucial question as it explains one of the least-understood doctrines. (Millet, *By Grace Are We Saved*)

Ignoring grace altogether or adding the phrase "after all we can do" are not the only ways Mormonism has drained it of its beauty. Instead of grace being a wonderful attribute of God, they have changed it into a power God gives them to save themselves.

> The main idea of the word is divine means of help or strength, given through the bounteous mercy and love of Jesus Christ . . . This grace is an enabling power that allows men and women to lay hold on eternal life and exaltation after they have expended their own best efforts. (*LDS Bible Dictionary*, p. 697)

> In short, *grace* refers to the gifts and powers of God by which men can be brought to perfection. To say that Jesus and all other men come to a fulness by moving from grace to grace or from gift to gift means simply that through obedience more and more power is given by the Father until they receive a fulness of his power. (*Doctrine and Covenants Student Manual*, p. 218)

As these statements illustrate, also in their view of grace, the idea of partnership between God and man occupies the foreground. The biblical doctrine that salvation by grace entirely excludes man's work is pushed completely out of the picture.

> Divine grace is needed by every soul in consequence of the fall of Adam and also because of man's weaknesses and shortcomings. However, grace cannot suffice without total effort on the part of the recipient. (*LDS Bible Dictionary*, p. 697)

> Therefore, acting alone, the grace of Christ is not *sufficient* for salvation. The works of man—the ordinances of salvation, the deeds of service and acts of charity and mercy—are *necessary* for salvation. (Millet, *By Grace Are We Saved*, p. 70)

> President Harold B. Lee wisely taught: "Spiritual certainty that is necessary to salvation must be *preceded* by a maximum of individual effort. Grace or the free gift of the Lord's atoning power, must be *preceded* by personal striving." (Millet, *By Grace Are We Saved*, p. 74, emphasis added)

After reading such statements, we are not surprised to hear scalding condemnations of the biblical teaching of salvation by grace alone.

> "One of the most fallacious doctrines originated by Satan and propounded by man is that man is saved alone by the grace of God; that belief in Jesus Christ alone is all that is needed for salvation." (Spencer W. Kimball, quoted in *Book of Mormon Student Manual*, p. 36)

> "Salvation by grace alone and without works," Elder Bruce R. McConkie explained," as it is taught in large segments of Christendom today, is akin to what Lucifer proposed in pre-existence . . . They both come from the same source; they are not of God." (Millet, *By Grace Are We Saved*, pp. 72f.)

> Ministers of false religions obtain the support of their congregations in large measure by flattery . . . Certain saved-by-grace-alone fanatics flatter their followers into believing they can be saved through no act other than confessing Christ with their lips. (McConkie, *Mormon Doctrine*, p. 287)

These statements remind me of the time that an LDS leader, after we had quite thoroughly discussed this all-important difference between Mormonism and Christianity, summarized our discussion by saying: "One of us is satanic, and one of us is of God." We naturally disagreed on who was who!

Forgiveness

God's forgiveness fares no better under Mormonism than his grace does.

> Peace comes only through forgiveness. But forgiveness has a high price. President Kimball tells us: "To every forgiveness there is a condition. . . . The fasting, the prayers, the humility must be equal to or greater than the sin. There must be a broken heart and a contrite spirit. . . . There must be tears and genuine change of heart. There must be conviction of the sin, abandonment of the evil, confession of the error to properly constituted authorities of the Lord." (*Gospel Principles*, p. 252)

> The Lord will not forgive us unless our hearts are fully cleansed of all hate, bitterness, and bad feelings against our fellow men [see 3 Nephi 13:14-15]. (*Gospel Principles*, p. 125)

> King Benjamin taught his people that they not only needed to *obtain* a remission of sins, but that they must also *retain* their sinless state (Mosiah 4:10-12). Forgiveness is a conditional gift that requires continued compliance with divine directives. (C. Max Caldwell, *Ensign*, April 1996, p. 32)

Complete forgiveness is reserved for those only who turn their whole hearts to the Lord and begin to keep all of his commandments—not just the commandments disobeyed in the past, but those in all fields. (McConkie, *Mormon Doctrine*, p. 295)

Just how far they thrust man into the foreground and push God into the background of forgiveness becomes evident in their interpretation of John 8:1-11:

Did the Lord forgive the woman? *Could he forgive her?* There seems to be no evidence of forgiveness. His command to her was, "Go and sin no more." He was directing the sinful woman to go her way, abandon her evil life, commit no more sin, transform her life. . . (*The Life and Teachings of Jesus & His Apostles*, p. 108, emphasis added)
Note that the Lord did not forgive the woman of her serious sin. He commanded quietly, but forcefully, "Go, and sin no more." *Even Christ cannot forgive one in sin.* The woman had neither time nor opportunity to repent totally. When her preparation and repentance were complete she could hope for forgiveness, but not before then. (Kimball, *The Miracle of Forgiveness*, p. 68, emphasis added)

Forgiveness for Mormons is a process—a long, drawn-out process.

"There is no royal road to repentance, no privileged path to forgiveness . . . There is only one way. It is a long road spiked with thorns and briars and pitfalls and problems." (Spencer W. Kimball, quoted in *Gospel Principles*, p. 123)

Your Heavenly Father has promised forgiveness upon total repentance and meeting all the requirements, but that forgiveness is not granted merely for the asking. There must be works—many works—and an all-out, total surrender, with a great humility and "a broken heart and contrite spirit."

It depends upon you whether or not you are forgiven, and when. It could be weeks, it could be years, it could be centuries before that happy day when you have the positive assurance that the Lord has forgiven you. That depends on your humility, your sincerity, your works, your attitudes. (Kimball, *The Miracle of Forgiveness*, pp. 324f.)

Even after expending all that effort, the Mormon god doesn't restore to people what they lost as a result of their sin.

Thus God will forgive the repentant sinner who sins against divine law, but that forgiveness can never restore the losses he sustained during the period of his sinning. (Kimball, *The Miracle of Forgiveness*, p. 311)

Kimball illustrates this with the Parable of the Prodigal Son. Not the father, not the younger son, but the elder son is the one who receives his praise! He is the one to whom the father says: "Son, thou art ever with me, and all that I have is thine" (Luke 15:31). Kimball interprets this to mean that only the elder son, because of his faithfulness, will go to the celestial kingdom. The younger son, although forgiven, lost that opportunity because of his waywardness.

The older son's being ever with his father is significant. If this parable is a reminder of life's journey, we remember that for the faithful who live the commandments there is a great promise of seeing the Lord and being with him always in exaltation. *On the other hand, the younger son could hope for no more than salvation as a servant.* (p. 310, emphasis added)

As you might have noticed, many of these quotes are from a book entitled, *The Miracle of Forgiveness*. Reading these excerpts, one wonders: where is the miracle in their concept of forgiveness? Many Mormons, however, have never asked that question. One young couple was genuinely puzzled as I tried to show them the problem I had with the idea of *earning* forgiveness. It took a fair amount of discussion before they even grasped the problem. Finally they saw that forgiving someone a debt wipes out all obligations to pay the debt. But even after seeing that, they hung onto their work-oriented view of forgiveness.

Faith

With such a demanding god, it is surprising that Mormons still talk about faith at all. We would think that faith wouldn't be a factor in a system based so much on a person's works. Nevertheless, the LDS church's Articles of Faith list faith as their very first principle.

Here again, however, we see that the meaning they attach to faith is different from the Christian meaning. The object of a Christian's faith is Jesus' saving work for us. The object of a Mormon's faith, however, is the LDS plan of salvation. They trust that the plan God has given them provides the way for them to save themselves.

That their faith rests in their plan rather than in Jesus is difficult to see because they often talk about believing in Jesus. By that, however, they don't mean trusting in his saving work. Even then the object of their faith is the plan of salvation. One manual simply defines *faith in Christ* as: "Commitment to keep his commandments" (*The Life and Teachings of Jesus & His Apostles*, p. 400). Others expand on this.

> First we should plant and nurture the seed of faith in the Lord Jesus Christ, our Savior and Redeemer. We each should develop the faith of Nephi to do the things the Lord has commanded [see 1 Ne. 3:7], knowing that all commandments are given for our good. (Elder Joseph B. Wirthlin, *Ensign*, May 1989, p. 8)

> Three things are necessary in order that any rational and intelligent being may exercise faith in God unto life and salvation.
> First, the idea that he actually exists.
> Secondly, a correct idea of his character, perfections, and attributes.
> Thirdly, an actual knowledge that the course of life which he is pursuing is according to his will. (*Sharing the Gospel*, p. 86)

> Primarily, and in a theological sense, we are considering faith as a living, inspiring confidence in God, and an acceptance of His will as our law, and of His words as our

guide, in life. (Talmage, *The Articles of Faith*, p. 100)

Faith, to a Mormon, means more than accepting the plan of salvation as good. It comes close to becoming synonymous with their idea of grace. As the following quotes illustrate, LDS faith also includes receiving the *power* to follow that plan.

> To those who have not begun the quest of comprehension, the word faith appears to be only a synonym for a kind of belief or conviction . . . It is a principle of power . . . Faith empowers the righteous to do anything Christ commands. (*Sharing the Gospel*, pp. 82, 84)

> Faith is an active force. If we have faith, we trust in Jesus Christ to help us find ways to live his commandments. (*Latter-day Saint Woman A*, p. 7)

Once again the pattern repeats itself of God's activity lying in the background while man's activity holds center stage. In fact, Mormons go so far as to teach that a person needs to be righteous before he can even attain faith. In addition, growing in faith depends on a person's good works.

> We must constantly nourish our faith through righteous works. *(Duties and Blessings of the Priesthood Part A*, p. 201)

> Faith is a gift of God bestowed as a reward for personal righteousness. It is always given when righteousness is present, and the greater the measure of obedience to God's law the greater will be the endowment of faith. (McConkie, *Mormon Doctrine*, p. 264)

In summary, the two main characteristics of LDS faith are:

1. *acceptance* of the plan of salvation rather than of salvation itself and

2. *power* God gives to resist sin and become perfect.

Repentance

Mormonism intricately intertwines repentance with faith. Repentance is their second principle of faith and immediately *follows* faith. To the Mormon, repentance is more than a change of mind; it is a mighty change of action. It is equated with *improving* one's life.

In some respects, LDS repentance resembles Christian sanctification or God-pleasing living. But there is one major difference between the two. When they speak of repentance, Mormons talk about completely abandoning sin.

> Repentance means not only to convict yourselves of the horror of sin, but to confess it, abandon it, and restore to all who have been damaged to the total extent possible; then spend the balance of your lives trying to live the commandments of the Lord so he can eventually pardon you and cleanse you. (Kimball, *The Miracle of Forgiveness*, p. 200)

> If we sincerely repent, we turn away from our sins and do them no more. We no longer have any desire to commit the sins. (*Uniform System for Teaching the Gospel*, p. 2-14)

If that is not depressing enough, they also teach that suffering is essential to repentance.

> There can be no forgiveness without real and total repentance, and there can be no repentance without punishment. *(Doctrine and Covenants Student Manual,* p. 224)

Justification and Sanctification

With the exception of grace, the terms we have looked at are ones familiar to most Mormons. They might not be able to define them precisely but they have a pretty good grasp of them. Justification and sanctification are two terms, however, that are not part of the average Mormon's vocabulary. They often respond with a shrug of the shoulders when you ask them what these terms mean.

This lack of familiarity is evident also in their literature. Rarely are justification and sanctification addressed . McConkie, in *Mormon Doctrine*, spends less than a page explaining justification. *Gospel Principles* doesn't mention it at all, not even in the glossary. The LDS Bible Dictionary also ignores it.

Sanctification fares a little better. McConkie spends a little more time on it; *Gospel Principles* has a brief sentence describing it in the glossary. But the *LDS Bible Dictionary* also ignores it.

Therefore, it is extremely difficult to get a handle on their definition of these two terms. What complicates matters even further is that when books do address them, they often don't agree. That alone indicates how unfamiliar these words are to Mormons.

After much sifting and sorting, one thing stands out about their view of justification, namely, that they equate it with a sense of fairness. Following is the statement cited most often in regard to justification.

> This law of justification is the provision the Lord has placed in the gospel to assure that no unrighteous performance will be binding on earth and in heaven, and that no person will add to his position or glory in the hereafter by gaining an unearned blessing. (DNTC, 2: 230.] (*The Life and Teachings of Jesus & His Apostles*, p. 319)

Note how this adheres to the pattern of emphasizing man's action. Instead of justification being God's loving and legal verdict declaring people "not guilty" because of Jesus' saving work, it becomes his strict confirmation of the merits or demerits of a person's own actions. There is no mercy in Mormon justification. Biblical justification, however, is filled with mercy.

> There is no difference, for all have sinned and fall short of the glory of God, and are justified freely by his grace through the redemption that came by Christ Jesus. (Romans 3:22-24)

The same thing emerges when we turn to the Mormons' view of sanctification. Here too the emphasis is on mankind. They see sanctification as people purifying themselves.

"I will put my own definition to the term sanctification, and say it consists in overcoming every sin and bringing all into subjection to the law of Christ." (Brigham Young, quoted in *Doctrine and Covenants Student Manual*, p. 41)

"Sanctification is a state of saintliness, a state attained only by conformity to the laws and ordinances of the gospel. The plan of salvation is the system and means provided whereby men may sanctify their souls and thereby become worthy of a celestial inheritance. . ."

"Those who attain this state of cleanliness and perfection are able, as occasion may require, to see God and view the things of his kingdom." (McConkie, quoted in *The Life and Teachings of Jesus & His Apostles*, p. 393)

Conclusion

No matter where you begin in Mormonism, you always end up in the same place. It always leads people back to themselves. It is a law-based, man-centered, work-oriented religion. In spite of Mormonism's high praise of Jesus and Heavenly Father, the facts prove that it keeps them in the background and, at times, pushes them completely out of the picture. Mormons don't know they are doing this; they will object strenuously to the idea that they are doing this.

They react in this way because they don't know anything better. They have never drunk from the well of God's grace. They have never experienced God's free and full forgiveness. They have never seen Jesus doing everything for them. *They* need to be told. *We* need to tell them.

> *How, then, can they call on the one they have not believed in? And how can they believe in the one of whom they have not heard? And how can they hear without someone preaching it to them? . . .*
>
> *Consequently, faith comes from hearing the message, and the message is heard through the word of Christ.*
> (Romans 10:14,17)

Key Concepts

Mortal: Mormons claim that mortality includes having the ability to bear children.

Adam's fall: Mormonism views it as a positive event because it made man mortal.

Sin: Mormons downplay sin. They see sin mainly in things that hurt them rather than anger God.

Five Major Sins of Mormonism: Apostasy, murder, sexual immorality, breaking the Word of Wisdom, refusal to bear children.

Atonement: Mormonism limits it to Jesus' overcoming physical death for mankind. LDS redemption is synonymous with it.

Salvation: In Mormonism, it is equivalent to physical resurrection. This is why Mormons can say Jesus saved them without any work on their part.

Jesus: Mormons view Jesus as a big brother who refinanced their loan for them, gave them more time to pay it back, and who set a good example for them.

Incarnation: The LDS church teaches that Jesus is the result of a physical union between Heavenly Father and Mary.

Grace: In Mormonism, not an attribute of God but a power God places within people.

Repentance: In Mormonism it means improving your life by abandoning the sin.

Faith: Mormons place their faith in their work-oriented plan of salvation.

Justification: Not God's loving verdict of "not guilty" but rather his strict accounting of merits and demerits.

100

CHAPTER FOUR: KNOW THEIR AUTHORITY

By now it is obvious that Mormons rely on a variety of authorities. Most Christians realize that Mormons regard the Book of Mormon as inspired, but few realize that it doesn't stop there. Mormons have a multitude of authoritative sources. Not only do they glean their belief from a number of written scriptures, they also look to the priesthood for guidance. Complicating matters even further, this priestly authority manifests itself in various ways and at various levels within the church. It is to this confusing array of authorities that we now turn our attention.

The Bible

We start with the Bible. To a Christian, the words "Scripture" and "Bible" are interchangeable. But not to a Mormon. The Bible is just one of four books that they consider scripture. The other three are the Book of Mormon, Doctrine and Covenants, and the Pearl of Great Price. These four books are also referred to as the "standard works".

In regard to the Bible, Mormonism's eighth Article of Faith states: "We believe the Bible to be the word of God as far as it is translated

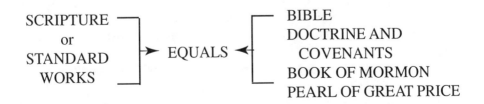

correctly." The crucial phrase obviously is "as far as it is translated correctly." Over the years, this phrase has effectively nullified the Bible's authority for most Mormons.

The key to understanding how it does that is seeing that they often include more in the definition of translation than they should. Dictionaries define translating as the process of rendering words from one language to another. But many times Mormons also include the transmission and preservation of the ancient biblical texts themselves in their description of translation. (The ancient texts are the copies of the original biblical books, in the original languages, on which modern translations are based.) In fact, the *transmission* of the ancient texts rather than the translation of those texts is what they emphasize. Worse yet, some Mormons even equate the *interpretation* of the Bible with its "translation."

They stress the transmission of the ancient texts because they believe that large portions of the Bible have been lost down through the ages. In addition, they feel that the remaining portions have been severely corrupted because of this supposed faulty transmission. They base this on the following passage from the Book of Mormon.

> Wherefore thou seest that after the book hath gone forth through the hands of the great and abominable church, that *there are many plain and precious things taken away from the book*, which is the book of the Lamb of God. (1 Nephi 13:28 emphasis added)

Mormons refer "the great and abominable church" to the Roman Catholic church. Most, however, think that the Roman Catholic church was in existence almost immediately after the apostles died. Many therefore date this corrupting process to the first few centuries after Christ. There are, however, a multitude, of biblical manuscripts that conclusively prove that the biblical texts were faithfully, even meticulously, transmitted during that time. Numerous books address this issue of the transmission of the biblical text quite thoroughly. One such book is *From God to Us: How We Got Our Bible* by Norman L. Geisler and William E. Nix.

But many Mormons have never seen such evidence and therefore have never questioned the truthfulness of the above passage. In fact, many have memorized the italicized portion of the quote. Therefore, the first thing that often comes to their minds when the discussion turns to the Bible, is that many plain and precious things have been taken from it. That is what the LDS church has pounded into them.

> "I believe the Bible as it read when it came from the pen of the original writers. Ignorant translators, careless transcribers, or designing and corrupt priests have committed many errors." (Joseph Smith, quoted in *Book of Mormon Student Manual*, p.14)

> Many passages and even whole books of scripture have been lost through the carelessness or wickedness of the record keepers . . . There is no more false or absurd doctrine than the sectarian claim that the Bible (or any other book for that matter) contains all of the word of God. (McConkie, *Mormon Doctrine*, pp. 453,455)

Another church leader, James E. Talmage, wrote with more restraint.

> The Church of Jesus Christ of Latter-day Saints accepts the *Holy Bible as the foremost of her standard works*, first among the books which have been proclaimed as her written guides in faith and doctrine. In the respect and sanctity with which the Latter-day Saints regard the Bible they are of like profession with Christian denominations in general . . . Nevertheless, the Church announces a reservation in the case of erroneous translation, which may occur as a result of human incapacity, . . . *both of translation and transcription of the text.* (*The Articles of Faith*, p. 236, emphasis added)

Note how he introduces the transcription or transmission of the text into his discussion of erroneous translation. When Mormons talk about the translation of the Bible, they almost invariably end up discussing its transmission.

Note also his use of and then explanation of the word "foremost." Mormons regard the Bible as the foremost of their scriptures because it is the oldest; not because they consider it their most reliable scripture. On the contrary, they deem it the *least* reliable of their four standard works.

> "When the Book of Mormon, Doctrine and Covenants, and Pearl of Great Price offer information relative to biblical interpretation, these should be given preference in writing and teaching . . ." [Editorial, *Church News*, 7 Dec. 1974, p. 16]. (quoted in *The Life and Teachings of Jesus & His Apostles*, p. 3)

In light of such statements, it is not surprising to discover that the Bible is an unfamiliar book to most Mormons. Why study something that is not reliable and is outdated? Many only know the few passages their church cites in an attempt to give biblical support to their teachings.

Surprisingly, nevertheless, a large percentage of Mormons still respect the Bible. It is not unusual for them to be genuinely puzzled over the meaning of a passage, or for them to try to reconcile that passage with their beliefs. Even though, according to their religion, they don't need biblical support for their beliefs, many are still bothered when their beliefs contradict the Bible. What has been more unusual in my experience is for them simply to disregard a passage as unreliable because of "erroneous translation." As will be demonstrated in the second half of this book, we can profitably use their respect for the Bible when we witness to them.

As we witness, it is good to remember that their official translation is the King James Version (KJV). This too is surprising since Joseph Smith authored his own translation, known as the Joseph Smith Translation (JST) or the "Inspired Version." But the JST is not widely used by Mormons. It was not even included in their official edition of the Bible until 1979. Even today it only contains excerpts of the JST and then only in footnotes or in the appendix.

The LDS Church explains its disregard of the JST by claiming Joseph Smith never completed it. Historical researchers, however, have found statements by Smith himself stating he had finished it. Be that as it may, the JST does not seem to be much of a factor in grass-roots Mormonism.

An interesting glimpse into the muddled view Mormons have of translating is seen in this description of Joseph Smith's "translating" method. "By translation is meant a revision of the Bible by inspiration or revelation" (*Doctrine & Covenants Student Manual*, p. 136). Thus "inspired revision" could serve as yet another LDS definition for translation.

104

The Book of Mormon

Unexpectedly, the Book of Mormon doesn't fare much better than the Bible. Although it is regarded much more highly, it is not used much more. I became convinced of that when, for a couple of years, I used it quite extensively in my witnessing attempts. I soon found out that very few Mormons could find their way around in it. Most missionaries and ward teachers had great difficulty finding verses I would mention. Once they found them, they had even greater difficulty explaining them.

Again, that is not to say that Mormons don't respect the Book of Mormon highly. They consider it nothing less than "another testament of Jesus Christ," as it is now subtitled. In a blatant misinterpretation, they say that Ezekiel 37 mentions it. They claim that the "stick of Judah" spoken of in that chapter refers to the Bible and the "stick of Ephraim" refers to the Book of Mormon. They then go on to say that this proves that the Book of Mormon deserves equal footing with the Bible. But the context clearly shows that Ezekiel 37 is not talking about the binding of two scriptures but about the uniting of true Israel (the church) under Jesus.

In addition, the LDS church is constantly urging its members to read the Book of Mormon.

> "No member of this Church can stand approved in the presence of God who has not seriously and carefully read the Book of Mormon." (Joseph Fielding Smith, quoted in *Ensign*, March 1990, p. 63)

> I witnessed that it is not sufficient that we should treasure the Book of Mormon, nor that we testify that it is of God. We must know its truths, incorporate them into our lives, and share them with others. I felt an overwhelming love for the people and an urgent desire that all would comprehend the value of the Book of Mormon. (Apostle Richard G. Scott, *Ensign*, March 1989, p. 9)

In light of such statements it is indeed surprising that more Mormons aren't better acquainted with it, surprising, that is, until one reads it. It doesn't take long to discover that the Book of Mormon doesn't mention, much less explain, many of Mormonism's unique teachings. It professes to be the history of three peoples that flourished in America centuries ago. These three people, the Jaredites, Nephites, and Lamanites, supposedly descended from Jews who had migrated to the Americas centuries before Christ. Much of the book deals with their wars and conflicts. One of its highlights is a supposed visit by Jesus to the Nephites after his resurrection (3 Nephi chapters 11-26). Other parts duplicate sections of the King James Version almost verbatim. For example, 2 Nephi quotes sixteen chapters of Isaiah nearly word for word. In all this, there is not much LDS doctrine.

Some observers of Mormonism are of the opinion that this is the very reason the LDS church encourages not only Mormons but also non-Mormons to read it. They feel that it serves as a nonthreatening introduction to Mormonism since it doesn't reveal the striking differences between Mormonism and Christianity. At the same time, moreover, it introduces the non-Mormon to the concept of additional scriptures. Mormons have made that very point. "The translation of the Book of Mormon assured from the birth of the Church an openness to scriptural texts outside the Bible" (*Ensign*, Feb. 1989, p. 9).

Because of the great claims made for it, the Book of Mormon has undergone close scrutiny by non-Mormons. The result is that both historical discrepancies and contradictions with other LDS scripture have been found in it. A number of books on the market detail these findings. Those by Jerald and Sandra Tanner are especially recommended.

But here again, most Mormons have not been exposed to such critical facts. They take on faith the unfounded and fraudulent claims that history and archaeology have proven its truthfulness. Nor are they accustomed to making critical comparisons between their various scriptures. In fact, such activity is vigorously discouraged.

> Recently the Council of the First Presidency and Quorum of Twelve Apostles issued a statement alerting members of the Church to the dangers of participating in circles which concentrate on doctrine and ordinances and measure them by the intellect alone. (Boyd K. Packer, *Ensign*, Nov. 1991, p. 21)

As a result, I have found it difficult to sit down with Mormons and try to have them look at the Book of Mormon objectively. Too often just the suggestion of doing that resulted in their putting up defenses and pulling back from me. Even if they don't read much of it, they still resent any attack against it. Even if it doesn't contain much LDS doctrine, they still consider it the bedrock of their faith. To most Mormons, "the Book of Mormon is the keystone of Mormonism" (*Sharing the Gospel*, p. 173)

Doctrine and Covenants

In some respects, it would seem more appropriate to call Doctrine and Covenants (D&C) the keystone of Mormonism. It is there that we find such teachings as baptism for the dead, celestial marriage, plurality of wives, plurality of gods, and the possibility of attaining godhood. It lays out the concept of missionary work in the spirit world. It is the "scripture" that contains the Word of Wisdom. Although D&C is not well-known to non-Mormons, it is basic to Mormonism.

Before we take a closer look at it, I would like to address briefly the dilemma Christians face in even talking to Mormons about their nonbiblical scriptures. On the one hand, we firmly believe that they are nothing but the work of Joseph Smith and thus the farthest thing from divine revelation. On the other hand, we want to be sensitive to the high regard in which Mormons hold both Joseph Smith and these books. In other words, we will always want to speak the truth in love (Ephesians 4: 15).

The best way I have found to address this dilemma is to honestly state it. I have told numerous Mormons that I wanted to speak to them with respect and love, but I also wanted to speak the truth. After explaining to them the dilemma as I saw it, most of our discussions turned out to be quite frank but also quite cordial.

D&C is a series of "revelations," each revelation forming one section of D&C. There are 138 revelations or sections in all, 133 of which were supposedly received by Joseph Smith. Although one does not want to speak flippantly of the man who means so much to Mormons, it soon becomes apparent to a person reading D&C that Smith grew in his use of revelation. The earliest revelations were often "given" to keep his followers in line and not to reveal new doctrine. For example, D&C Section 19 is purportedly a revelation from the Lord to one of Joseph Smith's followers, Martin Harris. There we read:

> And again, I command thee that thou shalt not covet thine own property, but impart it freely to the printing of the Book of Mormon, which contains the truth and the

word of God . . .

Impart a portion of thy property, yea, even part of thy lands and all save the support of thy family.

Pay the debt thou hast contracted with the printer.

The great majority of the revelations are of similar nature. Over 75% of them are from the five-year span (1829-1833) when Smith was founding the LDS church. Of all these, however, only two break major new doctrinal ground. Section 76 deals with the three kingdoms of heaven, while Section 89 spells out the Word of Wisdom.

After 1833 Joseph used "revelation" much more judicially. It appears that he became tired of having people ask him for a revelation addressing even the smallest of matters. In his own preface to Section 63 he wrote:

In these infant days of the Church, there was a great anxiety to obtain the word of the Lord upon every subject that in any way concerned our salvation.

Also towards the end of that five-year span he has the Lord say: "Therefore let them cease wearying me concerning this matter" (D&C 90:33). Shortly after that the number of "revelations" granted him dropped off sharply.

The quantity of his revelations is not the only thing that changed. So also did their nature. He increasingly used them to introduce new teachings. In 1841 he delivered the revelation espousing baptism for the dead (Section 124). In 1842 he gave two more detailed revelations on that same subject (Section 127, 128). In 1843 he revealed the following: the physical body of God (Section 130), the doctrine of celestial marriage (Section 131), and the teachings on plurality of wives and exaltation (Section 132). If he had not been killed in 1844, the LDS church might be promulgating even more exotic teachings.

One section Mormons like to refer to is Section 87. This is Joseph Smith's "prophecy" concerning the Civil War. He says that wars will shortly come to pass, beginning at the rebellion of South Carolina, which will eventually terminate the death and misery of many souls.

He also says that the southern states would call on Great Britain for help. Since this is what happened, Mormons claim that this proves

Smith was a true prophet of God seeing that he received this revelation in 1832, close to thirty years before the beginning of the Civil War.

He, however, was not the only one saying such things at that early date. It didn't take too astute a political observer to realize that trouble was brewing between the states and that South Carolina was a flash point. The LDS church also conveniently ignores the fact that in this same prophecy he says that "war will be poured out upon all nations, beginning at this place." That part of the "prophecy" never did come true.

The last three sections of D&C consist of "revelations" given to other presidents of the church. Of these three, Section 138 is the most important. It introduces and explains the concept of missionary work in the spirit world.

Appended to D&C are two official declarations. Although they are not labeled as "sections," these are just as binding and authoritative as the rest of D&C. The first one deals with the discontinuation of plural marriages. The second one deals with a revelation that church president Spencer W. Kimball supposedly received in 1978, allowing black males to receive the priesthood.

While Joseph Smith used the Book of Mormon to introduce the idea of additional revelation, he used D&C to capitalize on that idea. It became his chief means of introducing new doctrines to his church. Consequently it is the most widely quoted of their four scriptures. Church president Joseph Fielding Smith wrote:

> In my judgment there is no book on earth yet come to man as important as the book known as the Doctrine and Covenants, with all due respect to the Book of Mormon, and the Bible, and the Pearl of Great Price, which we say are our standards in doctrine. The book of Doctrine and Covenants to us stands in a peculiar position above them all.
>
> I am going to tell you why. When I say that, do not for a moment think I do not value the Book of Mormon, the Bible, and the Pearl of Great Price, just as much as any man that lives; I think I do . . . but the Bible is a history containing the doctrine and commandments given to the people anciently. That applies also to the Book of Mormon. It is the doctrine and the history and the commandments of the people who dwelt upon this

continent anciently.

But this *Doctrine and Covenants contains the word of God to those who dwell here now.* It is our book. It belongs to the Latter-day Saints. (*Doctrine and Covenants Student Manual*, p. 2, emphasis added)

The Pearl of Great Price

If Doctrine and Covenants is the scripture Mormons use the most, the Pearl of Great Price is the one they use the least. It is not a book at all, but rather a collection of five brief works totaling only 60 pages. Because of its brevity, it is published together with D&C in one volume.

The first work is the Book of Moses. This is Joseph Smith's reworking of the first five chapters of Genesis. In it he stresses man's agency and greatly expands the story of Enoch. Here he also states that Adam was baptized.

The second work is the Book of Abraham. Smith claimed to have translated it from Egyptian hieroglyphics written on some papyri he obtained from a traveling exhibition show. After his death, his widow sold these papyri, and they subsequently disappeared from sight. In 1967 they were discovered in the Metropolitan Museum in New York. It was quickly ascertained that the hieroglyphics described burial rites and bore no resemblance to Smith's Book of Abraham. The Tanners and others detail this entire story very well.

As earth-shattering as we would expect this to be to Mormons, it isn't to most. Many aren't even aware of this story, and even when they are, they usually don't pay much attention to it. Only a few become bothered by it. Even then, some of those who were initially troubled accept the church's explanation that Smith translated the hidden meaning of the hieroglyphics.

The Book of Abraham is the vehicle Smith used to explain and expand his teaching concerning the plurality of gods. In it he talks about preexistence and introduces Kolob, "the planet nearest to the celestial, or residence of God" (McConkie, *Mormon Doctrine*, p. 428).

The third item in the Pearl of Great Price is entitled "Joseph Smith-Matthew." It is his translation of Matthew chapter 24. It introduces no new doctrine.

"Joseph Smith-History," the fourth work, contains a couple of brief excerpts from his history of the church. The main selection is a description of the vision he claimed to have received as a youth. In this vision the Lord supposedly told him not to join any of the existing churches since they were all corrupt.

> I was answered that I must join none of them, for they were all wrong; and the Personage who addressed me said that their creeds were an abomination in his sight. (*Joseph Smith-History* 1:19)

The LDS Church points to this "vision" as proof that Joseph Smith was a true prophet of God. Because of that claim, non-Mormons have researched it intensely with the result that numerous historical problems have been found with it.

The LDS church's thirteen Articles of Faith complete the Pearl of Great Price. They give a false impression of Mormonism since they do not mention any of its unique teachings. They are often printed on small cards or bookmarks and handed out to interested individuals.

This sketch of the Pearl of Great Price completes our review of LDS scriptures. To Christians, the idea of having multiple scriptures is confusing and frustrating. Many Mormons, however, feel that it is only natural that God would not limit his revelation to one book. Not only do they see this as being logical but also as being very attractive. The more divine revelation they feel they have, the more enriched they think they are.

Going hand-in-hand with that thinking is their belief that God did not complete his revelation with these scriptures, but that he is still directly revealing his will to men today. In fact, they maintain men not only can but should expect to receive direct revelations from God. Even more startling, *Mormons value such direct revelations more than they do their written scriptures.* We will now explore the far-reaching implications of this.

The Priesthood

This belief in continual revelation is rooted in the LDS concept of the priesthood. There are two different priesthoods in Mormonism: the Aaronic and the Melchizedek. The Aaronic is the lesser priesthood while the Melchizedek is the greater one.

The Aaronic Priesthood administers the temporal matters of the Church and the Melchizedek Priesthood

> administers the spiritual. The Aaronic brings a person into the church of God upon the earth and the Melchizedek brings a person into the presence of God through the gospel and ordinances restored to the Church. (*Church News*, June 24, 1989)

Unlike Roman Catholicism or other religions with priests, LDS priesthood holders are not full-time church workers. (They prefer the term "priesthood holders" to "priests.") In fact, every male member in good standing holds the priesthood. Women cannot hold the priesthood. Worthy boys enter it at the age of twelve, when they become members of the Aaronic priesthood. While adult male converts also enter the Aaronic priesthood, they quickly progress to the Melchizedek priesthood.

The Aaronic priesthood has three offices through which the boys progress: deacon, teacher and priest.

Deacons are boys twelve and thirteen years old. They usher at sacrament meetings and keep up the church grounds. They also help distribute the sacrament each Sunday. (The bread and water are on small trays, which these boys pass down the aisles. We will be taking a close look at their sacrament meetings in the next chapter.)

When a boy becomes 14, he becomes a teacher, perhaps better called a "home teacher." Home teachers are paired off, and each pair of home teachers is assigned some member homes to visit each month. During these visits they are to teach lessons to the members of that household. But that is not to be their main emphasis.

> "We are to be thinking of a new name instead of teacher attached to these priesthood visitors. The word teaching suggests that they are to go there to teach a gospel message, and that primarily isn't what we expect the home teachers of today to do. They are home visitors; they are priesthood home visitors to inquire into the health of the family and to see if they are doing their family duties, and if they are assuming their Church responsibilities." (Harold B. Lee, quoted in *To Make Thee a Minister and a Witness*, p. 62)

To accomplish this purpose, all levels of the priesthood participate in home teaching. Often a young boy is paired with an experience man. Not only does this system give members regular personal contact with representatives of the church, but it also serves as a good training ground for future missionaries.

At the age of 16, a young man is eligible to become a priest. In addition to his responsibilities as a teacher, a priest can baptize and administer the sacrament. He administers the sacrament by praying the "sacramental prayers" over the bread and water before they are distributed.

At the age of 18 or 19, he can progress to the Melchizedek priesthood. The offices in this priesthood are elder, seventy, high priest, and patriarch. Progression within the Melchizedek priesthood is determined by worthiness rather than by age.

All holders of the Melchizedek priesthood belong to the office of elder. The other offices within this priesthood are specialized. A "seventy" concentrates on mission work. "Seventy" is a title and not the number of men in this position. It is derived from the incident, recorded in Luke 10, of Jesus sending out the seventy to spread the gospel.

High priests are the leaders in the church.

Patriarchs give special patriarchal blessings to members. Each territorial division, called a "stake," has only one patriarch. Members usually receive their patriarchal blessing in their late teens. This one-time blessing supposedly tells them from what tribe of Israel they have descended. (We will look at the significance of that in the next chapter.) It supposedly also offers them insights into their talents and even their future. These patriarchal blessings are naturally highly treasured.

In 1957 the First Presidency of the Church explained that the patriarchal blessing contains an inspired declaration of lineage . . . which tells us through which tribe of Israel we receive our blessings . . . Because a patriarchal blessing is personal and sacred, . . . its content should only be shared with those who are close to us and as we are directed by the Spirit. (*Duties and Blessings of the Priesthood A*, p. 74)

Our patriarchal blessing can also give us insight and help us find direction. Often we can find answers to our problems through studying this special blessing. (*Latter-day Saint Woman B*, p. 126)

A patriarchal blessing from an ordained patriarch can

give us a star to follow, which is a personal revelation from God to each individual . . . By their very nature, all blessings are conditional upon worthiness regardless of whether the blessing specifically spells out the qualifications. (James E. Faust, *Ensign*, Nov. 1995, p. 63)

Within each ward, priesthood holders are organized into quorums that meet each Sunday. Each quorum is headed by a presidency that consists of a president and his two counselors. These weekly quorum meetings are a crucial linchpin in keeping the ward running smoothly.

The priesthood is vitally important to Mormons because they feel it endows them with God's *authority* and *power*.

The priesthood, therefore, is the *authority of God* given to men to act in all things for the salvation of mankind. (*Duties and Blessings of the Priesthood A*, p. 1, emphasis added)

The priesthood is the greatest power on earth. It is not only the *power of God* given to men on the earth to do his work, but it is the same power by which our Heavenly Father and Jesus Christ perform their work. *(Duties and Blessings of the Priesthood B*, p. 19, emphasis added)

Mormonism teaches that the priesthood was gone from the earth from the days of the apostles until it was restored at the time of Joseph Smith. Mormons say that John the Baptist appeared to Smith and Oliver Cowdery in 1829 and conferred on them the Aaronic priesthood. About a month later, Peter, James, and John supposedly appeared to these same two men to confer on them the Melchizedek priesthood. In addition, Mormons claim that Smith was later visited by Elias (who, they feel, is a different person from Elijah), Moses, and Elijah, who each bestowed on him additional "keys" or authority. They assert that these keys are now being passed down through the priesthood. Consequently, they believe that the LDS church and only the LDS church has authority and power from God. Therefore they believe it is the only true Church.

The position that The Church of Jesus Christ of Latter-day Saints is the only true Church upon the face of the earth is fundamental . . . It is not merely an admission; it is a positive declaration. It is so fundamental that we cannot yield on this point. (*Sharing the Gospel*, p. 54)

Such beliefs have numerous ramifications. Mormons feel, for example, that only those baptisms performed by a member of their priesthood are legitimate. The same holds true for all other religious rites and activities. To be valid in their sight, they must be administered by a member of the LDS priesthood.

Because they feel that the priesthood gives them not only authority but also power, they believe that priesthood holders can even perform miracles.

Explain to the children that through the priesthood and faith in Jesus, we ca·. have miracles in our lives. (*Walk In His Ways B*, p. 31)

Priesthood is more than authority. It is also the power of God. Priesthood holders can perform God's work with spiritual power. They can perform miracles if they are worthy and have faith and if the Lord wills it. (*Discussion for New Members*, p. 3-6)

One ritual that they especially feel will produce miracles is the anointing of the sick. Many LDS elders carry small vials of olive oil just for that purpose. It is not uncommon to hear them telling how an emergency anointing saved a person's life. And that is just one of the numerous such rituals. It is difficult for non-Mormons to comprehend how all-important and how all-pervasive the priesthood is in Mormonism.

Not only do Mormons feel the priesthood gives them power and authority from God, most important, they believe it also allows them to receive direct revelation from God. As was mentioned above, closely connected with the priesthood are the "keys." Sometimes these keys are defined as delegated authority, but other times they are defined as the right to communicate with God.

President Joseph F. Smith said: "What is a key? It is the

right or privilege which belongs to and comes with the priesthood to have communication with God." (McConkie, *Mormon Doctrine*, p. 410)

Mormons believe that every priesthood holder has the right to communicate with God. Even holders of the Aaronic priesthood have

the keys of the ministering of angels, which means that those who hold it, and are worthy and faithful, have the keys to actually receive the visitation of angels from heaven. (*Ensign*, July 1989, p. 76)

But mostly members of the Melchizedek priesthood receive revelations. For example, they believe a father can receive direct revelation about his family.

Elder Franklin D. Richards told of a young father who was awakened one night by a voice that clearly told him to get up and go downstairs. He heeded the warning, and in going into the kitchen he found one wall in flames. Hurriedly, he awakened his family and called the fire department . . .

There was no question in his mind that this warning was a manifestation of the protection the Holy Ghost can give to those who keep their lives in harmony with the Spirit. (*Duties and Blessings of the Priesthood A*, p. 225)

Mormons manuals and magazines are filled with similar stories. This belief that God communicates to them in direct revelations plays an important part in their lives. I remember sitting in one of their sacrament meetings (church services) as a man exhorted his fellow members to make more use of this right to receive divine revelation

One significant limitation to receiving revelation, however, is that they can receive revelations *only concerning their sphere of authority*. A man, for example, could not receive revelations about another family or about teachings that would affect the whole church. If, however, he was a leader of one of the quorums in his ward, he and he alone could receive revelations affecting that quorum.

Every person properly appointed and sustained to act in

an official capacity in the church is entitled to the spirit of revelation to guide the particular organization or group over which he presides. (*Doctrine & Covenants Student Manual*, p. 187)

Within the Church there is an established pattern for receiving revelation and instructions. We need to be reminded that anyone claiming to receive direction or revelation for others should be held suspect. This is especially true when the content is believed to have relevance for areas, regions, stakes, or wards in the Church for whom the person has no particular responsibility. (Marvin J. Ashton, *Ensign*, Nov. 1990, p. 22)

This arrangement gives some men tremendous authority. On the local level, for example, the bishop (the leader of the ward) has a great degree of authority.

The bishop is our best earthly friend. He will hear the problems, judge the seriousness, then determine the degree of repentance and decide if it warrants an eventual forgiveness. (*Doctrine & Covenants Student Manual*, p. 334)

Mothers have a responsibility to teach their children to sustain and support their local priesthood leaders. They should never criticize priesthood leaders or say unkind things about them. *Criticizing our leaders endangers our own salvation.* (*Latter-day Saint Woman B*, p. 111, emphasis added)

An important difference between a Mormon bishop and a Christian pastor is that one of the bishop's main responsibilities is to act as a judge of people's worthiness.

Explain the role of bishop. Especially note his role as judge, who determines worthiness through interviews. (*Discussion for New Members*, p. 3-8)

As has been indicated, each judge in the Lord's kingdom has authority only over those within the boundaries of his ecclesiastical jurisdiction. Within those boundaries their responsibility to act as judges falls into two main categories:

(1) Determining worthiness for certain blessings and opportunities in the Lord's church, and

(2) Determining appropriate consequences for sin. (*Doctrine & Covenants Student Manual*, p. 407)

To judge the members' worthiness, not to teach them LDS doctrine, is the main role of LDS bishops. That is why it is not important for them to have theological training. In fact, bishops receive no specialized training. They are called from within the ward membership and serve an average of five years. While serving as bishops they continue to work in their secular occupations.

To enable bishops to serve as judges, Mormonism teaches that God gives them the ability to read hearts.

In order to help them in these duties, the Lord has promised bishops and branch presidents the gift of discernment (see D&C 46:27).

The gift of discernment enables a bishop or branch president to know truth, to understand the differences between good and evil, *and even know what is in a person's heart.* (*Duties and Blessings of the Priesthood A*, p. 60, emphasis added)

As a result, Mormons have high respect for and often fear of bishops. This was impressed upon me one day when a bishop gave me a tour of the local genealogical library. As we entered a room where a number of people were working, they reacted as if the President of the United States had entered. Their respect bordered on awe. That is not surprising when one realizes that bishops are looked upon as being almost perfect.

Every soul should develop the same spirit of devotion and

dedication to the work of the Lord as the bishops . . . enjoy. Most often theirs is near total devotion. (Kimball, *The Miracle of Forgiveness*, p. 202)

The authority that bishops enjoy on the local level is enjoyed worldwide by men called "General Authorities." They are also known as the "Brethren." They are called General Authorities because their authority is not limited geographically, but is worldwide. These men comprise the leadership of the LDS church. They receive lifetime callings except for members of the Second Quorum of Seventy.

This leadership of the LDS church is structured as follows: The General Authorities are headed by the First Presidency of the church, which consists of the President of the Church and his two counselors. (This pattern of president and two counselors is repeated at every level and in every organization of the church.) When a president dies, the apostle with the most seniority becomes the new president. He then selects his own counselors. Incidentally, Mormons teach that Peter, James, and John comprised the First Presidency of the early church.

Immediately below them in authority is the Quorum of the Twelve Apostles. They are followed by the Presidency of the Seventies, which consists of seven men who preside over two Quorums of Seventies. The First Quorum is comprised of men who serve to age 70. In October 1997 there were 47 men in this quorum. The Second Quorum are men who serve from three to five years. In October 1997 there were 30 men in this quorum. Finally, the three men of the Presiding Bishopric are also considered General Authorities.

These men's words are authoritative throughout the entire church—so much so that Mormons look upon the first presidency and the apostles as infallible prophets.

> "Now, brethren, I think there is one thing which we should have exceedingly clear in our minds. Neither the President of the Church, nor the First Presidency, nor the united voice of the First Presidency and the Twelve will ever lead the Saints astray or send forth counsel to the world that is contrary to the mind and will of the Lord." (Joseph Fielding Smith, quoted in *The Life and Teachings of Jesus & His Apostles*, p. 54)

> Latter-Day Saints sustain the first presidency, the twelve apostles, and the patriarch, as prophets. However,

> when we speak of "the prophet of the Church," we mean
> the President of the Church who is President of the High
> Priesthood. (*Gospel Principles*, p. 48)

As that last quote indicates, they single out the President of the Church as the one living prophet. Therefore we need to take special note of him.

The Living Prophet

Mormons believe that a sign of the true church is that it will always have a living prophet. As proof they site Amos 3:7: "Surely the Lord God will do nothing, but he revealeth his secret unto his servants the prophets." They claim that, with these words, God is insuring that he will send new prophets to every generation. They reason that if he didn't send such prophets, he couldn't do anything—for he says that he will always reveal his secrets to his prophets.

Amos 3:7 is set in the midst of one of God's condemnations of Israel for their unfaithfulness. In the surrounding verses, God is showing that nothing happens by chance, including Israel's coming defeat by Assyria. Rather it would be God's judgment on them—something he is now warning them about through the prophet Amos. The point God is making in Amos 3:7 is that, in his love, he warns before he punishes.

Today we have God's words and warnings in the Bible. That is where God has revealed his will for all generations. Since we now have the Bible, we no longer need a continual stream of prophets. The Bible is all we need. Paul reminded Timothy of that:

> from infancy you have known the holy Scriptures, *which
> are able to make you wise for salvation* through faith in
> Christ Jesus. All Scripture is God-breathed and is useful
> for teaching, rebuking, correcting and training in
> righteousness, so that the *man of God may be thoroughly
> equipped for every good work.* (2 Timothy 3:15-17,
> emphasis added)

The Bible makes us wise for salvation. It thoroughly equips us for every good work. But, as we have seen, Mormons do not believe the Bible is either trustworthy or complete. Therefore, they still feel a need for prophets and direct revelation. The one man who especially fits the bill for them is the president of their church. He is their "living prophet." He supposedly receives direct revelation for the whole church.

Naturally this prophet is highly respected. Respect is too weak a term, however, to describe how Mormons regard him. It would be difficult to overstate their esteem of him. Consider these statements:

> "*Next unto God and Christ,* in the earth is placed one unto whom the keys of power and authority of the Holy Priesthood are conferred, and unto whom the right of presidency is given. *He is God's mouthpiece* to His people, in all things pertaining to the building up of Zion, and to the spiritual and temporal salvation of the people. *He is God's vice-regent*; I do not hesitate to announce this truth; for it is His Word, and therefore it is true." (Joseph F. Smith, quoted in *Achieving A Celestial Marriage,* p. 147, emphasis added)

> President Gordon B. Hinckley now wears the mantle given to the Prophet Joseph Smith. He was foreordained to this high and holy calling in premortal councils. (David B. Haight, *Ensign,* May 1995, p. 36)

> "I desire to call your attention to the principle of loyalty, loyalty to the truth and loyalty to the men whom God has chosen to lead the cause of truth. I speak of 'the truth' and these 'men' jointly, because it is impossible fully to accept the one and partly reject the other." (Marion Rommey, quoted in *Old Testament Manual I,* p. 122)

If the church president is "God's mouthpiece" and "God's vice-regent," if he and the truth go hand-in-hand, then the logical conclusion is that his words must be on the same level as scripture. The LDS church, however, goes beyond that. It says the words of the living prophet are *more important* than scripture!

> "The older I get the closer the contact I have with the President of the Church, the more I realize that the greatest of all scriptures which we have in the world today is current scripture." (President Henry D. Moyle, quoted in *Teachings of the Living Prophets,* p. 19)

> When prophets, who are inspired by the Holy Ghost, speak, their words take precedence over other statements on the same issue. (*Teachings of the Living Prophets*, p. 18)

In 1980, Ezra Taft Benson gave a speech at Brigham Young University entitled, "Fourteen Fundamentals in Following the Prophet." In it, he clearly spelled out the superiority of the living prophet over their scripture. For example, his second and third points were: (2) The living prophet is more vital than the standard works. (3) The living prophet is more important to us than a dead prophet. Some Mormons try to downplay this speech but a church manual currently being used not only lists all fourteen fundamentals, but also quotes extensively from it. Following are two of numerous such excerpts:

> Beware of those who would pit the dead prophets against the living prophets, for the living prophets always take precedence. (*Teachings of the Living Prophets*, p. 20)

> Because he gives the word of the Lord for us today, his words have an even more immediate importance than those of the dead prophets. (*Teachings of the Living Prophets*, p. 41)

Ezra Taft Benson is not alone in saying that the living prophet is to be preeminent.

> If we do not sustain the living prophet, whoever he may be, we die spiritually. Ironically, some have died spiritually by exclusively following prophets who have long been dead. (President James E. Faust, *Ensign*, August 1996, p.5)

> President Wilford Woodruff recalled a meeting at which the Prophet Joseph Smith said to Brigham Young, "Brother Brigham I want you to take the stand and tell us your views with regard to the written oracles and the written word of God." Brigham Young is reported to have laid the scriptures, one by one, before him and then indicated he felt the words of the living prophet were

more important than the writings before him because the words of the living oracles convey the word of God to us in our day. President Woodruff went on to say, "When he was through, Brother Joseph said to the congregation: 'Brother Brigham has told you the word of the Lord, and he has told you the truth.'" (H. David Burton, *Ensign*, November 1995, p. 43)

It follows, therefore, that the writings Mormons are directed to study are not so much their scriptures, but rather the words of their living prophet.

This inspired counsel comes to members of the Church at least two ways. First, every six months a general conference is held during which inspired counsel is given by the Lord's servants. The Lord warns those who do not heed this instruction that they "shall be cut off from among the people" (D&C 1:14). Second, the Saints should read what the prophets have written (see D&C 52:9,36), including not only the scriptures but such things as conference talks, the message of the First Presidency in the *Ensign*, and special bulletins which are mailed to priesthood leaders to be read to the Saints in the stakes of the Church. (*Doctrine & Covenants Student Manual*, p. 390)

"The most important prophet, so far as we are concerned, is the one who is living in our day and age . . . Therefore, the most crucial reading and pondering which you should do is that of the latest inspired words from the Lord's mouthpiece. That is why it is essential that you have access to and carefully read his words in current Church publications." (Ezra Taft Benson, quoted in *Teachings of the Living Prophets*, p. 19

Many practice what Benson preaches. They clear their calendars every six months so that they can listen to the general conference. These conferences are held for two days each April and October in Salt Lake City. They consist of a series of talks given by the General Authorities. These conferences are beamed to LDS meetinghouses throughout the world. To receive these and other such talks, many of their meetinghouses have satellite dishes. In this way Mormons all over the world receive "their marching orders."

> "A general conference of The Church of Jesus Christ of Latter-day Saints is far more significant than most people realize. . . It is one of the most important events of the present day. Many do not so regard it, even among the Latter-day Saints. But for those who appreciate its true significance, it is of transcending importance, for in it PROPHETS OF GOD SPEAK, living prophets."

> "When God gives a message to mankind, it is not something to be lightly cast aside. Whether He speaks personally, or through His prophets, He himself said, it is the same.

> "And in this conference HIS PROPHETS SPEAK." (Mark E. Petersen, quoted in *Teachings of the Living Prophets*, p. 63)

In addition, to being broadcast worldwide, these speeches are printed in the following month's issue of *Ensign*, the Mormon's official magazine. Even if they have already heard the speeches, Mormons are encouraged to study them thoroughly in their written form.

> Three thousand miles from this pulpit lives a family who will again do a very special thing following this conference. When the *Ensign* arrives with the conference addresses at their home, the family will immediately read the messages, with the older children reporting on selected addresses.

> But they will do more than read. In family home evenings they will select family and personal goals based upon the conference messages . . . Is there any wonder why the father says: "Our family regards general conference as the Lord's list of things we should be concentrating on. It has meant more to us and our children than words can say." (*Duties and Blessings of the Priesthood B*, p. 153)

"The way I have enjoyed studying the prophet's words," reports Frank Perri, "is getting audiocassette tapes of conference and keeping them in my car. Since I drive a lot in my work, I can listen to inspirational talks again and again. This not only feeds my soul as I go about my daily work, *it keeps me current on the Lord's word to me as it comes through the Brethren.*" (*Ensign,* March 1989, p. 54, emphasis added)

This emphasis on the words of the "living prophet" helps us understand why many Mormons aren't familiar with their own scriptures. Because they have a living prophet, they don't have to know their scriptures. Rather than reading their scriptures, they can listen to their living prophet!

That is an arrangement most find quite attractive. Not only does it take less work, but they feel it is also more practical. An LDS acquaintance made that point to me one day as he was extolling the virtues of having a living prophet. He stressed how beneficial it was to have someone who received direct guidance from God for even the most recent of developments. He implied that I was to be pitied because all I had was the Bible. In that he was echoing his church.

Conditions are so different in the world today that a church without daily revelation cannot make the change necessary to meet those new conditions. How would the modern church know what stand to take with reference to the use of tobacco, or coffee, or the atomic bomb, or motion pictures, or television, or a thousand things that were not so much as known to men in Peter's day? (*Teachings of the Living Prophets*, p. 101)

The Church of Jesus Christ of Latter-day Saints is a theocracy. It is ruled by the God of heaven through direct revelation. (*D&C Student Manual*, p. 439)

This respect for the words of their church president is not restricted to spiritual matters either.

All Latter-day Saints should understand clearly that the earth and the fulness thereof belong to the Lord and that his prophet, who is President of the Savior's church on the earth, is to speak on any topic the Lord directs him to speak on . . . Elder Widstoe went on to say, however, that the "unofficial expressions [of a prophet] carry greater weight than the opinions of other men of equal or greater gifts and experience but without the power of the prophetic office . . .

. . . The unofficial views and expressions of such a man with respect to any vital subject, should command respectful attention." (*D&C Student Manual*, p. 390, 391)

How important, then, is the living prophet to Mormons?

Until the members of this church have that conviction that they are being led in the right way, and they have a conviction that these men of God are men who are inspired and have been properly appointed by the hand of God, they are not truly converted. (*Duties and Blessings of the Priesthood A*, p. 85)

Our eternal salvation may very well rest on how well we listen to these divinely appointed guides who show us the way of truth, the way to salvation. (*Church News*, March 25, 1989, p. 16)

It becomes increasingly apparent that the greatest external authority in Mormonism is the living prophet. This makes it extremely difficult to "attack" Mormonism's changing doctrine, since the idea of changing doctrine is built right into their system by this emphasis on current revelation.

"It is the latest word from God that must be heeded, in preference to any former revelation, however true. The same God who says do thus and so today, can repeal that commandment tomorrow, without being changeable or inconsistent." (Orson F. Whitney, quoted in *Teachings of the Living Prophets*, p. 20)

That which a living prophet tells us will always be in harmony with the standard works, but this is not to say he is limited by them. Although a prophet speaking under the influence of the Holy Ghost will never contradict principles found in the standard works, he will expand, or even go beyond them. A prophet may also give or take away principles or programs, according to the spiritual readiness of the people. (*Teachings of the Living Prophets*, p. 18)

"The most important prophet in any age is the living prophet . . . To follow the living prophet, the interpreter of the past, is the essence of wisdom. The very strength of the Church lies in the doctrine of continuous revelation through a living prophet." (John A. Widsoe quoted by H. David Burton, *Ensign*, November 1995, p. 43)

Consider, for example, Spencer Kimball's 1978 declaration allowing black males to enter the priesthood. This contradicted statements by past "living prophets," including Joseph Smith; it even went contrary to the Book of Mormon. Some Mormons found this troubling. But we didn't witness a mass exodus leaving the church. The majority were satisfied with Kimball's explanation that God had decided the black had suffered enough.

That incident illustrates how Mormons are conditioned not to do critical thinking about spiritual matters. Although many LDS are highly educated, their minds seem to switch off when the subject turns to religion. This is understandable when we remember that many Mormons consider questioning their leaders as the first step on the road to apostasy. In 1945 the statement was made: "When our leaders speak, the thinking has been done" (*Improvement Era*, June 1945, p. 354). The LDS church no longer uses this statement and does not like it to be publicized. That it still encourages blind obedience, however, cannot be denied.

President George Q. Cannon explained the spiritual dangers of turning away from the prophets: "God has chosen His servants, He claims it as His prerogative to condemn them, if they need condemnation. He has not given it to us individually to censure and condemn them. No man, however strong he may be in the faith, however high in the Priesthood, can speak evil of the Lord's anointed and find fault with God's authority on the earth without incurring His displeasure. The Holy Spirit will withdraw itself from such a man, and he will go into darkness. This being the case, do you not see how important it is that we should be careful? However difficult it may be for us to understand the reason for any action of the authorities of the Church, we should not too hastily call their acts in question and pronounce them wrong." (*Doctrine & Covenant Student Manual*, 4)

Elder Russell M. Nelson testifies that "once you stop putting question marks behind the prophet's statements and put exclamation points instead, and do it, the blessings just pour." (*Ensign*, March 1990, p. 55)

In summary, through the priesthood—starting with the father in the home, proceeding through the bishop in the ward, and culminating with the living prophet in Salt Lake City—Mormonism holds the tight reins that control its members. In chapter six we will see that these tight reins are placing numerous Mormons under tremendous strain.

Feelings

Instead of *thinking* about spiritual matters Mormons rely heavily on their *feelings*.

They look upon their feelings as the vehicle the Holy Ghost uses to give them inspiration and guidance.

The Holy Ghost speaks with a voice that you *feel* more than you *hear*... Revelation comes as words we *feel* more than *hear*. (Boyd K. Packer, *Ensign*, Nov. 1994, p. 60)

Many times, therefore, it is their own feelings that constitute their greatest and highest authority. (The living prophet is their greatest *external* authority.)

"How shall we know when the things they have spoken were said as they were 'moved upon by the Holy Ghost?' "I have given some thought to this question, and the answer thereto so far as I can determine, is: We can tell when the speakers are 'moved upon by the Holy Ghost' only when we, ourselves, are 'moved upon by the Holy Ghost.'

"In a way, this completely shifts the responsibility from them to us to determine when they so speak." (J. Reuben Clark Jr., quoted in *Doctrine & Covenants Student Manual*, p. 144)

I remember spending one entire afternoon talking to an elderly LDS man. During the course of our conversation, I had successfully neutralized the authority of the Book of Mormon, Joseph Smith, and even the living prophet. But all that was to no apparent avail, since he closed by saying, "I know Mormonism is true because Jesus appeared to me after I joined the church and told me it was true!"

This reliance on feelings and experiences is stressed already when people are introduced to Mormonism. Their missionary manual repeatedly instructs the missionary to ask investigators (i.e., prospective members) how they *feel* about the various topics under discussion. One of the first things they encourage investigators to do is read the Book of Mormon. When giving this encouragement, they stress this passage:

> And when ye shall receive these things, I would exhort you that ye ask God, the Eternal Father, in the name of Christ, if these things are not true and if ye shall ask with a sincere heart, with real intent, having faith in Christ, he will manifest the truth of it unto you, by the power of the Holy Ghost. (Moroni 10:4)

They believe God fulfills this promise of manifesting the truthfulness of the Book of Mormon through a "burning in the bosom." This expression comes from D&C 9:8. There we hear the Lord supposedly saying:

> But, behold, I say unto you, that you must study it out in your mind; then you must ask me if it be right, and if it is right *I will cause that your bosom shall burn within you; therefore, you shall feel that it is right.* (emphasis added)

Mormons equate this burning in the bosom with the promised revelation from the Holy Ghost mentioned in Moroni 10:4. *In other*

129

words, what we would call a feeling, they would call a revelation.

Interestingly, they have difficulty describing this burning in the bosom. Apostle Dallin H. Oaks explained it this way:

> I have heard adult members of the Church claim they do not have a testimony because they have never experienced a "burning in the bosom."

> If I thought this scriptural "burning" only referred to caloric heat, I would have to say that I have never had a burning in the bosom either . . . In this usage, it does not seem to refer to heat but rather to an *intensity of feeling.*

> For me, the witness of the Holy Ghost is an *intense feeling* of serenity or well-being. (*Church News*, April 29, 1989, emphasis added)

As his words reveal, even among Mormons there is unclarity concerning its exact nature. Nevertheless, there is universal agreement that it is a feeling. It is this feeling, rather than any facts, that assures them of the truthfulness of the Book of Mormon.

> But the great and conclusive evidence of the divinity of the Book of Mormon is the testimony of the Spirit to the honest truth seeker. (McConkie, *Mormon Doctrine*, p. 99)

Nearly every issue of *Ensign* has a story describing how someone received this burning in the bosom upon reading the Book of Mormon. The following is representative of such accounts.

I found myself using all my spare hours to search through the Book of Mormon. I found something else, too: a promise by an ancient prophet named Moroni—a bold declaration that I could know the truth of the book by asking God to reveal it to me. . . .

> Then it happened. It was a Thursday night in October, before a general conference of The Church of Jesus Christ of Latter-day Saints. I came home from work with a peculiar feeling growing inside me—a feeling I had never before experienced. I did not know what to make of it. It slowly grew in intensity. What a marvelous feeling! . . .

Then came the testimony—that sureness of the missionaries that had bothered me in the past. I *knew*. Joseph Smith *had* been in the presence of the Father and the Son. Indeed, he had been visited by angels. I knew. Yes, indeed, I knew. (*Ensign*, April 1990, p. 65)

This story introduces another important word in Mormonism, the word "testimony." Often Mormons want to "bear you their testimony." Although their individual testimonies vary slightly, most of them are quite standard. Most contain the following points: (1) they *know* that Jesus is the true Son of God, (2) they *know* that Joseph Smith was true prophet of God, (3) they *know* that the Church of Jesus Christ of Latter-day Saints is the true church on earth, and (4) they *know* that the Book of Mormon is true. Carefully note that this knowledge is not based on facts but on their feelings. One of their manuals described receiving a testimony this way: "when your heart begins to tell you things that your mind does not know, then you are getting the Spirit of the Lord" (*Sharing the Gospel*, p. 131). Similarly, one of their prophets wrote:

Every man who can say knowingly that Jesus Christ is the Son of God, and the Savior of men, is a prophet. This knowledge comes only through the testimony of the Holy Spirit. Men may *believe* Jesus to be the Christ, but to *know* it requires revelation from the Holy Ghost. (Joseph Fielding Smith, *The Way to Perfection*, p. 158)

Mormons view their testimony as having supernatural power. Many times when they didn't know how to answer, they would bear their testimony to me. It seemed their reason for doing that was more to "protect" themselves that to "witness." This observation appears to be valid in light of the following:

Our testimonies will sustain us throughout our lives when difficulties and trials come. At such times, we cannot be sustained by the testimonies of others, but will have to stand on our own testimonies in order to endure our trials in faith. (*Duties and Blessings of the Priesthood A*, p. 190)

Burnings in the bosom and bearing of testimonies are just two of a number of different ways Mormons rely on their feelings rather than on the facts. One other prominent way this reliance on feelings manifests itself is in their concept of prayer. They believe that their prayers are answered when they feel good.

> After making the choice, we approach the Lord in prayer and ask if the decision is right. If the decision is right, the Holy Ghost will confirm the decision by giving us a peaceful, reassuring feeling that our decision is right (see D&C 6:22-23). Sometimes we will even get a "burning in the bosom" (see D&C 9:8).

> If for some reason we have not chosen correctly, the Lord will reveal that our decision is wrong by leaving us with an uncomfortable feeling or serious doubt. (*Duties and Blessings of the Priesthood B*, p. 189)

Their manuals and magazines are filled with story after story exhibiting this same philosophy of prayer.

> I had never been able to show emotion through tears and humility, but the next thing I remember I was on my knees pleading with my Heavenly Father for help for the first time in 19 years. As I prayed, an overwhelming feeling of love and compassion and happiness filled my being, and the Holy Ghost encompassed me with such power that I sobbed convulsively for a considerable time. When I arose, I felt good. Gratitude and thankfulness filled my heart. Never in my life had I known such a feeling of warmth, and an inner burning filled my entire being with such intensity that I thought I was going to be consumed.

> I went to our bedroom and awakened my wife. I was still crying, and she asked me what was wrong. I told her of my desire to change my life and encompass the gospel of Jesus Christ, and she told me instantly that she would support me. From that moment I have never had a desire for a cigarette, a drink of any type, or a cup of coffee. (*Duties and Blessings of the Priesthood* A, p. 210)

There was only one problem: the new job required him to work on Sunday. But he needed money to support his family.

He knew that the Lord is not always displeased when people have to work on Sunday, so he prayed that the Lord would approve of his work on the Sabbath. But the Lord gave him the feeling that, in his case, he should not work on Sunday. (*Duties and Blessings of the Priesthood B*, p. 247)

An Acute Awareness of Spirits

One final outgrowth of their dependence on feelings is the acute awareness of spirits many of them have. But this awareness of the spirit world goes beyond that of feelings. Many claim, especially while they were in the temple, to have seen a deceased ancestor. They also testify of supernatural help given them. The following is quite typical:

Because the handwritten and typewritten records are sometimes faint, some names are illegible. When encountering an unreadable name, the extractors pray for help. Upon returning to the record, they often find that the name can be read easily. (*Ensign*, July 1990, p. 27)

Conclusion

This reliance, not only on their standard works and their living prophet, but especially on their feelings, can make it difficult to talk with them. Ken Mulholland, an observer of Mormonism, put it well:

They are, in fact, an *ethnos* (people) in a cultural sense, and they do have a very different way of conceptualizing truth than we do as Christians . . .

"Don't confuse me with the facts, I already know what I believe." . . . Hence, the court of final appeal—the human emotion—has passed judgment. This is the bedrock of LDS theology. ("LDS Evangelism Seen As A Cross-

Cultural Mission," pp. 1,2)

Note especially how he labels Mormonism a culture. In the next chapter, we will see a variety of reasons for labeling it as such.

Key Concepts and Terms

Scriptures: Mormonism has four scriptures: Book of Mormon, Doctrine and Covenants, Pearl of Great Price, and the Bible. They also consider the words of their living prophets as scripture.

Translation of the Bible: Many times Mormons use this phrase in reference to the transmission of the text of the Bible, rather than its translation.

Joseph Smith Translation: Also called the Inspired Version. The church claims Smith never finished it, therefore they don't use it much. Excerpts from it are given in the footnotes and appendix of their edition of the KJV.

Standard works: Another name for their four scriptures.

Book of Mormon: The supposed history of three ancient peoples in the Americas. It does not contain many unique LDS beliefs.

Doctrine and Covenants: A book containing "revelations" given mostly to Joseph Smith. It contains more LDS doctrine than the other three standard works combined.

Pearl of Great Price: A collection of five short works. Even though it is one of Mormonism's standard works, it is not familiar to many Mormons.

Priesthood: Mormons identify it with the power and authority of God. They believe that the priesthood was lost from the earth and restored at the time of Joseph Smith. There are two priesthoods in the LDS church: Aaronic and Melchizedek. Because of the priesthood, they feel they can receive revelations from God.

Bishops: The leaders in the LDS wards (local congregations). Their main responsibility is to judge the worthiness of members. They are called from within the membership and are not theologically trained. They serve for an average of five years.

General Authorities: The title for the leaders of the international church. They consist of the Presidency of the Church, the Quorum of the 12 Apostles, the first and second quorums of Seventies, and the Presiding Bishopic. They are also called the Brethern.

Living Prophet: The President of the Church. They believe his words take precedence even over their written scriptures.

Revelation through feelings: Feelings, not facts, are important to Mormons. Their testimonies are based on feelings. One of the greatest things that can happen to them is getting a "burning in the bosom."

134

CHAPTER FIVE:
KNOW THEIR
CULTURE

Mormonism is more than a religion; it is also a culture. It is not just their unique beliefs that distinguish them from all other peoples. Mormons also have a unique lifestyle.

We have already encountered some of Mormonism's cultural traits in previous chapters. Consider Mormons' language, and think of the numerous examples of how they define words uniquely. Think of how they equate the ability to bear children with mortality or how they equate revelation with a feeling. Think of how they define salvation, justification, damnation, and a host of other words.

Not only do they define words uniquely, they also employ words that are uniquely Mormon. A good example of this is "deseret," a word from the Book of Mormon that supposedly means honeybee. Nowhere is it used except in Mormonism. But there it is commonly used. A number of LDS enterprises employ it in their name (e.g., Deseret bookstores). Or think of the words "telestial" and "Lamanites." They too are unique to Mormonism, as are other expressions such as "burning in the bosom" and "bearing their testimony." It is no exaggeration to talk about the language of "Mormonese." (The glossary contains a much fuller look at Mormonese.)

LDS culture traits, however, go well beyond their language. In respect to food, we have seen their distinctive position concerning the sinfulness of drinking coffee and tea. With clothing, they have their distinctive temple garments. Even when they do something non-Mormons also do, they often do it uniquely. For example, instead of folding their hands to pray, they cross their arms. As we will see in this chapter, they have their own distinctive mythology, centered especially around the stories in the Book of Mormon and around Joseph Smith and the Mormon pioneers. Mormonism is not just a religion, it is a culture.

As with any culture, these cultural traits tend to isolate Mormons from non-Mormons. Their nonuse of coffee or caffeine products often serves as a barrier to developing casual relations with non-Mormons. Their sacred undergarments can make them stand out as different in locker rooms. Their use of "Mormonese" contributes to poor communication between Mormons and non-Mormons.

To reach Mormons, we need to bridge these cultural gaps. This chapter aims to lay the groundwork for doing that. Here we will be looking at some of the major characteristics of LDS culture. As we look at the individual traits, the picture can get somewhat confusing. It is much like looking at the individual patches of a patchwork quilt. But when we put them all together, they combine to form the fabric of LDS culture.

Church Structure

Isolation is both a characteristic of and a result of that culture. And this isolation is not confined to the heartland of Mormonism in the intermountain West. Even in its outposts, LDS culture often effectively isolates Mormons.

Many factors contribute to this isolation. The largest single contributor is that the Mormon church, by its very structure, encourages isolation. As one stake president stated: "We have a virtually self-sufficient world, physically, intellectually, spiritually, and socially, within the ward boundary" (*Idaho Statesman*, June 26, 1983). That statement does not exaggerate much. A Mormon's world revolves around the church. It does even though in recent years the church has been encouraging its members to become more involved with non-Mormons.

A Mormon can easily become all wrapped up in the church because it offers so many programs. Every day of the week their meetinghouses are beehives of activity. There are service groups, craft groups, self-improvement classes. Nearly every ward sponsors its own Scouting troop. Mormons also are very strong on athletics. Many of their meetinghouses have well-equipped gyms and lighted softball fields, with the result that they often have their own leagues in basketball, volleyball, and softball.

They especially try to center the world of their youth on the church. Their young people can participate in many of the above activities and others. For example, Friday night commonly is dance night at the ward.

136

Most important, every school day, high school students are to attend "seminary." In contrast to the common usage of this word, an LDS seminary does not train future full-time church workers. Rather it applies Mormonism to the teenage years for the high-school students. In areas with a strong LDS population, the Mormon church will build a seminary building right next to the public high school. These buildings soon become places where their youth gather and socialize before and after school. In the heartland of Mormonism, many public high schools also accommodate the LDS church by offering "early bird" classes. By taking these classes before the normal school day begins, LDS students have a free period during the day in which they can go to the seminary building for their seminary class. This practice naturally reinforces isolation.

In a similar way, the LDS church has built "institute" buildings, the college equivalents to seminary, adjacent to the campuses of many secular colleges. Such institutes offer up to twelve courses each day: courses on the various LDS scriptures, on genealogy work, on celestial marriage, on leadership. All instructors must have a master's degree or its equivalent. In addition, institutes offer many social and service activities. An LDS sorority and fraternity program even exists within the structure of this institute program.

As might be expected, the seminaries and institutes often establish very strong ties between Mormonism and its youth.

> "I am convinced that the seminaries and institutes can do much to get young people into the mission field and into temple marriage and, finally, into exaltation." (Spencer Kimball, quoted in *Achieving A Celestial Marriage*, p. 180)

In addition to all these group-oriented activities, every family is to make every Monday night "family home evening." The church is careful never to schedule any activities for Monday evening. On that night, the family stays together for family studies and fun. Single persons are urged to find others with whom to hold these evenings. These family home evenings not only bind them together but again tend to isolate them from their non-Mormon friends. Monday night becomes another time when you can't get together with them.

Ideally, home teachers also visit every family each month. If there is a woman in the home, female "visiting teachers" also visit her. This regular contact in their homes is another thread binding Mormons to the LDS church and culture.

Taken together, all this activity tends effectively to isolate them. It also keeps them busy as bees. In fact, being busy is another of the cultural traits of Mormonism.

Busy as a Bee

It is no accident that Utah is known as the beehive state. "Right from the beginning, the beehive was a symbol of the church" (Church spokesman Ted Johnson, in *Idaho Statesman*, July 3, 1983). Being busy is an integral part of the LDS faith.

> "Our Heavenly Father loves us so completely that he has given us a commandment to work. This is one of the keys to eternal life." (Howard W. Hunter, quoted in *Ensign*, May 1989, p. 8)

> Man's goal is to become as God is, and the Lord has said "*there is no end to my works*" [Moses 1:38, emphasis added]. To enter into the "rest" of the Lord means to enter into a fulness of God's glory (see D&C 84:24) where one will rest from the cares and sorrows of mortality. It does not, however, mean that one will cease to work. (*D&C Student Manual*, pp. 360,361)

> Elder Bruce R. McConkie commented on the necessity of work: "Work is the law of life; it is the ruling principle in the lives of the Saints. We cannot, while physically able, voluntarily shift the burden of our own support to others. Doles abound in evils. Industry, thrift, and self-respect are essential to salvation." (*Lay Hold Upon the Word of God*, p. 83)

As that last comment illustrates, when Mormons talk about the importance of work, they are not just speaking of doing morally good works. They are talking about physical labor. In more ways than one, their gospel centers on work. In keeping with that emphasis, they prize worldly success very highly.

How highly they value a good work ethic and worldly success can be seen in the makeup of their leadership. The General Authorities are not theologians. Rather they were successful bankers, doctors, lawyers, business executives, and politicians. For example, Ezra Taft Benson, a past church president, was the Secretary of Agriculture in President Eisenhower's administration.

> Perhaps the most vigorous tradition transmitted by Joseph Smith was the identification of God with material prosperity . . . Financial wizardry has come to be looked upon as equally important with spiritual excellence among the qualifications for church leadership. (Fawn Brodie, *No Man Knows My History*, p. 403)

This pattern is usually repeated on the local level. The following was said in a discussion of bishops and branch presidents:

> As the Church continues to grow, more and more worthy priesthood holders are being called to these responsible positions of leadership. Many of them have little church experience and gospel knowledge. But they are humble, and they need the faith, prayers, and support of the members they serve. (*Duties and Blessings of the Priesthood A*, p. 58)

Note that, according to his quotation, many bishops do not hold their office because of their knowledge. They have little gospel knowledge! What makes them worthy, more often than not, is not only their moral living but also their worldly success. It is the successful business leader or professional person who most often becomes the bishop. Mormons look upon worldly success, if it is earned by hard work, as a sign of spirituality. They learn this work ethic at a very young age.

> Thou shalt not refuse to take part in any work of the Church, for by thy work shall thou be known. (*Talks for Tots*, p. 48)

Because of this emphasis on work, bishops and other church leaders donate many hours each week to their church callings. But the leaders are not the only ones who are expected to work in the ward. According to an article in the October 1990 issue of *Ensign*, there are 330 church positions in an average ward. Admittedly, many of these positions are of a minor nature and not very time-consuming. Yet, even the minor positions can regularly remind them of the importance of work.

I didn't realize how closely Mormons identify themselves with hard work until an LDS leader asked me if I was trying to convert Mormons to Christianity because I was afraid of their busyness and hard work. The surprising thing to me was that he still felt that way after I had explained to him on different occasions my motivation for reaching out to Mormons. In spite of my spelling out to him my concern for his and other Mormon's souls, he still thought that it was their work ethic I found threatening.

Not only do they emphasis working hard, they also stress self-sufficiency. Every Mormon is to strive to become increasingly self-sufficient. Girls and women are to sew and cook; men are to be handy around the house. This emphasis is reflected in their manuals, which routinely talk about such subjects as gardening and homemaking.

This emphasis on being self-sufficient is tied in with their belief that, before Christ returns, the world will become so ravished that they will need to fend for themselves. It is the duty of every family to prepare for that by having a year's supply of food in storage. That is why many Mormons have large gardens. That is why many were pioneers in the area of freeze-dried food.

> "The revelation to store food may be as essential to our temporal salvation today as boarding the ark was to the people in the days of Noah." (Ezra Taft Benson, quoted in *Achieving A Celestial Marriage*, p. 258)

> "We affirm the previous counsel the Church has always given, to acquire and maintain a year's supply—a year's supply of the basic commodities for us . . . We encourage families to have on hand this year's supply, and we say it over and over and over and repeat over and over the scripture of the Lord where He says, 'Why call ye me, Lord, Lord, and do not the things which I say?" (Spencer W. Kimball, quoted in *Latter-day Saint Woman B*, p. 210)

But they are to have not only a year's supply of food stored away. Material to make clothes, generators and other sources of power, medicine, and blankets are also to be gathered.

> In addition to the storage of food items, there are other things to consider. If possible, a reserve of fuels, such as coal, oil, or wood, should be part of the storage plan. Various types of supplementary heating and cooking units, some of which are portable, are available on the market. It is wise to select those that would, in an emergency, serve both for the preparation of food and for warmth. Items such as first-aid articles, soaps or cleansing agents, and matches, may be considered. A reserve of bedding should be included. (*Come Unto Me*, p. 230)

Still another activity that keeps them busy is keeping a journal. Each day they are to write in their journals, stressing especially how following the principles of Mormonism has helped them. Their journal is to serve as their testimony to their posterity. In the following quote note that keeping a journal is not optional; it is part of obeying the prophet:

> Tell the children that the prophet Spencer W. Kimball spoke of the need for a journal in the following statement: "Get a notebook, my young folks, a journal that will last through all time, and maybe the angels may quote from it for eternity . . ." Explain that obedience to the counsel of the prophet is a very important reason for keeping a journal. (*Walk in His Ways B*, p. 187)

Their missionary program reveals still another facet of this emphasis on work and self-sufficiency. In 1997 they had over 53,000 full-time missionaries in the field. The majority of these were young men and women, but an increasing number are retired individuals and couples. Young men serve for two years, while young women serve for 18 months. We will be looking at the missionary program in depth in chapter twelve. I mention it here as just another illustration of the LDS gospel of work.

No matter where a Mormon is—whether at home, on the job, or at church—he is busy. As one of their church presidents, Joseph Fielding Smith, said:

Membership in the Church is not for the idler. He who seeks an easy road to salvation must go elsewhere, it is not to be obtained in the Church. (*The Way to Perfection*, p. 149)

Morally Good

Along with the idler, there is no room in the LDS church for the blatant sinner.

Besides murder, other reasons for losing LDS membership would include conviction on a felony charge, adultery, child or wife abuse, and the practice of plural marriage. (Scharffs, *The Truth about the Godmakers*, p. 335)

Morality has become a prominent characteristic of Mormonism. One of the first things that comes to most people's minds about Mormons is that they are good people.

Many critics of Mormonism have attacked this image of morality and have tarnished it. To prove their claim, they often cite Utah state statistics on drug abuse, teen pregnancies, and a number of other such problem areas, which are higher than the national average. The LDS rebuttal is that there are many non-Mormons living in Utah, That is true, but the 70% Mormon population of Utah should have some bearing on the state's statistics.

Nevertheless, many Mormons live good moral lives. Many make good employees and good neighbors. They work hard on projecting that image. From the cleanliness of the Temple Square in Salt Lake City to their clean-cut missionaries scattered around the world, Mormonism projects an image of wholesomeness.

Hand-in-hand with this upright image, most Mormons are fiercely patriotic and politically conservative. In fact, they believe that the Constitution of the United States was divinely inspired.

And for this purpose have I established the Constitution of this land by the hands of wise men whom I raised up unto this very purpose, and redeemed the land by the shedding of blood. (*Doctrine and Covenants* 101:80)

"To me . . . that statement of the Lord, 'I have established the Constitution of this land,' puts the Constitution of the United States in the position in which it would be if it were written in the book of Doctrine and Covenants itself. This makes the Constitution the word of the Lord to us." (J. Reuben Clark, quoted in *Doctrine and Covenants Student Manual*, p. 244)

Their welfare program also has contributed to their positive public image. Over the years, their welfare program has received extensive publicity so that it has also undergone intensive scrutiny. Critics of Mormonism claim that it is not the shining example of charity it is portrayed to be. In their carefully-researched book, Heinerman and Schupe go so far as to talk about "The Myth of Mormon Welfare." (For their treatment, see pp. 180-195 in *The Mormon Corporate Empire*.) They claim that it never was very effective and is diminishing in importance each year. As proof they point to the dwindling number of stake welfare production committees, bishops' storehouses, and church-owned farms: all of which serve as the backbone of the system.

Less controversial are their Deseret Industries, which are patterned after Goodwill Industries. They employ handicapped and impaired persons who recondition and repair donated items. These items are then sold in outlet stores.

Family-oriented

Closely connected with the Mormons' image of being moral is that of being family-oriented. In the preceding chapters we have seen the theological reasons for this emphasis. Not much needs to be added at this point. Suffice it to say, they have emphasized family to the point that it has become one of their cultural traits. As a result, most people associate Mormonism with concern for the family.

Although this emphasis on the family is not unique to Mormonism, there are still some uniquely LDS aspects to it. For one, their motivation for having children is unique. As we saw in a previous chapter, one of their main motivations for bearing children is to provide bodies for spirit children. Having children is a good work. Such thinking results in some Mormons placing more importance on the act of having children than on the children themselves.

Another unique aspect of their family emphasis is their stress on genealogy work. Because of their theology, family history is extremely important to them. They can't understand and are shocked, at times, by a non-Mormon's casual attitude toward family history. Ancestors play a significant role in Mormonism.

Sunday Schedule

Another important patch in the quilt of LDS culture is their Sunday activity. Here again we see elements that are found in other religions, mixed with elements that are uniquely Mormon. Similar to some Christian churches, Mormons equate Sunday with the Sabbath.

> "There seems to be an ever-increasing popularity in disregarding the centuries-old commandment to observe and respect the Sabbath day. For many it has become a holiday rather than a holy day of rest and sanctification. For some it is a day to shop and buy groceries. The decision of those who engage in shopping, sports, work, and recreation on the Sabbath day is their own, for which they alone bear responsibility." (James E. Faust, quoted in *Lay Hold Upon the Word of God*, p. 99)

On Sunday they are expected to spend three hours at their meetinghouses. One hour is devoted to a sacrament meeting, which is their equivalent of a worship service. Another hour is devoted to Sunday School for all ages. During the third hour, the men go to their respective priesthood meetings, the women attend Relief Society, and the children go to Primary (similar to Sunday school). A church wide curriculum is used for Sunday School, Relief Society, and priesthood meetings. They are not to deviate from this curriculum or the manuals that present the individual lessons.

Often two wards share one building. One ward meets for three hours on Sunday morning and the other one meets for its three-hour block of time on Sunday afternoon. Each year the wards will switch schedules, and the members must switch schedules along with their wards. They can't switch wards if, for example, they prefer always going in the morning. Each ward covers a certain geographic area and all members within that area belong to that ward.

Although the heart of their Sunday observance is this three-hour block of time, they are to keep the whole day sacred.

144

"The Sabbath is a holy day in which to do worthy and holy things. Abstinence from work and recreation is important but insufficient. The Sabbath calls for constructive thoughts and acts, and if one merely lounges about doing nothing on the Sabbath, he is breaking it. To observe it, one will be on his knees in prayer, preparing lessons, studying the gospel, meditating, visiting the ill and distressed, sleeping, reading wholesome material, and attending all the meetings of that day to which he is expected. To fail to do these proper things is a transgression on the omission side." (Spencer W. Kimball, quoted in *Ensign*, Nov. 1991, p. 34)

President Ezra Taft Benson listed some activities that are not in harmony with the spirit of the Sabbath.

•Overworking and staying up late Saturday so that you are exhausted the next day . . .
•Doing gardening and odd jobs around the house.
•Taking trips to canyons or resorts, visiting friends socially, joy riding, wasting time, and engaging in other amusements . . .
•Playing vigorously and going to movies.
•Engaging in sports and hunting "wild animals" which God made for the use of man only "in times of famine and excess of hunger . . ." (See D&C 89:15)
•Shopping or supporting with your patronage businesses that operate on Sunday, such as grocery stores, supermarkets, restaurants and service stations. (*Lay Hold Upon the Word of God*, pp. 99,100)
Our observance of the Sabbath is an indication of the depth of our conversion and our willingness to keep sacred covenants. (Earl C. Tingey, *Ensign*, May 1996, p. 12)

As stated before, the core of their Sunday activity is the time they spend at their wards, at the heart of which is their sacrament meetings. Since they have no ordained ministers, each week the bishop assigns talks to individual members. During each sacrament meeting there will be a handful of such talks. These talks usually do not center on LDS teachings. More often the assigned speaker will speak on morality or will tell how some aspect of Mormonism benefitted them greatly in their lives.

During the sacrament meeting they also sing hymns. Many of their hymns are common to Christianity; others are uniquely Mormon. What is revealing is how small but subtle changes have often been made in the hymns common with Christianity. At times a verse is left off; other times a phrase is reworded. Many times it changes because the common wording would have contradicted LDS teaching. By using these Christian hymns, however, they strengthen the impression that they are Christian.

An integral part of each sacrament meeting is the distribution of the sacrament, consisting of bread and water. Before it is distributed, the sacrament prayers must be spoken over the elements by one of the young men in the priesthood. These prayers, from Section 20 in D&C, must be spoken exactly as printed, before the sacrament can be distributed. Some Mormons have related stories to me of times when a boy would get flustered and would have to repeat the prayers five times before he got them right. After the sacrament is blessed, the deacons (12-to 14-year-old boys) distribute it to the congregation. Even toddlers partake of it. The purpose of the LDS sacrament is not to receive forgiveness from God; it is to remind them of their obligations to God.

> To keep his saints in constant remembrance of their obligation to accept and obey him—or in other words, to eat his flesh and drink his blood—the Lord has given them the sacramental ordinance. (*Life and Teachings of Jesus & His Apostles*, p. 93)

On the first Sunday of the month, the sacrament meetings are known as fast and testimony meetings. Instead of assigned speakers, any member is welcome to come forward and bear his or her testimony. The common theme of such testimonies is how following the principles of Mormonism has helped them. After sitting through a couple of such meetings, one begins to understand how hearing a number of their peers sing the praises of Mormonism can easily strengthen a person in Mormonism.

On this Sunday they are to fast. Spencer W. Kimball went so far as to say: "Failing to fast is a sin" (quoted in *Doctrines of the Gospel*, p. 34).

146

> "The law to the Latter-day Saints, as understood by the authorities of the church, is that food and drink are not to be partaken of for twenty-four hours, 'from even to even,' and that the Saints are to refrain from all bodily gratification and indulgences." (Joseph F. Smith, quoted in *To Make Thee A Minister and a Witness*, p. 116)

They are to donate the money they save from fasting as their fast-offering for the poor, but they don't collect this or any money during their sacrament meetings. That is not to say, however, that giving is not important. As was noted in a previous chapter, tithing is one of the requirements they have to meet before they can enter the Temple. In addition, members meet with their bishop once a year for their tithing settlement. Tithing is essential to Mormonism.

> Accordingly, tithing becomes one of the great tests of the personal righteousness of the church members. "By this principle," President Joseph F. Smith says, "the loyalty of the people of this Church shall be put to the test. By this principle it shall be known who is for the kingdom of God and who is against it . . . There is a great deal of importance connected with this principle, for by it shall be known whether we are faithful or unfaithful." (McConkie, *Mormon Doctrine*, p. 797)

Mormons just don't collect tithes and offerings during the sacrament meeting. Instead, each member hands them directly to the bishop or one of his counselors. In addition to tithes and fast offerings, they are encouraged to give other gifts such as missionary offerings. Thus faithful Mormons contribute substantially more than 10% of their income to the church.

In this section I have intentionally shied away from using the word worship. I did that because numerous Mormons and ex-Mormons throughout the years have expressed difficulty with the concept of worship. As one put it: "How can you worship someone who hasn't really done anything for you?" Or as another wrote:

> "Mormons don't grovel before God, prating their unworthiness and imploring mercy. They are not slaves! They are men, made in the image of God! They proudly

> stand, hold their heads high, and put out their hands to shake that of God in greeting, as any worthy son would be expected to respectfully but proudly stand before a wise and good father." (Joseph H. Weston, quoted in *Shadow and Reality*, p. 564)

Such comments are not surprising in light of the content and structure of their sacrament meetings. The closest things resembling worship are their songs and prayers, and even most of them focus on the Mormons themselves. They spend the vast majority of time encouraging each other to be good and moral. Rarely do they mention what God has done for them. This is not just my observation either. At a general conference, Apostle Dallin H. Oaks reported the following:

> I quote from a recent letter I received from a member in the United States. He described what he heard in his fast and testimony meeting:

> "I sat and listened to seventeen testimonies and never heard Jesus mentioned or referred to in any way. I thought I might be in [some other denomination], but I supposed not because there were no references to God, either . . .

> The following Sunday, I again attended church. I sat through a priesthood lesson, a Gospel Doctrine lesson, and seven sacrament meeting speakers and never once heard the name of Jesus or any reference to him. (*Ensign*, Nov. 1990, p. 30)

Mormonism, because it is a thoroughly man-centered religion, has no true concept of worship. True worship is foreign to LDS culture.

Mormon Mythology

One striking patch in the quilt of LDS culture is Mormon mythology. By that I mean stories both from the Book of Mormon and from their church's early history. Although they would vehemently object to these stories being called myths, I feel that mythology best describes, for the non-Mormon, how these stories are used in the LDS

148

community. They don't just know them, they treasure them. They pass them down from generation to generation. They refer to them often. For many Mormons, this mythology is one of the strongest bonds binding them to Mormonism.

They revere especially stories about Joseph Smith. Many incidents in his life have become so embellished that it is often difficult to separate the facts from the fiction. No incident better illustrates this than the one known as his first vision.

According to Smith, Heavenly Father and Jesus appeared to him in the spring of 1820 and told him not to join any existing church because "all their creeds were an abomination in his [Heavenly Father's] sight" (*Joseph Smith-History*, 1:19). Although most non-Mormons view this whole incident as a figment of Smith's fertile imagination, *all Mormons* view it as nothing less than epoch-making. That they have included this account in the Pearl of Great Price, thus giving it the status of scripture, already illustrates that. Even more revealing is the following statement-the gist of which runs through their manuals:

> The key to a testimony of the gospel is Joseph Smith's
> first vision. All that we believe hinges on this account. .
> . . The greatest event that has ever occurred in the world
> since the resurrection of the Son of God from the tomb
> and his ascension on high, was the coming of the Father
> and the Son to that boy Joseph Smith, to prepare the way
> for the laying of the foundation of His kingdom. (*Sharing
> the Gospel Course Manual*, pp. 33,34)

Mormons consider the first vision such a great event because they believe

> 1. it marked the end of the great apostasy and signaled
> the return of the true church to earth, and
> 2. it proved that Joseph Smith was a true prophet of God.

Because they place such great stock in it, it has been intensely scrutinized by non-Mormons. This scrutiny has uncovered many problems with Smith's story. The Tanners, among others, have done yeoman's service detailing such problems.

Along with the first vision, Mormons also treasure the account of Joseph Smith's death. That account, like his account of the first vision, has the status of scripture (Section 135 in D&C). In June of 1844 he and three other LDS leaders were arrested in a wave of anti-Mormon sentiment and taken to jail in Carthage, Illinois. On June 27, a mob rushed the jail, killing Joseph and his brother Hyrum. Mormons today refer to this as his martyrdom.

Many other incidents from his life, even the ones based on proven fact, are often embellished. Other stories go beyond embellishment. Let one example suffice.

> "He [Joseph] called upon the Lord in prayer, the power of God rested upon him mightily, and as Jesus healed all the sick around Him in His day, so Joseph, the Prophet of God, healed all around on this occasion. He healed all in his house and dooryard; then, in company with Sidney Rigdon and several of the Twelve, went among the sick lying on the bank of the river, where he commanded them in a loud voice, in the name of Jesus Christ, to rise and be made whole, and they were all healed." (Wilford Woodruff, quoted in *Truth Restored*, pp. 65f.)

All of this has made Joseph Smith bigger than life to most Latter-day Saints. For example, they believe that he, along with other great prophets, participated in creation.

> Enoch, Noah, Abraham, Moses, Peter, James, and John, Joseph Smith, and many other "noble and great" ones played a part in the great creative enterprise. (McConkie, *Mormon Doctrine*, p. 169)

They also say that his coming was prophesied in the Book of Mormon (See 2 Nephi 3). As Moslems have elevated their prophet Mohammed next to God Himself, so Mormons have elevated Joseph Smith.

> Joseph Smith, the Prophet and Seer of the Lord, has done more, save Jesus only, for the salvation of men in this world, than any other man that ever lived in it. *(Doctrine and Covenants,* 135:3)

> "No man or woman in this dispensation will ever enter into the celestial kingdom of God without the consent of

Joseph Smith. From the day that the Priesthood was taken from the earth to the winding-up scene of all things, every man and woman must have the certificate of Joseph Smith, junior, as a passport to their entrance into the mansion where God and Christ are—I with you and you with me. I cannot go there without his consent." (Brigham Young, quoted in *Sharing the Gospel Course Manual*, p. 40)

It is next to impossible for a non-Mormon to understand just how essential a role the "mythology" of Joseph Smith plays in Mormonism. They talk about Joseph Smith, not Jesus Christ, at their sacrament meetings. Numerous hymns extol his virtues. Respect for Joseph is one of the first things Mormon children learn.

An angel came and spoke to man
About the everlasting plan,
That God would send again to earth
The same as at the Savior's birth.
Our prophet Joseph was the one
God chose, and with his holy Son,
Told him the things that he must do
To bring the truth to me and you.

So children grown, and children small,
It is God's hope that one and all
Will listen, learn, and work and pray,
To follow this, the only way.
(*Talks for Tots*, p. 38)

Whole books have been written examining Joseph Smith's life. Since such great claims have been made about him, he and his life have been thoroughly examined by critics of Mormonism. Their work has resulted in exposing much of the myth that surrounds him. Fawn M. Brodie's book, *No Man Knows My History*, is considered by many the classic in the field. Many, then, use these facts as their main weapon when talking to Mormons.

Although the facts uncovered by this research are extremely valuable, it is my opinion that it is better first to bring God's law and gospel to bear on a Mormon. I believe that the subject of Joseph Smith can be profitably addressed only after Mormons have been exposed to the drastic difference between how Mormonism and Christianity describe the attaining of perfection. Part two of this book explains this approach in depth.

Not all Mormon mythology is tied up with Joseph Smith. They also idolize Brigham Young and the pioneers that followed him west. Stories of the 1846-1847 "Great Trek" west are especially treasured. They compare it with the Exodus and Utah with the Promised Land.

> President Anthony W. Ivins explained the similarities and differences between the exodus of the Saints to the West and the exodus of ancient Israel. He pointed out that the trek west for the Saints was a *greater accomplishment* for those people than was the exodus from Egypt for the ancient Israel.

> Recognizing the hopelessness of reconciliation with their neighbors, determined to find a place where the Saints could worship the Lord without molestation, this modern Moses [Brigham Young] and his associates turned their faces westward, and after a *journey unparalleled in the history of the world* found asylum in these mountain valleys, where the body of the Church now resides. (*D&C Student Manual*, p. 351, emphasis added)

In line with this, the biggest holiday in Salt Lake City and its surrounding areas is Pioneer Days, commemorating the pioneers' arrival in the Salt Valley. It is a point of great pride to be related to one of these early pioneers. Many issues of *Ensign* contain at least one story extolling the pioneers' virtues, especially their spirit of sacrifice. These pioneers are held up before the eyes of even the smallest children.

> The pioneers of long ago
> Were strong and brave and true
> They earned many blessings
> For themselves, for me, and you.

> They worked hard as they struggled
> To make new homes in the West.
> They kept the Sabbath holy;

Of all days they loved it best.
(*Talk for Tots*, p. 44)

We cannot deny that this journey from the banks of the Mississippi to the mountains of Utah was a great accomplishment. Neither can we deny that many who made the trip in subsequent years demonstrated great courage. But it also cannot be denied that many of these stories have become embellished over the years. Just like fictional stories about George Washington have developed over time (e.g., his cutting down the cherry tree) so also here. At times, these pioneers, like Joseph Smith, have become bigger than life. For example, they say that when Brigham Young became President of the church, he was transfigured to look like Joseph Smith. (For the story, see *Latter-day Saint Woman B*, pp. 105-107.)

Another prominent piece of Mormon mythology, based on various sections of Doctrine and Covenants, revolves around Christ's second coming. Mormons believe that when he returns he will return both to Jerusalem and Independence, Missouri (Jackson County), which they consider Zion. (The LDS concept of Zion is very confusing. Sometimes it refers to Independence; other times to Salt Lake City; still other times to a condition in their heart.) For this reason, the temple plot in Independence, Missouri has special significance for them.

> Since this revelation (D&C 103:11-14) was given, many leaders of the Church have discussed the future return to Jackson County, Missouri, including Elder Orson F. Whitney, who said: "Will our mission end here [in Utah]? Is the State of Utah the proper monument of the 'Mormon' People? No . . . the monument to 'Mormonism' will stand in Jackson County, MO. There the great City will be built: There Zion will arise and shine, 'the joy of the whole Earth,' and there the Lord will come to His temple in his own time, when His people shall have made the required preparation." (*D&C Student Manual*, p. 249)

Because of their belief concerning the ten lost tribes of Israel, the Mormons believe Jesus will return to both Jerusalem and Independence. They believe that, at Christ's return, the lost tribes will come forward and their capital will be Independence, while the capital of Judah will be Jerusalem.

For from both these centers the Lord shall judge. Jerusalem shall be rebuilt and become a holy city, the capital for Judah, and Zion shall be the capital and city of our God, for Ephraim and his fellows. Both shall be seats of government in unison with each other, and the Lord shall dwell in both. *(D&C Student Manual,* p. 339)

In fact, they often refer to their mission activity as the preliminary "gathering of Israel." They believe that most Mormons today are from the tribe of Ephraim.

"The great majority of those who become members of the Church are literal descendants of Abraham through Ephraim, son of Joseph." (Joseph Fielding Smith, quoted in *Ensign,* Jan. 1991, p. 53)

They go so far as to say that, at the moment of conversion, the Holy Ghost will change a person's blood to make him a literal descendant of Abraham. They identify this change with the new creation we become in Christ.

"The effect of the Holy Ghost upon a Gentile, is to purge out the old blood, and make him actually of the seed of Abraham. That man that has none of the blood of Abraham (naturally) must have a new creation by the Holy Ghost." (Joseph Smith, quoted in *Doctrines of the Gospel,* pp. 57f.)

Mormons also believe, based on D&C 116, that immediately before Jesus returns, Adam will return and preside over a great council at Adam-ondi-Ahman. Adam-ondi-Ahman is north of Independence and was, according to Joseph Smith, the site where Adam lived after he was driven out of the Garden of Eden. The world and even most Mormons will not be aware of this council; only a select few will know about it.

The LDS church also teaches a millennium. During this time, they believe the veil separating this world from the next will become very thin, making it much easier for the spirits to aid the people on earth with their genealogical work. So, they believe, the temple work will be corrected and completed during the millennium.

Or consider the following:

Those worthy parents who have lost a child in this life have the promise that they may rear their child after the Resurrection during the Millennium. "Joseph Smith declared that the mother who laid down her little child, being deprived of the privilege, the joy, and the satisfaction of bringing it up to manhood or womanhood in this world, would, after the resurrection, have all the joy, satisfaction and pleasure, and even more than it would have been possible to have had in mortality, in seeing her child grow to the full measure of the stature of its spirit." (*Learn of Me*, p. 68)

The LDS church promulgates numerous other beliefs in connection with Christ's return, all of which contribute to Mormon mythology. I cite just one more example, the belief that when Christ returns the continents will be rejoined.

President Joseph Fielding Smith added to the Saints' understanding of the last days: "If, however, the earth is to be restored as it was in the Beginning, then all the land surface will again be in one place as it was before the days of Peleg, when this great division was accomplished. Europe, Africa, and the islands of the sea including Australia, New Zealand, and other places in the Pacific must be brought back and joined together as they were in the beginning." (*D&C Student Manual*, p. 340)

One more prominent strand of Mormon mythology remains, namely, all the stories contained in the Book of Mormon. Even though I am labeling them as mythology, it is important to keep in mind that Mormons view them as scriptural truth. We are talking about them here because they are not only part of LDS religion, they are also part of its culture. In fact, since the Book of Mormon teaches few distinctive LDS doctrines, Book of Mormon stories are more a part of their culture than their religion.

Even though many Mormons are not very familiar with the Book of Mormon, they are familiar with some of its stories. Even as many non-Christians know about Noah, Moses, and David and Goliath, most Mormons are familiar with the stories of Nephi, Alma, Mosiah, Mormon, and Moroni. Similarly, many know about Lehi and his family leaving

Jerusalem, sailing across the ocean, and coming to the Americas centuries before Christ; about Jesus' appearance to the Nephites in America after His resurrection; and about the great battle fought at the hill of Cumorah. In addition, they still use Book of Mormon expressions in their everyday conversations. Previously I mentioned the word "deseret." Still today Mormons often refer to native American Indians as Lamanites. Even the names of numerous towns in Utah are taken from the Book of Mormon (e.g., Bountiful, Manti, Nephi). In these and many other ways, Mormon mythology illustrates that it is more than a religion. It is also a culture.

> All observers, scholars and journalists alike, agree that Mormon subculture is unique. Probably the closest comparison could be made to the individual colonies of religious sects that fled Old World persecution to settle on the Eastern seaboard of North America in the seventeenth and eighteenth centuries. Each possessed its own distinctive theology and civic style, consciously keeping itself different from others.

> . . . It has its own heroes and icons, holidays, and traditions, and even its own vocabulary. In many ways Mormonism is still a colony marking time in modern America. (Shupe, *The Darker Side of Virtue*, p. 14)

Controlled

The thread that ties together the various patches of this cultural quilt is the control the LDS church exerts over its people. From top to bottom, it is a highly structured organization:

The President of the Church

The Quorum of the Twelve Apostles

The Other General Authorities (who supervise 20 worldwide areas)

The areas are divided into districts (regions)

The districts contain a number of stakes

The stakes contain a number of wards

The local wards and branches (mission churches)

Through this structure, the church's influence permeates every corner of a Mormon's life. The church has set policies and procedures on matters from how to garden to what to teach in Sunday School, from who is eligible to play on a ward softball team to who is eligible to enter the temple. From daily seminary classes to monthly visits from the home teachers, the church is constantly in their lives.

Add to that the mind set of never questioning priesthood authority and you have a carefully controlled society. As we will see in the next chapter, some find this attractive while others find it oppressive.

Key Concepts

Mormonism: A religion of work: their salvation depends not only on "doing good works" but also on physical labor.

Sacrament Meetings: Their "worship" services. Each week they partake of the sacrament (water and bread). Instead of hearing sermons, members give talks and personal testimonies.

Sacrament: Stresses their obligation, not God's forgiveness.

First Vision: Heavenly Father and Jesus supposedly appeared to Joseph Smith and told him all existing churches were corrupt. Mormons view this as proof that Smith was a true prophet of God.

Joseph Smith: Mormons view him not only as the founder of their religion but as having done more than anybody else, except Jesus, for the salvation of mankind.

Mormon Pioneers: They regularly hold up the early Mormons as examples of work and sacrifice.

CHAPTER SIX: KNOW THEIR ATTRACTIONS/ STRESSES

M ormonism is one of the fastest growing religions in the world, gaining over a quarter of a million converts each year. Lyle Schaller, a prominent observer of religious trends, has gone so far as to describe it as the first worldwide religion to emerge since Islam.

This chapter lists some of the reasons behind its appeal. Since many of these reasons have been thoroughly discussed in previous chapters, this won't require much more than a quick enumeration. Of much greater importance is seeing that there is another, and opposite, side to its appeal. For many of its members, the LDS church is not a little bit of heaven on earth. It is, instead, a source of great stress. That is where we want to focus our attention. The more points of stress we can uncover in the lives of our LDS friends, the more pointed our witness to them can be.

Attractive Teachings

But first we want to look briefly at some of the things that attract people to Mormonism. Heading the list is its emphasis that people must win their way back into God's favor. Sometimes Christians forget just how attractive a teaching this is. After seeing the eternal life Jesus completely won for us and God freely gives us, we wonder why anybody would want to try to work their way into heaven.

We, however, need to remember that this is how all people think by nature. Everybody was born with that idea ingrained in them. Thinking that we have to earn eternal life is inherent in having a sinful nature. In addition, most people have had that idea pounded into them from birth. From every direction, they are told there are no free rides in life. Therefore, most people look upon it as a given that it is all up to them to work themselves back into God's good graces. As evidence of such thinking, note that all religions, with the exception of Christianity, are founded on that very premise.

But Mormonism has taken it one step further. Instead of just gaining heaven by hard work, it says people can attain godhood itself! Nothing caters to people's pride and challenges them more than being told that they can become gods. Over the years, millions have accepted this challenge.

Another attractive LDS teaching is their belief that very few persons will spend their eternity in outer darkness. As anyone knows who has ever done much witnessing, one of the biblical doctrines most troubling to non-Christians is that all unbelievers, even "good" people, will go to hell. When told this, they often view it very negatively, labeling it as unthinkable and barbaric. It often becomes a roadblock, preventing them from doing any further study of Christianity. By all but abolishing hell, Mormonism has removed that stumbling block.

Similarly, many find Mormonism's work of redeeming the dead appealing. That everyone receives this chance to hear and accept "the truth" is in tune with people's sense of fair play. This teaching is especially enticing to someone who is religious but whose parents weren't. Such people frequently would give anything to help their parents especially if they are feeling guilty about not talking to their parents about religion before they died. Mormonism gives them, and their parents, a way out.

Still another teaching that serves as a magnet, drawing people to Mormonism, is their emphasis on having eternal families. In the early 1980's, the church started promoting its family image more than its doctrine. According to newspaper interviews of some local Mormon leaders. It did so on the basis of market surveys that revealed this is what non-Mormons found attractive about Mormonism.

Surprisingly, however, that is not what numerous individuals who had converted to Mormonism pointed to when I asked them what attracted them to the LDS church. Far more commonly, they said they were drawn to Mormonism because it was the only church that made God understandable. Often they would go on at length explaining how they had previously struggled with the doctrine of the Trinity. They would talk about their great frustration in trying to understand it and the

159

satisfaction they experienced with the LDS explanation.

The more I have encountered this, the more I have wondered if their recollections were not skewed somewhat by their later exposure, as members, to this emphasis. But even if that is the case with some, the following two conclusions seem warranted:

1. Many LDS doctrines, on the surface, cater to human reason. That is attractive to human nature.

2. Centering our witness attempts around the nature of God by contrasting the biblical teaching with LDS teaching is attacking one of their strong points, not one of their stress points. As I will demonstrate shortly, I think it is much better to find them and concentrate on those areas where Mormonism is producing stress in Mormons.

In summary, Mormonism offers many people what they want. It gives them a chance to earn heaven (even godhood) themselves, without having the threat of eternal punishment hanging over their heads. It gives them a chance to be with their extended family forever, even giving them the opportunity to save some of their families. And it gives them a god after their own image: one who once was a man, who remains an exalted man.

Attractive Practices

Coupled with these appealing teachings are some appealing practices. The LDS church with its many rules and regulations removes much of the decision-making from life. As we will see shortly, some find this oppressive. But others find this quite attractive. Kevin Bond, a former Mormon, put it this way:

I felt a real security in Mormonism. Everything was spelled out for me. Everything was either black or white. (*Ex-Mormons—Why We Left*, p. 120)

The varied activities that the LDS church sponsors also serve as drawing cards for many people. They keep their craft groups, youth activities, sports leagues, and the like, open to non-Mormons. It is estimated that 50% of the people who make use of their genealogical libraries are non-Mormons. These non-threatening initial exposures to Mormonism have drawn many non-Mormons slowly but surely into full-fledged church membership.

As has already been touched on, Mormonism's high profile on family issues attracts many troubled families. So does its image of being morally and politically conservative. To parents and/or teenagers who are despairing of the evils of society, Mormonism appears to be a safe haven in which to weather out the storm. (Many times, it is the teenagers who are being attracted by the LDS image of morality.)

Still another appealing aspect of Mormonism is its image of being a caring community. If a non-Mormon needs help, whether it is legal, financial, or just help around the house, Mormons are often right there. Countless are the stories of Mormons bringing over meals to families in times of sickness, or of doing odd jobs for the elderly.

Finally, the LDS emphasis on emotions and feelings as a source of revelation strikes a responsive cord in many people. We live in a world whose motto many times is: "If it feels good, do it." Mormonism has capitalized on that emphasis with the result that it feels good for many people.

It feels good initially. But much of the beauty of Mormonism is only skin—deep. Underneath lurks a hideous monster that has slowly enslaved and now is steadily tormenting many Mormons. Few religions better fit Jesus' picture of false prophets as ferocious wolves wearing sheep's clothing. In order to understand our LDS friends-in order to feel compassion for them—in order to witness pointedly to them—we need to become acquainted with the beast behind the beauty.

The Stress of Being Obsessed with Perfection

Throughout the preceding chapters, we have repeatedly encountered the tremendous emphasis Mormonism places on perfection. We have observed Matthew 5:48 being cited time and again. We have seen how Mormons equate repentance with abandoning the sin and, in that connection, have listened as one of their prophets said:

> "Nor is repentance complete when one merely tries to abandon sin . . . To try is weak." (Spencer Kimball, quoted in *Sharing the Gospel Manual*, p. 94)

We have met their "Savior," who saved them by becoming their friendly creditor, assuming their loan and conquering physical death for them in order to give them "eternities" to pay him back. (See *Gospel Principles*, pp. 68-71.) Hand-in-hand with that, we learned that their god doesn't forgive—not in the true sense of the word. Instead he demands full payment with interest.

> "To every forgiveness there is a condition . . . The fasting, the prayers, the humility must be equal to or greater than the sin." (Spencer Kimball, quoted in *Gospel Principles*, p. 252)

> It depends upon you whether or not you are forgiven, and when. It could be weeks, it could be years, it could be centuries before that happy day when you have the positive assurance that the Lord has forgiven you. That depends on your humility, your sincerity, your works, your attitudes. (Spencer Kimball, *The Miracle of Forgiveness*, p. 325)

We have also seen how Mormons must be worthy before they can hold any church position or participate in any temple rites. We have found that one of the biggest LDS words is the little word "if," it being attached to every blessing and promise. "All blessings are conditional. I know of none that are not" (Spencer Kimball, quoted in *Remember Me*, p. 23). In short, we have seen that Mormonism has an obsession with perfection.

Even though Mormons try to temper this obsession with saying that a person has "eternities" to progress to perfection, it still puts many of them under stress to the breaking point. A recent visit to an LDS bookstore revealed that some of their best-selling books were: *Stress Reduction for Mormons; If the Gospel Is True, Why Do I Hurt So Much?*; and *Sanity Strategies for Everyday Mormons*. Even more revealing, the promotional blurbs for each of these three books specifically mentioned coping with perfectionism.

There is much more evidence that this passion for perfection is a monster eating many Mormons alive. That idea permeates their own literature. The following are just three of many examples.

> Perhaps no idea creates more emotional stress for some of us than the idea that we need to be perfect right now-

or soon! . . . And when we fail to achieve perfection in some area, we criticize ourselves harshly, even to the point of despair. (Jan Underwood Pinborough, *Ensign*, Sept. 1990, p. 50)

Their efforts to force those around them into perfection often results in conflict, estrangement of family members, deep unhappiness, anger and a sense of futility. (Morris, *If The Gospel Is True, Why Do I Hurt So Much?*, p. 65)

When I was a bishop, it was my privilege to counsel with many faithful members like Janet who were struggling, often valiantly, to escape soul-destroying cycles of discouragement and despair that came when they failed to overcome their imperfections. (Jeffery C. Jacob, *Ensign*, Jan. 1991, p. 66)

But the full horror of how devastating this obsession can be doesn't hit home until you personally witness a Mormon struggling to be perfect. It is heartrending to watch someone frantically trying to do it all, while all they end up doing is destroying themselves and their families. Yet, many Mormons are doing just that. They are struggling to be the perfect family or spouse or child. All the while, however, many LDS families and individuals are falling apart.

If we want to speak the truth in love to Mormons, it is essential that we come to grips with the magnitude of this obsession with perfection. It is also essential we understand that no single aspect of Mormonism places stress on every Mormon. We should see that there are many different sides to LDS perfection, each one hitting each Mormon differently. Through careful listening and observation, we need to discover the particular points of Mormonism that are placing our particular LDS friend under stress. The following paragraphs describe some of the aspects of Mormonism that weigh heavily on many Mormons.

The Many Faces of LDS Perfection

Mormonism's glorification of work makes many Mormons feel as if they are being slowly squeezed to death. In the last chapter we saw how being busy as bees is an integral part of being Latter-day Saints. Both men and women are to be handy around the house. As a family they are to have a year's supply of necessities stored away. Everyone is to take time for daily scripture reading and journal writing. Every Monday evening they are to hold a family home evening. Not only are they to be working regularly on their genealogies, but they also are to be attending the Temple frequently to perform vicarious work for the dead. In addition, they are to be active in the various activities in their ward. It goes on without letup. No wonder one person described her Mormon neighbor by saying she drives up herdriveway at 35 mph and runs into her house even faster.

Zane Nelson, an LDS psychologist, put it this way:

Many LDS people wrongly think that consistently accomplishing a great checklist of righteous activities constitutes righteousness. LDS women seem especially vulnerable to pressure regarding this never-ending list. (*Sanity Strategies for Everyday Mormons*, p. 1)

In another place he quotes from a book by Scott Peck:

Nonetheless, as soon as we believe it is possible for man to become God, we can really never rest for long, never say, "OK, my job is finished, my work is done." We must constantly push ourselves to greater and greater wisdom, greater and greater effectiveness. (*Sanity Strategies for Everyday Mormons*, p. 55)

The emphasis on having as many children as possible also weighs heavily on many Mormons. In chapter three we saw that refusing to have children is regarded as a serious sin. The following statements, quoted in currently used manuals, reveal that the pressure is still on.

"There are couples in the Church who think they are getting along just fine with their limited families but who will someday suffer the pains of remorse when they meet the spirits that might have been part of their posterity. The first commandment given to man was to multiply and

164

replenish the earth with children." (Ezra Taft Benson, quoted in *The Life and Teachings of Jesus & His Apostles*, p. 284)

"There are multitudes of pure and holy spirits waiting to take tabernacles, now what is yourduty?--To prepare tabernacles for them: to take a course that will not tend to drive those spirits into the families of the wicked, where they will be trained in wickedness, debauchery, and every species of crime. *It is the duty of every righteous man and woman to prepare tabernacles for all the spirits they can.*" (Brigham Young, quoted in *Achieving A Celestial Marriage*, p. 230, emphasis added)

"When people have found their companions, there should be no long delay. Young wives should be occupied in bearing and rearing their children. I know of no scriptures where an authorization is given to young wives to withhold their families and go to work to put their husbands through school." (Spencer W. Kimball, quoted in *The Life and Teachings of Jesus & His Apostles*, p. 365)

Such statements weigh heavily on many Mormon couples who already have children. But imagine the pressure they place on those who are infertile. Although the LDS church speaks gently to such people, this emphasis on bearing children is difficult for some to reconcile with their condition.

The most difficult aspect of infertility to overcome was the effect that it had on my feelings of self-worth. During those pain-filled years, I mistakenly felt that because I could not have children, I must be of no worth. The resulting depression and despair only made my feelings of worthlessness worse. (Janet Nelson Christensen, *Ensign*, August 1996, p. 53)

But it's not only married couples who feel this pressure. The LDS church also urges single men to find wives as quickly as possible so that they too can start having children.

No man who is of marriage age is living his religion who remains single. (*Achieving A Celestial Marriage*, p. 181)

"Let me say again, marriage is honorable. It is a plan of God. It is not a whim, a choice, a preference only; it is a must." (Spencer W. Kimball, quoted in *D&C Student Manual*, p. 106)

"If a man refuses to take upon himself the responsibilities of married life, because he desires to avoid the cares and troubles which naturally will follow, he is taking a course which may bar him forever from the responsibilities which are held in reserve for those who are willing to keep in full the commandments of the Lord. His eternal progression will thus be limited." (Joseph Fielding Smith, quoted in *Achieving A Celestial Marriage*, p. 175)

Not only does the LDS church encourage large families, it also frowns on mothers working outside the home. Although it has weakened its stand on this in recent years, it still comes out quite strongly against it.

We urge you to do all in your power to allow your wife to remain in the home, caring for the children while you provide for the family the best you can. (President Howard W. Hunter, *Ensign*, Nov. 94, p. 51)

"This divine service of motherhood can be rendered only by mothers. It may not be passed to others. Nurses cannot do it; public nurseries cannot do it; hired help cannot do it—only mother, aided as much as may be by the loving hands of father, brothers, and sisters, can give the full needed measure of watchful care." (The First Presidency of Heber J. Grant, J. Reuben Clark, Jr., and David O. McKay, quoted in *The Life and Teachings of Jesus & His Apostles*, p. 365)

166

Find a large family living on a single income, and many times you will find some stress. But then add the LDS glorification of worldly and financial success, and things often get much more tense. Finally, throw in large money and time commitments to the church, and you have a recipe for nervous or family breakdowns. Heinerman and Shupe comment:

> Mormon middle-class families have difficulty maintaining the lifestyle held out to them as a goal (particularly if they tithe) unless the woman works as well as the man. At a time when the Church still encourages large families and condemns birth control, both the demands on single-income families and the opportunities open to women are enormous. Yet the Church chooses to instill guilt and to blame all manner of social problems on working mothers instead of realistically dealing with the bind in which many Mormon families find themselves. (*The Mormon Corporate Empire*, p. 229)

Statistics support the observation that all is not well in many LDS households. Regularly Utah is above the national average in such categories as suicide, divorce, prescription drug abuse, abuse of family members, and the like. The LDS church routinely shrugs these statistics off with the disclaimer that many non-Mormons live in Utah. But more and more of their own members aren't discounting them. For example, a popular LDS author, Carroll Morris, writes:

> While the statistics do not indicate the number of Latter-day Saints living in Utah who might be affected by domestic violence, the high percentage of Church members in Utah population (an estimated 77.2% in 1991-1992) makes them pertinent to any discussion of dysfunction in an LDS context. (*If the Gospel Is True, Why Do I Hurt So Much?*, p. 14)

She then cites a 1987 study entitled, "In Search of a Peculiar People: Are Mormons Really Different?" This study, which was done at their own Brigham Young University, concluded that Mormons are no different when it comes to social problems. They experience physical, sexual, or emotional abuse at the same rate as any other social group.

In spite of their popular image as being family-oriented, this really shouldn't surprise us. As we saw earlier, many people initially joined the church because they wanted help for their families. But once they were members, they discovered to their dismay that the LDS church couldn't give them any lasting help. (I make that statement from the conviction that the church which is devoid of the gospel cannot address, much less solve, the root problems of life.) Therefore, they still have the problems — but often intensified by the additional pressures of Mormonism. In this regard, I found it interesting that the majority of ads in a regional LDS magazine were for groups who worked with troubled teens.

Another reason these statistics shouldn't surprise us is that many Mormon couples feel forced into having large families. Since they can't take their resentment out on the church, some take it out on their children.

The trouble in many LDS families is evidenced also by more openness about "unrighteous dominion." This is a popular Mormon expression used to describe a person who acts like a tyrant. In most cases, it applies to a domineering, even abusive, husband or father. The extent of the problem became evident when Gordon Hinckley of the First Presidency addressed it publicly in General Conference.

> I have in my office a file of letters received from women who cry out over the treatment they receive from their husbands in their homes. They tell of the activity of some of these men in Church responsibilities. They even speak of men holding temple recommends. And they speak of abuse, both subtle and open. They tell of husbands who lose their tempers and shout at their wives and children. They tell of men who demand offensive intimate relations. (*Ensign*, May 1990, p. 52)

Similarly, the authority wielded by the priesthood causes some Mormons stress. Even if an LDS husband is not exercising "unrighteous dominion" over his wife, she still might, at times, chafe under the complete authority he wields. One area of

168

concern common to many LDS wives is the thought that their husbands might not call them from the grave at the resurrection if they fail to please them. Many wives view that as a sword continually dangling over their outstretched necks — even if their husbands are not using it in that way.

This uneasiness with priesthood authority isn't confined to the family. Since the main function of LDS bishops is to act as judges, many Mormons are scared of them and scared to meet with them. This is such a deeply embedded feeling that it still occasionally arises in former Mormons when I, as their pastor, ask if I can meet with them. As one Mormon told me: "When the bishop asks to meet with me it is either to examine my worthiness or give me a job to do. Being examined is nerve-racking, and I can't refuse the job." In that, she was echoing her church.

> We support our leaders when we accept Church callings willingly and fulfill them faithfully, realizing that a call from the priesthood is a call from the Lord. (*Latter-day Woman A*, p. 96)

> "If the Bishop, who is a common judge in Israel, tells a person to restrain this gift, or any other gift, it is the duty of that person to do it. The Bishop has a right to the gift of discernment, whereby he may tell whether these spirits are of God or not, and if they are not they should not have place in the congregations of the Saints. No man or woman has a right to find fault with the Bishop for restraining him or her in any of these matters. The Bishop is the responsible party, and it is his privilege to say what shall be done under his presidency." (Abraham O. Woodruff, quoted in *Doctrines of the Gospel*, p. 45)

It is not just the bishop's authority either that some Mormons find stifling. Some also chafe under the absolute authority wielded by the living prophet. This is the case not so much in regard to doctrinal issues, but more with issues that hit close to home. Then, frequently, the grumbling starts.

Having such thoughts, moreover, makes sincere Mormons

feel even more guilty and thus increases their stress. They realize it is wrong for them to question priesthood authority. But what can they do? They can't run to Heavenly Father for forgiveness. They hesitate to share their feelings with a fellow member. Many end up slowly being eaten alive by guilt and stress.

In the previous paragraph, I mentioned still another factor creating stress for many Mormons; namely, that many hesitate to share any of their negative feelings. They hesitate because they are supposed to be strong. I saw just how far some carry this when a former Mormon gave me her journal to read. She warned me, however, not to expect to receive a whole lot of insight into her life since she avoided writing down her negative thoughts. She knew her journal would serve as a testimony to her children, and she wanted to leave them a positive witness.

This is a widespread feeling. Troubled Mormons, therefore, go to their meetings only to hear, from peer after peer, how much they have been blessed by living the principles of Mormonism. As they sit there, they can easily become convinced that they are the only ones with problems or doubts.

> I know of sisters who have gone home after some Relief Society lessons and literally withdrawn into lethargy, only to go back the next week to feel more inadequate! (Nelson, *Sanity Strategies for Everyday Mormons*, p. 56)

> Church members who are striving unsuccessfully to create a "forever family" feel separated from thosewhose family lives are healthy and happy. They are plagued by grave doubts about themselves and their Church. They listen with heavy hearts to testimonies, to missionary farewell speeches, and to Mother's and Father's Day talks. The words of hope, love, and happiness seem directed to everyone else but them. (Morris, *If the Gospel Is True, Why Do I Hurt So Much?*, p. 8)

This can happen in other churches as well. Many churches have difficulty establishing and then maintaining a climate of trust that encourages people to open up and share their problems. But there's a difference. While most churches are striving to develop such a climate, the LDS church stifles such a climate with their obsession with perfection. When it comes to spiritual problems, the LDS church is not a very caring community. One clear evidence of that is the complete absence of any type of support group in LDS wards. The absence of such groups becomes all the more glaring in light of the many types of activities they do sponsor.

This naturally has a debilitating effect on numerous Mormons. Not only are many stressed-out, many are struggling with serious problems such as "Word of Wisdom problems" (i.e., alcoholism). Yet, most have no place to turn for help. Numerous Mormons, therefore, resemble a pressure cooker with no outlet for steam. Instead of admitting their problems and confessing their sins, they try to hide them by keeping them inside. Eventually the pressure gets too great, and they blow up.

Otherwise they maintain a fragile grip on life by becoming complacent about being hypocrites. (Hypocrisy is the inevitable result of any religion that demands perfection from its members.) Instead of confessing their sins, they try to hide them or rationalize them. As a result, you find the Mormon who has, for years, been getting up every night at 2:00 to sneak a cup of coffee. Or the young LDS wife who has a headache each day so she can have tea for "medicinal purposes." Or the bishop who realizes that he really can't read a person's heart, so he has become adept at reading body language. Or the missionary who is trying to convince the investigator of the importance of getting a burning bosom, never admitting that he himself has never experienced it. Such hypocrisy doesn't bother many of them. But it does bother a significant group, people who are miserable because of the hypocrisy in their lives.

No matter where you turn, you see another facet of LDS perfection and the stress that accompanies it. This has just been a sampling. There's more. At every turn, Mormonism brings stress to many Mormons while offering them no solutions. The books written by Mormons to Mormons on stress reduction do nothing but parrot secular counseling techniques. They are filled with such things as values clarification, the need to fight co-dependency, transactional analysis, and self-respect models. Never do they talk about a Lord who forgives sin and removes guilt.

The more a person looks beneath the sheep's clothing of Mormonism, the more ugly it becomes. The more a person knows of Mormonism, the more he or she realizes how desperately

Mormons need someone to tell them the good news of the Savior who was already perfect for them. How to do that is the theme of the second part of the book.

Key Concepts

1. A List of Some Attractions
Teaching that you have to earn eternal life
Teaching that hardly anybody goes to outer darkness
Teaching that persons get a second chance in the
    spirit world
Teaching that makes God understandable.
The emphasis on the eternal family
Its many rules and regulations.
Its many and varied activities
Its image of being a caring community
Its emphasis on emotion and feeling
Its image of wholesomeness

2. A List of Some Stresses
Their obsession with perfection
Its many rules and regulations
Constant busyness
The emphasis on having as many children as possible
Time and money pressures
The complete authority wielded by the priesthood
The discouragement from showing weakness

PART II

REACH MORMONS

CHAPTER SEVEN: REACH MORMONS WITH THE POWER OF GOD'S WORD

Witnessing to Mormons can be an extremely frustrating experience. In the previous chapters we have identified a variety of reasons for that. We have seen how they define many words differently, with the result that it is easy to talk past each other. Their interpretations of individual Bible verses and stories is so different that it is difficult to find common ground on which to build a discussion. Causing further difficulty, they base their faith on their feelings. In addition, their unique cultural traits build walls that are difficult to surmount. These and other reasons can make effective witnessing to Mormons appear to be a mission impossible.

I'm convinced, however, that much of this frustration is avoidable. We can learn their language; we can become sensitive to their culture. But mainly we just need to witness to them. I believe that the greatest reason why witnessing to Mormons is so often maddening is that many times we don't actually witness to them. Instead we debate with them.

That's what I did for a number of years. After moving to Idaho, I tried to talk with as many Mormons as I could. I would even stop LDS missionaries on the street and invite them over to my house. I would frequently spend all afternoon debating with them about the nature of God, or about the truthfulness of the Bible and the Book of Mormon, or about the character of Joseph Smith. Many times, however, I never got around to sharing the gospel with them. I would touch on it, but I wouldn't focus on their need for a Savior and how Jesus fully fills the need. More often I debated Mormonism with them than I witnessed to them about what Jesus had done for them.

We need to emphasize Christ's saving acts. Whenever we don't focus on them, we shoot ourselves in the foot. I say that for a couple of reasons. First, most Mormons will view quite negatively anything we say about Joseph Smith or the Book of Mormon. No matter how hard we try not to come across as attacking them, that is how they often feel when we talk to them about their religion. And when people feel attacked, they put up their defenses and close their ears.

> "The greatest harm, though, was done by well-intentioned Christians who actually attacked the Mormon church and its doctrines in my presence. They were a great stumbling block for me, especially when they held my beliefs up to ridicule.
>
> That did nothing but make me angry, and make me protective of the church. It made no difference in my mind at that point whether or not what they were saying was correct: I felt that they were attacking me as well as my church." (Sheila Garrigus, quoted in *Ex-Mormons, Why We Left*, p. 111)

No matter what we do, we won't be able to avoid completely the impression that we are attacking them. No matter what we do, they usually will interpret *any* witness on our part as an attack against them. It is almost inevitable. But we can lessen that feeling considerably and, in the process, lower their defenses measurably, if we focus on perfection and how to obtain eternal life. Those are topics that lie near and dear to most Mormon hearts.

When those topics are discussed, they often prick up their ears instead of closing them. This holds true especially if they are experiencing stress because of Mormonism's obsession with perfection. When that is the case, we often hit a nerve when we talk about the impossibility of their being perfect. Even more important, this opens the door to talk to them about Jesus and his being perfect for them.

Stressing what Jesus has done for them through his perfect life and sacrificial death makes us much more effective. Not only does that address an area of great stress in their lives, but that message is the only thing powerful enough to bring them to faith in Jesus.

The Bible testifies to that with crystal clarity. Paul wrote: "I am not ashamed of the gospel, because it is the power of God for the salvation of everyone who believes" (Romans 1:16). Note how he says that the gospel is the power of God for the salvation of not some, but of *everyone* who believes. If a person believes in Jesus, it is because the gospel worked on him. Or, approaching it from a different angle, no one comes to faith without exposure to the gospel.

Too often we forget that. Instead we think we have to "reason" Mormons out of Mormonism. We try to do that in a variety of ways. We alert them to the many contradictions between their various scriptures. We show them the numerous changes that have occurred in the Book of Mormon. We dig up the skeletons in Joseph Smith's closet. We even try to win them by reason when we debate with them about the nature of God or how many gods there are. The common denominator of all these approaches is that they rely on the power of rational argumentation to convince Mormons that Mormonism is false.

And, at times, we succeed in doing that. By seeing its various contradictions, or by seeing the changes in the Book of Mormon, or by seeing something else we have pointed out to them, some Mormons have seen Mormonism's errors. Since it claims to be a reasonable religion, we can use arguments from reason to demolish that claim.

However, although this can be effective and proper, it can easily backfire on us. When we demonstrate how Mormonism goes against reason, we too often demolish much more than a person's faith in Mormonism. It is my opinion that this reliance on rational argumentation has caused many ex-Mormons to abandon not only the LDS faith but all faith. After examining Mormonism to see if it is reasonable, they use the same criteria on Christianity and also find it lacking. The following letter is representative of how many ex-Mormons think:

> It is quite obvious from the accurate letters that Margaret Ramshaw has written on Mormonism that she has done extensive investigation of it. This has led her to do what any prudent investigator would do, i.e., reject it.

It is equally obvious that she has not applied the same principles of investigation to Christianity, for if she had she would do what any prudent investigator would do, i.e., reject it. (*Idaho Statesman*, Oct. 10, 1991)

Getting people out of Mormonism, but not getting them into Christianity, does them no good. They still are on the way to hell. Yet, that is where many ex-Mormons are today. They are in a spiritual limbo, often because they have never wrestled with the gospel. Since much of the discussion often centers on the negatives of Mormonism rather than the positives of Christianity, they aren't attracted to Christianity. They become turned off by Mormonism, but they don't become turned on to Christianity. They are frequently left with the impression that the major conflict between Christianity and Mormonism is over the nature of God, not over the way to obtain eternal life.

Only the wonderful news that eternal life is God's gift can attract them to Christ. Instead of trying to pull them out of Mormonism by stressing its negatives, we need to push Mormonism out of them by filling them up with the positives of Christianity. Otherwise, all too often they are left in a spiritual vacuum, giving up on all religion and becoming agnostics.

It is vital for us to see that a reliance on arguments from reason, although very appealing, can easily become a fatal attraction. It becomes fatal especially when we put too much faith in such arguments and then go the next step by trying to reason someone into Christianity. Doing that is nothing less than deadly. In the first two chapters of 1 Corinthians, Paul emphasizes that trying to reason people into Christianity is hazardous to their spiritual health. There he emphasizes that human wisdom is an *obstacle*, not an aid, to conversion. He convincingly shows that the gospel works not *with*, but *against* human wisdom, to bring people to Christ. To witness effectively to Mormons, we need to be completely convinced of how the gospel works. A closer look at Paul's words will do just that.

1 Corinthians 1:18--2:16

Although Paul never uses the word gospel in these verses, the gospel obviously is his main topic. In 1:18 he talks about "the message of the cross"; in 1:23 he speaks about preaching "Christ crucified"; in 2:2 he says: "I resolved to know nothing while I was with you except Jesus

178

Christ and him crucified." These phrases not only show us that Paul's subject is the gospel, they also supply us with a good description of the gospel. Proclaiming the gospel is not "talking religion" or debating the nature of God. It is speaking the *specific message* of Christ crucified for us. That, and that alone, constitutes the power of God for the salvation of everyone who believes.

Paul brings that out forcefully in this section. He does that by demonstrating the total incompatibility between human wisdom and God's wisdom (i.e., the gospel), especially in the area of conversion. They are not just opposites; they violently conflict with each other. They cannot be reconciled with each other. Therefore, relying on rational arguments or mixing such arguments with the gospel to reach Mormons is a formula for failure.

Paul demonstrates this by giving a devastating critique of the role human wisdom plays in spiritual matters. First, in 2:9,10 he shows that a human being cannot learn about salvation apart from God's revelation. We can't learn about it from nature: "no eye has seen, no ear has heard." We can't discover it through our own thinking processes: "no mind has conceived." We can learn about salvation only from God's revelation. "But God has revealed it to us by his Spirit."

Paul doesn't stop there. Not only can't we learn about salvation through careful observation of nature or complicated mental gymnastics, we aren't wise enough to accept the truthfulness of God's revelation even when it hits us right in the face.

> The man without the Spirit does not accept the things
> that come from the Spirit of God, for they are foolishness
> to him, and *he cannot understand them*, because they are
> spiritually discerned. (2:14), emphasis added)

This passage is all the more striking when we realize that Paul employs a word that the Greeks had constantly used to describe man at his natural best. The term translate "without the Spirit" is psuchikos" and was "continually used as the highest [part of man] in later classical Greek literature . . . constantly employed in praise" (Trench, *Synonyms of the New Testament*, p. 268). Man, at his *natural best*, cannot discern the wisdom of the gospel. We just aren't smart enough. "Reason is incapable of discovering and incompetent to judge religious truth" (Becker, *The Foolishness of God*, p. 7)

Instead, as this verse states, natural man views the gospel as foolishness. Paul repeatedly returns to this thought (i.e., 1:18,21,23,25). He wants to leave no doubt about it. Instead of being attracted to the gospel, human wisdom is repulsed by it.

> Reason knows only the religion of works. Human reason is not able to free itself from the habitual and permanent opinion that man's righteousness is an active, personal uprightness, rather than the passive righteousness bestowed freely for Christ's sake, proclaimed in the gospel, and accepted by faith. (Becker, *The Foolishness of God*, p. 56)

Because of human wisdom's innate opposition to the gospel, God does nothing less than destroy and frustrate it in matters of spiritual discernment.

> I will destroy the wisdom of the wise;
> the intelligence of the intelligent I will frustrate. (1:19)

Those are startling words. Those are harsh words. This is a devastating critique of any and all methods that rely on human wisdom and reason to convert people. Note well that limitation. God does not frustrate all uses of human wisdom. It is when we place it above the Bible, or when we try to "reason" people into Christianity, that God frustrates and destroys it.

In those areas, there are no exceptions. All types of human wisdom come under his condemnation. In 1:19-20 Paul employs four different words to describe human wisdom. First he mentions wisdom. The Greek word for this is *sophia*, which "is mental excellence in its highest and fullest sense" (Trench, *Synonyms of the New Testament*, p. 283).

Paul then speaks of intelligence (Greek: *sunesis*). This word is especially pertinent to our discussion because it deals with man's reasoning abilities. It literally means a junction of streams or roads.

> Applied to the mind it would be a junction of thoughts and ideas, and thus, clearly to be able to separate the different ideas running together on a subject and discern the right idea. *A logical mind is meant.* (Wenzel, *Commentary on the Gospels*, p. 62, emphasis added)

180

This is supported by the passage Paul quotes, namely, Isaiah 29:14. Isaiah employs the Hebrew word, *bin*. *Bin* refers

> to knowledge which is superior to the mere gathering of data . . . *Bin* is a power of judgment and perceptive insight and is demonstrated in the use of knowledge. (*Theological Wordbook of the Old Testament, I,* p. 103)

In 1:20 he adds two more descriptions of human wisdom when he mentions the scholar and the philosopher. The Greek word for scholar (*grammateus*) is most often used in the New Testament in reference to Jewish scribes. Although called scribes, they were religious scholars and thus were highly respected for their knowledge. The Greek philosopher (*suzetetes*) held similar highly respected positions in their society.

By describing human wisdom with these four words, Paul is making clear that his comments apply to all types of human wisdom. They apply to the highest and the best type of human wisdom, to logic and perceptive insight, to the wisdom of the Jewish scribe and the Greek philosopher. When it comes to spiritual discernment, human wisdom is a tremendous liability.

> Summing up what Paul writes, we may say that it is the gravest and most dangerous error to promulgate the Gospel by means of the wisdom of the world, whether it be the wisdom of our present or of any previous age. (Lenski, *I & II Corinthians*, p. 85)

> There is no greater danger in all the world than a highly gifted reason which seeks to deal with spiritual matters. . . . *Reason is the greatest impediment to faith.* (Becker, *The Foolishness of God,* pp. 157, 160, emphasis added)

What human wisdom cannot accomplish, however, the gospel does. "God was pleased through the foolishness of what was preached to save those who believe" (1:21). The gospel succeeds where reason fails because it is nothing less than the power of God (1:18) and the Spirit-filled word (2:4-5). Thus it is "wiser than man's wisdom" and "stronger than man's strength" (1:25).

All Scripture says the same thing. Whenever it talks about

conversion, it highlights the gospel's vital role. Consider the series of rhetorical questions Paul asks in Romans 10:14:

> How, then, can they call on the one they have not believed in? And how can they believe in the one of whom they have not heard? And how can they hear without someone preaching to them?

These questions conclusively demonstrate that conversion does not happen apart from God's Word. As Paul himself concludes: "faith comes from hearing the message" (v.17).

Peter said the same thing: "For you have been born again, not of perishable seed, but of imperishable, through the living and enduring word of God" (1 Peter 1:23). Countless other passages could be cited. From beginning to end, the Bible emphasizes that the gospel "is the power of God for the salvation of everyone who believes" (Romans 1:16)

Since the Bible states this so emphatically, it seems that it would be easy for us to believe it wholeheartedly and then to implement it effortlessly. But we experience otherwise. Too often we still try to fight Mormonism with the toy sword of human reason, rather than with the double-edged sword of God's Word. Our sinful nature is constantly trying to turn us away from complete reliance on the gospel. And we often are quick to listen to human reason, especially when it appears as if God's Word is having no effect.

Even Paul had to wrestle with this. Reliance on the gospel didn't come naturally to him. He wrote: "I *resolved* to know nothing while I was with you except Jesus Christ and him crucified" (1 Corinthians 2:2, emphasis added). Paul was extremely well-educated. In addition, he was in a Greek city, preaching to people who took great pride in human wisdom. The temptation must have been strong to meet them on their own terms, especially since he had the ability to do that. But he *consciously* fought doing that. He *resolved* to rely on the power of the message of Christ crucified.

The more we know of Mormonism, the greater the temptation will be for us to concentrate on its manifold contradictions and historical inaccuracies. Like Paul we need to consciously resolve not to do that. Like Paul we need to rely on the foolishness of the gospel.

It will help our resolve when we remember that faith is something God creates in us, rather than something we make a conscious decision about. Consistently in this section of Corinthians, and throughout

Scripture, God does the converting. Not man, but God does the calling and the choosing. As Paul says in 1:30: "It is because of him that you are in Christ Jesus." Becker succinctly sums up the biblical teaching when he writes: "Faith is something done to us rather than by us" (*The Foolishness of God*, p. 155)

Rather than chafing under this teaching, appreciate it. See it as another example of God's wisdom (See 1 Corinthians 1:21). See it as God's way of taking the pressure off us. This teaching reassures us that a person's conversion is not contingent on how eloquent or persuasive we are. In fact, this teaching demonstrates that we do not convert anyone. That is not our responsibility. Our sole responsibility is to spread the gospel. It is God's responsibility to work through the gospel to bring people to faith.

Furthermore, when we immerse ourselves in the gospel in order to share it effectively with our LDS friends, we ourselves are strengthened by it. The more we see the extent of God's love for us, the stronger our own faith becomes. And the more contact we have with his love, the more motivated we will be to love, rather than ridicule or even despise, our LDS friends. "We love because He first loved us" (1 John 4:19).

The gospel is the key. It is the *truth* we need to share with our LDS friends. It is the *power* motivating us to speak that truth in love to them. The next two chapters detail some ways to do that.

Discussion Questions

1. What makes witnessing to Mormons frustrating and difficult?

2. Instead of witnessing, what do most people tend to do when speaking to Mormons? Why?

3. How does 1 Corinthians 1:18ff. help us understand the importance of sharing the gospel with Mormons rather than employing logical argumentation?

CHAPTER EIGHT: REACH MORMONS WITH THE HARD-HITTING LAW

S ome might find the title of this chapter startling, especially since the last chapter ended by saying the gospel is the key to reaching Mormons. And it is. But people need to be prepared for the gospel by seeing that they are in trouble. A man who thinks he can swim to shore doesn't call for help. He does that only when he realizes he is drowning.

Mormons are drowning in their sins, but they don't know it. They realize that reaching the shore of the celestial kingdom won't be easy, but many think they can make it — if they follow the LDS plan of salvation. They view its cornucopia of laws as a heavy but manageable burden. How well they think they are carrying that burden determines where they are sitting on the following scale.

Self-righteous Mormons naturally don't think they are in much danger. They will need a heavy dose of God's law to convict them of that. In contrast to the gospel, which consists of God's promises, the law spells out God's commands. And those commands expose a person's sinfulness:

> Therefore no one will be declared righteous in his sight by observing the law; rather, through the law we become conscious of sin. (Romans 3:20)

The law reveals our sinfulness by demanding the impossible of us. This is a vitally important concept to understand. Contrary to popular opinion, God did not give his commandments as a way for people to gain heaven. That is not only popular opinion, however, that is also Mormonism.

> Although God's laws are exact and immovable, they are revealed and given to mankind for one specific purpose-- to bring to pass their ultimate joy . . . God gives laws and commandments to his children to provide the only possible means whereby they may become like him. (*D&C Student Manual*, pp. 393, 394)

That is in direct opposition to the Bible. Rather than being a means for us to save ourselves, the commandments show us the utter impossibility of doing so. Who can love God wholeheartedly? Who can love his neighbor as himself? Who can keep himself free of every greedy, lustful, selfish thought? No one can! "There is no one who does good, not even one" (Romans 3:12). That we are not good is what God wants us to see when we encounter his commandments. God gave us the law so that we would despair of trying to save ourselves.

God's law reveals the extent of sinfulness, and it lays out sin's dire consequences.

> All who rely on observing the law are under a curse, for it is written: "Cursed is everyone who does not continue to do everything written in the Book of the Law." (Galatians 3:10)

Note how all-inclusive that statement is. It includes *everyone* who does not *continue* to do *everything.* No matter how good people think they are, if they are not *perfect,* they are under God's curse; they are guilty of breaking the whole law (James 2:10); they have earned the eternal death of outer darkness (Romans 6:23).

All Mormons, including stressed-out ones, need to hear this. Even stressed-out Mormons don't realize the serious consequences of sin. No matter how much stress they are experiencing, no matter how much they think they are failing to live their religion, they still believe that they will end up in one of the kingdoms of heaven. The idea that their sins will cause God to banish them to outer darkness doesn't even enter their minds. Why should it? According to Mormonism, a person is in danger of going to outer darkness only by becoming an apostate (i.e., leaving the LDS church). Mormonism teaches that everyone else, no matter how evil they are, will go to heaven.

Therefore, all Mormons need to hear God's law. They need to have close encounters with its spirit, rather than a superficial acquaintance with its letter. They need to have their self-righteousness shattered by its blows. They need to see that they are hopelessly lost in their sins and are on the road to outer darkness.

We need to bring them that message. If they view Mormonism as a heavy but manageable burden, we need to make that burden so heavy it crushes them. We need to keep on adding weight until they cry out for mercy. We need to pound them into the ground with the law before we can lift them up with the gospel.

This is not easy to do. It is not a pleasant task to impale people on the spear of God's law. But it is an essential task. If they don't see the extent and seriousness of their sin, they won't be interested in seeing their Savior.

What makes this even more difficult is that it usually involves more than a one-time effort. We have to persist. Our LDS friends will often try to wiggle off the hook of the law, but we can't let that happen. A common mistake Christians make is to focus on the gospel before the law has done its work. Note that I said "focus" on the gospel. The gospel will naturally come up in our discussions, and we will want to share it. But self-righteous Mormons especially will need a hefty dose of God's law before they are ready to concentrate on the gospel.

Complicating matters even further is that most Mormons, even if they are stressed-out, won't readily admit their stress. They have been conditioned not to share their doubts and weaknesses with anybody. At all times, they are to put on a happy face.

Even their degree of involvement in the church isn't an accurate indicator of where they are sitting on the self-righteous/stressed-out scale. I have met jack Mormons (i.e., inactive Mormons) who were very self-righteous. On the other hand, I have met some who were inactive just because Mormonism had stressed them out. They realized that it was an impossible religion to live and, therefore, had quit trying. Likewise, I have met some self-righteous leaders and stressed-out leaders. Rather than approaching them with preconceived notions, we need to listen actively to them and observe them carefully. Only then will we get a handle on whether they need the hammer of God's law or the soothing balm of his gospel.

Luther once remarked that anybody who rightly applies the law and the gospel deserves to be called a doctor of theology. His comment underscores the difficulty of what we have been talking about. But don't let that keep you from reaching out to Mormons. The stakes are too high. Nothing less than their eternal destiny is at risk. Because of that, carefully but confidently witness to them. Do it carefully, mindful of the great stakes. Do it confidently, mindful that the Holy Spirit can and does work through the Word, even though we may feel we have mumbled and bumbled our witness.

Following are some specific suggestions on how to confront Mormons with God's law.Because of Mormonism's unique interpretations of specific passages or its redefining of specific terms, many of the traditional ways of talking about sin do not hit home with them. Here, then, are ways I have found that reach Mormons where they are:

Hold Up God's Law by Talking about Outer Darkness

One of the first things I like to discuss with Mormons is the subject of hell or outer darkness. Since Mormonism uses the term hell to describe either a temporary state of suffering in the spirit world or a partial state of suffering in heaven, I prefer using the expression outer darkness. It is the LDS expression that best approximates the biblical teaching of an eternal and complete hell. When you talk to a Mormon about outer darkness, the message of eternal punishment comes through loud and clear. (Because of terminology differences, I also avoid talking about damnation.)

The reality of eternal punishment is something they need to struggle with. As mentioned above, Mormons believe that 99.99% of all people will go to heaven. We need to prove them wrong. One passage that shakes their confidence is Matthew 7:13, 14:

> Enter ye in at the strait gate: for wide is the gate, and broad is the way, that leadeth to destruction, and many there be which go in thereat: Because strait is the gate, and narrow is the way, which leadeth unto life, and few there be that find it. (KJV)

They aren't familiar with this passage and , therefore, can't explain away its reference to the destruction of many. I remember one conversation I had with two LDS missionaries and a seminary teacher. I cited this passage and asked them what it meant. After huddling together for over ten minutes, they said it referred to the destruction of the family.

Still, it is not good enough to show them that the Bible says many will experience eternal destruction. We need also to state clearly that we know they will experience eternal destruction if they remain in Mormonism. Until they understand that, they will not view our discussion with the same sense of urgency that we do. At best, they might view the differences between Mormonism and Christianity as serious but not as catastrophic. For their sakes, we need to speak plainly and tell them that they are on the road to outer darkness.

Often, however, we hold back. We think that if anything will make them close their ears to what we have to say, that will. But I have not experienced so. In the last couple of years, I have consciously striven to make that point early in any discussion with a Mormon. Although they react with great shock, most don't break off the conversation. Instead they press me, wanting to know why I say that. And that, in a natural way, leads into a presentation of God's law and gospel.

I remember one conversation I had while flying back from Salt Lake City. The man across the aisle noticed I was reading an LDS manual and asked if I was a member of the Mormon church. When he found out I wasn't, he asked why I was reading that manual. I explained to him that I wanted to learn more about LDS teachings since I was very concerned about Mormons. Naturally he asked why I was concerned. I told him it was my heartfelt conviction that they were going to outer darkness. Instead of ending the discussion, that stimulated it. We talked the entire flight. In fact, he followed me to the baggage claim area, asking me questions all the way.

Granted, not all have reacted that way. Some have tried to end the conversation as quickly as they could. But such reactions have been rare. Telling Mormons they are going to outer darkness has opened the door for more profitable witnessing discussions than anything else I have ever said.

The important thing is to say that as *lovingly* as we can. I realize that suggesting we, in a loving way, are to tell people they are going to hell sounds like a contradiction in terms. But it isn't. It is loving to warn people of danger. It is not loving to let people go their merry way to an eternity of suffering, especially when we have the only thing that can save them from that horrible fate. Not warning them is like a doctor who, because he doesn't want to be the bearer of bad news, refuses to tell a patient he needs a lifesaving operation!

Because this is such shocking news, and because they expect to be "bashed" for their beliefs, Mormons don't readily see that we are coming to them out of concern for them. We need to convince them of that. The best way I have found to do so is to talk about my feelings. I tell them that I don't expect them to believe me immediately. I tell them that I know what I will say will shock them and maybe even anger them. But I ask them, even if they disagree with what I say, not to doubt my motives. I try to convey to them as sincerely as I can that I don't want to "bash" them, but rather save them. I often use the above illustration of the doctor. In other words, I don't assume that they know I'm concerned about them; I spell it out for them. When I do that, most will listen to what I have to say.

As I said, telling Mormons that they are on the road to outer darkness has led to numerous profitable witnessing opportunities. But even when it doesn't, that doesn't mean we have failed . The possibility of their going to outer darkness has been planted in their minds. And that might be the seed of doubt that will spur them on, sometime in the future, to study the differences between Mormonism and Christianity.

In addition, when we do not mention the seriousness of their situation, it becomes much easier to fall into the trap of debating Mormonism with them rather that witnessing Christ to them. For these various reasons, therefore, I am convinced that talking about their going to outer darkness is one of the best ways we can approach our LDS friends.

Hold Up God's Law by Emphasizing Matthew 5:48

This also sets the stage for discussion of Matthew 5:48 with them. As mentioned above, they often react to being told that they are on the road to outer darkness by asking: "Why do you say that?" I like to answer by saying: "Because I take seriously what God says in Matthew 5:48: 'Be ye therefore perfect, even as your Father which is in heaven is perfect'" (KJV).

There are certainly other ways of introducing Matthew 5:48. But no matter how we lead into it, I'm convinced that thoroughly discussing this passage is the most effective way of bringing God's law to bear on a

Mormon. There are four reasons for that:

> 1. It is perhaps the most quoted Bible passage in Mormonism. Mormons know it and respect it. It is one of the few passages that serves as common ground on which to build a discussion.
> 2. Trying to be perfect is the greatest point of stress for most Mormons. (See chapter six.) By talking about perfection, there is a much greater chance that they will listen to what we have to say. Many are looking for all the help they can get in this area.
> 3. It summarizes God's law as few passages do. Fewer things reveal our sinfulness more then being *commanded* to be as perfect as our heavenly Father.
> 4. It leads easily into a discussion of Hebrews 10:14, which points to the perfection of Christ for us, and thus is one of the best passages to bring the gospel to a Mormon. (In the next chapter we will take a closer look at Hebrews 10.)

More important than seeing why to use Matthew 5:48, is seeing how to use it. Everything hinges on the little word "be" and the fact that it is a present tense. The point we need to make with Mormons is that Jesus commands us to *be* perfect, not to *become* perfect as Mormonism teaches.

Even though "become perfect" is what Mormonism teaches, that is not what Joseph Smith translated. He retained the thought of "be perfect" by translating: "ye are therefore commanded to be perfect." In fact, Apostle Russell M. Nelson wrote, "Those words were given additional intensity in the Joseph Smith Translation." (*Ensign*, November 1995, p. 88) Neither does the Book of Mormon introduce the concept of becoming perfect. 3 Nephi 12:48 says: "Therefore I would that ye should be perfect, even as I, or your Father who is in heaven is perfect."

The combination of Matthew 5:48, Joseph Smith's translation, and 3 Nephi 12:48 serves as a powerful witness to Mormons. All their lives they have been told they need to become perfect. They assumed that is what the Bible and the Book of Mormon said. Even though they have heard Matthew 5:48 many times, they are conditioned to think of becoming perfect when they hear it. Although the word "be" is there in black and white, it often takes a lot of effort on our part just to make them see that. They need to be confronted with these three references and challenged to show on what basis they believe that they can become perfect.

Even then, they frequently don't grasp what we are getting at. Mormons have great difficulty understanding the tremendous difference between "being" and "becoming." Therefore it is beneficial to proceed very slowly. I ask them what it means if I tell my children to be good. Does that mean that I want them to be good immediately or in ten years? I ask them what the boss means when he tells people to be on time. These and similar illustrations can demonstrate the vast difference between being and becoming.

Even after all that, however, they often shrug this passage off. They just are not accustomed to *studying* the Bible. All their lives they have treated it in a slipshod manner. Therefore, we have to be like a pit bull, tenaciously clamping on the little word "be" and not letting go. If we keep focusing on it, slowly but surely they start seeing the light.

One way they reveal they are beginning to understand the point we are making is by asking us if we are perfect. I have found it quite effective to answer with a resounding yes and nothing else—which usually is met with quite dubious looks. They then ask: "Are you telling me that you never do anything wrong?" By this time I have tweaked their curiosity so much that they listen very attentively as I witness to them about how God has declared me, a person who sins constantly, perfect because Jesus was perfect for me and wiped my sins away with his death.

The next chapter explains this more fully. And some will be ready for full exposure to this good news. But the majority won't. Instead they will need to be softened up some more with God's law. This becomes apparent by their reaction. It has been my experience that most react to this initial presentation of the gospel with disbelief. They will make such statements as: "I just can't believe that we don't have to do anything to be saved."

When that happens, they need to be confronted again with "be perfect." We need to show them that God hasn't lowered his entrance requirements for heaven. "Be perfect," not "become perfect" is clearly what he requires.

To underscore that point we can refer to James 2:10. "For whosoever shall keep the whole law, and yet offend in one point, he is guilty of all" (KJV). Note that this describes a person who offends, that

191

is, stumbles at just one point, who sins unintentionally. He is still guilty of breaking the whole law. Just as a single pinprick completely destroys the balloon, so one sin completely destroys us. When it comes to getting to heaven by keeping the law, it is all or nothing.

Or we could refer to Matthew 19:21. There Jesus told the rich young man: "If thou wilt be perfect, go and sell that thou hast, and give to the poor, and thou shalt have treasure in heaven" (KJV). If they want to be perfect, they had better sell everything they have.

Still another passage we can refer to is 1 Nephi 3:7 from the Book of Mormon. It says that when the Lord gives people a command, he gives them the ability to keep that command.

> I know that the Lord giveth no commandments unto the children of men, save he shall prepare a way for them that they may accomplish the thing which he commandeth them.

Citing this is effective because it is well-known. It is often quoted to spur them on to greater deeds as the following illustrates:

> Ask a child to read and explain 1 Nephi 3:7. Stress the concept that with God's help we can obey every commandment we receive. (*Walk in His Ways B*, pp. 34,35)

But even more enlightening is the fact that the LDS church links this passage with the command to be perfect.

> Perfection is a word that causes different reactions from many people. Some people say, "Perfection? Why that is impossible!" Others say, "Perfection! I get discouraged just thinking about it!"

> Yet would the Lord give us a commandment that was impossible for us to keep? And when he gives a commandment, doesn't he, *as Nephi said*, prepare a way for us to accomplish what he commands? The Sermon on the Mount is the Lord's blueprint for perfection. (*The Life and Teachings of Jesus & His Apostles*, p. 57, emphasis added)

Linking the command "be perfect" with 1 Nephi 3:7 paints Mormons into a corner that they have great difficulty getting out of.

By now you might be wondering if the LDS church has supplied its members with any rebuttals to this approach. I know of three, but rarely has a Mormon cited any of them to me. Almost without exception, they have not known how to respond. They have tried to change the subject, they have attempted to ignore the implications of "be perfect," but they haven't come up with a good argument against it. That's understandable because even the rebuttals offered by the church are weak.

One that I thought they would cite more often would be the argument that later prophets explained "be perfect" to mean "become perfect." For example, I thought they might quote the following statement of Brigham Young:

> "If the . . . passage I have quoted is not worded to our understanding, we can alter the phraseology of the sentence, and say, 'Be ye perfect as you can,' for that is all we can do." (Quoted in *The Life and Teachings of Jesus & His Apostles*, p. 412)

After puzzling over why this and similar statements were not used in response, I think I know why. It is obvious that most Mormons aren't familiar with them because the LDS church downplays them. It downplays them because such statements relieve the pressure and thus the grip the church has on its members. Much more common are statements like this:

> Yes, I said, but we are commanded to be supermen. Said the Lord, "Be ye therefore perfect, even as your Father which is in heaven is perfect." (Matt. 5:48) We are gods in embryo, and the Lord demands perfection of us. (Spencer W. Kimball, *The Miracle of Forgiveness*, p. 286)

Therefore, even though they know their church teaches that a person becomes perfect, most can't cite any authoritative statement saying that. And we can't let them off the hook by allowing them to cite anything less than an authoritative statement. If, for example, they say their bishop said they are to become perfect, I reply by quoting a statement like Kimball's and asking: "Whose words are more binding:

193

your bishop's or one of your prophets?"

Once in a while, they cite the footnote in the LDS edition of the Bible which says that perfect means being "complete, finished, fully developed." That need not faze us because our main focus is on the word "be." Instead of arguing with them over the meaning of perfect, we can simply ask them if they, right now, are as complete, finished, fully developed, as Heavenly Father. Or are they still gods in embryo? What is important is that the Bible says "be," not "become."

A final argument I have seen, but have never personally encountered, is one offered by Gilbert Scharffs: "The Greek word 'be' in 'be ye perfect' is in future tense, hence 'become perfect'" (*The Truth About the Godmakers*, p. 93)

This is a case of a little knowledge being a dangerous thing. It is true that the Greek word (*esesthe*) is a future tense. But it is also true that this form of the future is commonly used in legal precepts as a substitution for the present imperative. (Imperatives are verbs of command.) A. T. Robertson, in his definitive study of Greek grammar, specifically cites Matthew 5:48 in this connection. Especially telling is that all translations uniformly translate it as a present, not as a future.

As I said, no Mormon has ever used this argument with me. If any would, I would just ask if that means that Joseph Smith erred in his translation of this verse, seeing he did not use a future tense. That, I think, would quickly end all discussion of Greek grammar.

In summary, we need to be like a broken record about being perfect. We need to repeatedly and persistently tell them that God demands perfection now. We cannot let them ignore that. They need to sweat over it. They need to lose sleep over it. They need to despair of trying to become perfect themselves. Then, and only then, will they be ready to look to Jesus for salvation.

Hold Up God's Law by Being a Mormon's Conscience

Another way we can show them the futility of trying to be perfect is by holding up before them all the various demands of Mormonism. Many Mormons either don't know or else conveniently ignore the rigorous demands of their religion. At times they resemble a child who thinks he can become a pro ballplayer without expending any effort. But they outdo that child. They think that, without a whole lot of trouble, they can become a god! Many don't have a clue to what their religion demands.

Cathy (not her real name) was a good example of that. She was raised in an active LDS family in a community that was predominantly LDS. No one had ever challenged her beliefs until she went off to college and met Ron, a Christian. He contacted me for help. After Ron laid some groundwork, I met with the two of them. The thing that readily became apparent was that Cathy was living a watered-down version of Mormonism *without realizing it.* She truly thought that she was fulfilling all its requirements. The realization that she had been *playing* at Mormonism rather than *practicing* it upset her greatly.

There are many Mormons like Cathy: Mormons who are playing rather than practicing their Mormonism, Mormons who have never come face-to-face with Mormonism's harsh demands.

Out of love, we need to make them aware of those demands. Take Cathy. Her idea of fasting was skipping Sunday breakfast. Needless to say, she was more than a little troubled when I confronted her with the following quote.

"The law to the Latter-day Saints, as understood by the authorities of the church, is that food and drink are not to be partaken of for twenty-four hours, 'from even to even', and that the Saints are to refrain from all bodily gratification and indulgences." (Joseph F. Smith, quoted in *To Make Thee a Minister and a Witness*, p. 116)

We explored various areas of her life in that way. After I left, she admitted to Ron that she was not living her religion.

For now, however, she has not thrown up her hands in despair and turned to Jesus for help. Rather she has bent her back to the plow and is trying all the harder to meet Mormonism's requirements.

Most respond initially in that way. Even though we have made the load heavier, they still think they can carry it. That is why we have to remain at their side. Not to help them carry the load or make it lighter for them, but to make it heavier! We need to be their consciences, regularly reminding them what is all involved in being a good Mormon.

Few things are more difficult than that. It is heartrending to stand by and watch people struggle, and then cause them to struggle all the more. It is difficult to increase people's stress intentionally.

But it needs to be done. The law has to break apart their stony hearts of self-righteousness first, before we can plant gospel seeds in it. Instead of letting them off the hook, we need to dig the hook in even deeper. We need to ask them if they are keeping up their genealogy records, if they are doing their temple work, if they are observing the Sabbath correctly. In this connection, I have found quite a helpful the following list from the priesthood manual, *To Make Thee a Minister and a Witness* (p. 59). It is a summary of what they should be doing.

Personal prayers
Regular family prayer
Regular family home evening
Home storage
Regular scripture study
Strict personal worthiness
Support of quorum, ward, stake, and general Church leaders
Tender concern for your wife and other family members
Family History
Patience and love
Honest work and integrity in your occupation
Exemplary grooming and dress
Regular attendance at and gaining strength from Church meetings and activitiesRegular temple
    attendance
Observance of the Word of Wisdom
Purity of thought

The more pointed we can make this, the better. If our Mormon friends are having trouble keeping the Word of Wisdom, that is what we have to talk to them about. If they are content with having limited families, that is what we need to confront them with. Where they are fudging in their religion is where we need to concentrate

Church leaders recently have identified two areas where they say members are falling short: Sabbath-keeping and home storage.

The Sabbath of the Lord is becoming the play day of the people. It is a day of golf and football on television, of buying and selling in our stores and markets. Are we moving to mainstream America as some observers believe? In this I fear we are. What a telling thing it is to see the parking lots of the markets filled on Sunday in communities that are predominately LDS. (Gordon B. Hinckley, *Ensign*, Nov. 1997, p. 69)

196

Acquire and store a reserve of food supplies that will sustain life. Obtain clothing and build a savings account on a sensible, well-planned basis that can serve well in times of emergency. As long as I can remember, we have been taught to prepare for the future and to obtain a year's supply of necessities. I would guess that the years of plenty have almost universally caused us to set aside this counsel. (Apostle L. Tom Perry, *Ensign*, Nov. 1995, p. 36)

These, then, would be two good areas to address with your Mormon friend.

Many people are repulsed by this strategy since it has the appearance of kicking Mormons when they are down. Many regard this as the farthest thing from treating Mormons lovingly.

I can identify with such feelings—until I remember the big picture and see Mormons suffering eternally in hell. Then I know that drastic measures are called for. Then I understand that, much like a surgeon, we have to hurt in order to heal. Being a conscience to Mormons, adding weight to their load until they realize they can't carry it, is painful for all involved. But it can't compare to the pain of hell. That is what we always need to keep in mind. Only then will we be moved to apply the scalpel of the law to LDS self-righteousness.

Hold Up God's Law by Stressing the LDS Concept of Repentance

Like so many other aspects of Mormonism, its teaching concerning repentance can hang like a huge black cloud over a Mormon's head. This happens because the major component of LDS repentance is "abandoning the sin." Put yourself in their shoes as you read the following statements:

"There is one crucial test of repentance. This is abandonment of the sin . . . The saving power does not extend to him who merely wants to change his life . . . Nor is repentance complete when one merely tries to abandon sin . . . To try is weak." (Spencer W. Kimball quoted in *Sharing the Gospel Manual*, p. 94)

This repentance must make such a mighty change in our hearts that we have no more disposition to do evil, but to do good continually. (*Sharing the Gospel Manual*, p. 95)

"Repentance must involve an all-out, total surrender to the program of the Lord. That transgressor is not fully repentant who neglects his tithing, misses his meetings, breaks the Sabbath, fails in his family prayers, does not sustain the authorities of the Church, breaks the Word of Wisdom, does not love the Lord nor his fellowmen. A reforming adulterer who drinks or curses is not repentant. The repenting burglar who has sex play is not ready for forgiveness. God cannot forgive unless the transgressor shows a true repentance which spreads to all areas of life." (Kimball, quoted in *Doctrines of the Gospel*, p. 41)

Understandably, many Mormons conveniently ignore such statements. But I have been surprised at the number who have echoed such thoughts. For example, one explained repentance this way. He said that if he had taken God's name in vain when he was 16 and repented of it, God would forgive him. But if he did it again when he was 17, he would not be forgiven, and he would also lose the former forgiveness. His repeating the sin had shown that he hadn't abandoned it and thus had not sincerely repented.

That is exactly what Mormonism teaches.

Those who receive forgiveness and then repeat the sin are held accountable for their former sins. (Gospel Principles, p. 253)

Here again, we need to hold before them the full implications of what their church teaches. When we see them repeating a sin, we need to confront them with these quotations and show them how impossible it is to live the Mormon religion.

Conclusion

Many Mormons are like the rich young man that came to Jesus

in Matthew 19. They think they have done enough, but they have a vague feeling that they have to do more. Carefully note what Jesus did. He didn't talk about his being the Savior. Neither did he mention faith. Rather he brought the law to bear on the young man in an attempt to show him his sin. And he did that in a very pointed way. He knew the man's weakness was his wealth, and that is what Jesus zeroed in on. He did that because he loved him (Mark 10:21).

That is how we need to treat our LDS friends. Lovingly, but firmly, we need to show them their sin and the impossibility of their being perfect. Once they see that, they will be ready to hear the wonderful news of the gospel.

Discussion Questions

1. How can you emphasis outer darkness to a Mormon on the basis of Matthew 7:13,14? What other passages might you also use to speak about outer darkness? How can you lead into a discussion of law and gospel?

2. Why is it important to show concern when speaking to a Mormon about the law? How can we show concern in the way we speak?

3. How can you use Matthew 5:48 in speaking the law to Mormons? Mormons emphasize becoming perfect. This passage says, "Be perfect." What's the distinction?

4. How can we hold up to a Mormon the "unreasonable" demands of Mormonism?

5. How can you use the teaching of repentance, as Mormons understand it, to "burden their conscience" under the law of God?

CHAPTER NINE: REACH MORMONS WITH THE SWEET GOSPEL

I n an attempt to witness to his LDS friend, John says: "I believe that Jesus is my Savior." His friend quickly agrees and says he believes the same thing. John isn't expecting that and is taken somewhat aback. He tries to explain himself by saying, "I believe that Jesus saved me by doing everything for me." Again his friend readily agrees. By now John is totally confused and is wondering if Mormons aren't Christians after all.

Many such conversations have occurred over the years. And countless Christians have gone away from them frustrated. The problem is not that Mormonism has been misrepresented and is truly Christian, but rather one of terminology. What Mormons mean by salvation and what Christians mean are two entirely different things, with the result that Mormons and Christians end up talking past each other.

Not just the word "salvation" creates problems either. "Grace," "atonement," "redemption," "justification" — they and other biblical words describing the gospel have been drastically redefined by the LDS church. Because of this, traditional presentations of the gospel and popularly used Bible passages often miss the mark. But when we are aware of these difficulties and tailor our witness to avoid them, we can experience the joy of bringing the gospel to our LDS friends in ways that hit home with them.

Besides avoiding the pitfall of terminology differences, we need to be aware of the obstacles thrown in our path by the Joseph Smith Translation (JST). It has drained some passages of their gospel content. For example, in Romans 4:5 Paul says that God "justifieth the ungodly," but the JST says that God "justifieth not the ungodly." Although many Mormons are not familiar with the JST, it is footnoted in their edition of the Bible and will be one of the first things many will check.

In what follows, I will show some ways to avoid the twin obstacles of terminology differences and mistranslations. It has been my experience that these get Christians and Mormons to talk to each other, not past each other.

We need to note a couple of other preliminaries. Although you will want to talk to Mormons about going to heaven, I have discovered that it is more effective to talk about "living with Heavenly Father." Mormons believe that nearly everybody goes to heaven, but only those who go to the celestial kingdom will live with Heavenly Father. Thus "living with Heavenly Father" comes closer to conveying to them the biblical concept of heaven.

Also, since the King James Version (KJV) is their official translation, we should use it when we talk to Mormons. Even though at times the KJV's archaic English makes witnessing more difficult, overall it helps our witness. Our use of it prevents them from disregarding what we say simply because of our choice of translations.

Talk to Mormons about Already Being Perfect in Christ

In my estimation, the one section of Scripture that most effectively presents the gospel to Mormons is Hebrews 10:10-18. This has proven effective because

1. It deals with perfection, a point of great stress and emphasis in Mormonism;
2. it does not employ many words that are defined differently by Mormons;
3. Joseph Smith did not alter it in his translation;
4. most Mormons have never heard it. Neither have I seen it cited in a church manual. Their unfamiliarity with it means that they have no canned response to it.

Hebrews 10:10-18 contains some powerful gospel statements. Three times the writer emphasizes that Jesus' one sacrifice was sufficient for all people (verses 10,12,14). Verses 17 and 18 wonderfully describe the result of that one sacrifice for us. "And their sins and iniquities will I remember no more. Now where remission of these is, there is no more offering for sin." The entire section shows us that "no more needs to be done, no more can be done" (Kretzmann, *Popular Commentary of the Bible, New Testament*, Vol 2, p. 475). Jesus did it all. This is the message that Mormons need to hear.

Verse 14 is the verse that especially hits home: "For by one offering he hath perfected for ever them that are sanctified." When witnessing to Mormons, the point we need to stress is that the tense of the verb "hath perfected" indicates that this is a *completed*, not a *future* action. More exactly, in the original Greek, it is a perfect tense which "expresses the continuance of completed action" (Robertson, *A Grammar of the Greek New Testament*, p. 893). In other words, we have already been perfected by Jesus' sacrifice on the cross.

Understandably, Mormons find this mind-boggling. But many Christians also have trouble with this teaching. They say: "That can't be true! I'm not perfect. I sin daily." What is vital for all to see is that God is talking about people's *status*, not their *state*. All people are still in a state of sin. Because of Jesus, however, believers have received the status of saints. That is what being justified by faith means. Justified means that God declares us righteous or perfect because Jesus kept the law perfectly for us and then washed away our sins on the cross. Therefore believers are now saints in God's sight. (See 2 Corinthians 1:1, Ephesians 1:1, Philippians 1:1.)

This is what our LDS friends so desperately need to hear. They need to hear that the way to being saints is not by being Latter-day Saints but by placing all their hope in what Jesus has already done for them. They need to see Jesus as their *substitute*, doing it all for them, not as their *example*, showing them what they need to do. They need to frolic in his perfection for them rather than struggle to become perfect themselves.

Because this is so foreign to them, they have great difficulty believing it. Therefore, we have to take our stand on Hebrews 10:14 and not be moved off it. If they don't accept our interpretation, we can ask them to give us an alternate interpretation that does justice to the text. We can personally witness to the joy, peace, and relief that is ours, knowing that Jesus was perfect for us. We can emphasize how this section abounds in past tenses with not a future tense in sight. Whatever we do, we need to keep the substitutionary nature of Jesus' life and death always before them. That is the good news that the Holy Spirit can so powerfully use to overcome their resistance and bring them to faith.

Before leaving this verse, we should briefly address its last phrase: "them that are sanctified" (KJV). Or as the NIV translates: "those who are being made holy." Don't be taken aback if they point to that as proof that people have to do something after all. Verse 10 shows us that this too is a result of Jesus' one sacrifice, and not a result of anything we do. "By the which will we are sanctified through the offering of the body of Jesus Christ once for all" (KJV). The following observation also proves helpful:

> The present tense "are being made holy" reminds us how one after the other the Spirit through the gospel sets men free from sin and for service to their loving God. (Lauersdorf, *Hebrews* in The People's Bible, p. 112)

Talk to Mormons about Forgiveness

Forgiveness is one word Mormonism hasn't redefined, as the following quote illustrates:

> How do you define forgiveness? (Overcoming the desire to punish someone who has offended you. Not being angry with him and *granting him complete pardon.*) *(Latter-day Saint Woman B,* p. 63, emphasis added)

Although Mormons haven't redefined forgiveness, they have badly twisted it. Most of the time they use it to describe their duty to each other. Rarely is it used to picture what God does for them. Therefore when Mormons hear the word forgiveness, they almost automatically think of something they have to do, rather than of a blessing they receive from God.

When they talk about God's forgiveness, they stress that it has to be earned. This is contrary to their own definition given above but is consistent LDS teaching. No place does this become more evident than in a book written by one of their prophets, Spencer W. Kimball, entitled *The Miracle of Forgiveness.* As one reads it, one wonders where the miracle is in LDS forgiveness. As you read the following excerpts, try to imagine how depressing it must be to believe what they say:

"There is no royal road to repentance, no privileged path to forgiveness. . . . There is only one way. It is a long road spiked with thorns and briars and pitfalls and problems." (*Miracle of Forgiveness*, quoted in *Gospel Principles*." p. 123)

"Peace comes only through forgiveness. But forgiveness has a high price. President Kimball tells us: 'To every forgiveness there is a condition . . . The fasting, the prayers, the humility must be equal to or greater than the sin. There must be a broken heart and a contrite spirit . . . There must be conviction of the sin, abandonment of the evil, confession of the error to properly constituted authorities of the Lord.'" (*Miracle of Forgiveness*, quoted in *Gospel Principles*, p. 252)

Your Heavenly Father has promised forgiveness upon total repentance and meeting all the requirements, but that forgiveness is not granted merely for the asking. There must be works—many works—and an all-out, total surrender, with a great humility and "a broken heart and contrite spirit."

It depends upon you whether or not you are forgiven, and when. It could be weeks, it could be years, it could be centuries before that happy day when you have the positive assurance that the Lord has forgiven you. That depends on your humility, your sincerity, your work, your attitudes. (*The Miracle of Forgiveness*, p. 324f.)

Against this dreary background, the biblical doctrine of forgiveness shines forth brilliantly. Before you introduce Mormons to what the Bible has to say, however, you do well to set the stage. You can do that by asking them what their definition of forgiveness is. They often hem and haw and say they have never thought about it. You might suggest looking up the definition in the dictionary. Or you might try to illustrate it. For example, you could say something like this: "Say that you owed me $10. But one day I came to you and said I have forgiven you that debt. What does that mean to you? Do you still owe me $10? Almost always such illustrations bring them to a proper definition of forgiveness.

The important thing is mutually to establish that definition before anything else. Once you have forgiveness defined, you can refer to the above quotes and ask them how they square these with their definition. You can ask them how they can talk about forgiveness and payment in the same breath. Either a bill needs to be paid or it is forgiven, but it can't be both.

Most become quite befuddled at this point. They don't know how to respond so they might try to change the subject. Instead of letting them do that, bring in Bible passages that speak of God's true forgiveness. Passages like Hebrews 10:17,18; Psalm 32: 1,2; Ephesians 1:7; Micah 7:19; and Psalm 103: 11,12 work quite well. Each of these passages emphasizes that when God forgives our sins, he doesn't expect us to pay him back. In fact, even attempting a payment becomes an affront to his love. Most Mormons have never heard these passages and are overwhelmed by them.

All this demands patience on our part. Most Mormons will struggle greatly to grasp our point. You need to realize that the biblical teaching of forgiveness goes against everything they have been taught. Don't get discouraged. Be confident that, by using these gospel passages, you are bringing the power of the Holy Spirit to bear on them. Be patient and give him time to work.

Talk to Them about Eternal Life

Eternal life, in Mormonese, is not living with God, but living as God. It is equivalent to exaltation. "Exaltation means the same thing as eternal life" (*Learn of Me*, p 72). Because of the problems that can be caused by these terminology differences, I prefer talking to Mormons about God's forgiveness and of Christ's perfection for them. However, speaking to them about eternal life can be effective too because:

> 1. many Mormons are sloppy in their definition of eternal life and do equate it with "going to heaven" (even a member of the local stake presidency did that in a conversation with me);

> 2. the focus of the discussion can be kept on how to obtain eternal life rather than on what is eternal life.

No matter how they define it, Mormons feel eternal life is

something they must obtain and thus is something that lies in the future. The Bible, however, describes eternal life as a *present condition* for believers. The passage that most effectively illustrates this to the LDS is John 6:47: "Verily, verily, I say unto you, he that believeth on me hath everlasting life" (KJV). The key word is "hath." This is archaic English for "has" and describes a present state. That will be the point on which you will want to focus. How can eternal life be a present state if it is something they need to obtain?

That this passage speaks about "everlasting life" rather than "eternal life" need not bother us because in the footnotes of the LDS edition of the KJV, everlasting life is referenced to eternal life and exaltation. In contrast, John 5:24 also describes everlasting life as a present state, but it has no reference to eternal life in the footnotes. For that reason, it is better to use John 6:47 with your LDS friends.

Probably the most familiar passage to Christians in this regard is Romans 6:23. "For the wages of sin is death; but the gift of God is eternal life through Jesus Christ our Lord" (KJV). Because Christians, in the past, have used this passage with Mormons, some Mormons are familiar with it and are ready to refute it. They say that eternal life is God's gift (although they still have to earn it!), but they won't receive it until some future time. Because some have this canned response to it, I prefer taking the path of least resistance and sticking with John 6:47, a passage they are not familiar with.

Talk to Mormons about Jesus Conquering Satan

Although I haven't found much evidence of this in their writings, some Mormons and former Mormons have told me that the spiritual presence they were most aware of was Lucifer. They felt he was constantly around trying to lead them astray. On the other hand, they thought of Heavenly Father as a distant deity.

Former Mormon Latayne Scott makes the same point in her book, *The Mormon Mirage*:

> As much as any religious group on earth, the Mormons are acutely aware of the reality of the being they refer to as Satan . . .
> Although God blessed water in the beginning of history, Mormons say He cursed it in the last days, and now the element of water is one that is the dominion of Satan.

206

. . . That is one of the reasons Mormon missionaries may not swim while on their missions, and why many older Mormons will not get near any body of water greater than that contained in a bathtub . . .

Many Mormons, in dwelling on the negative forces that they believe surround them on this earth where the devil also abides, have become downright superstitious. (pp. 178-180)

This sensitivity to Lucifer's presence, coupled with their belief that they must resist him entirely by themselves, causes many Mormons much anxiety. For example, one ex-Mormon told me that his biggest fear as a Mormon was that Satan would call his wife out of the grave by her secret name before he could, with the result that she would be married to Satan for all eternity.

With such a Mormon, Bible passages like Hebrews 2:14 and 1 John 3:8, which stress that Jesus has already conquered the devil, can prove effective.

Talk to Mormons about James 2:14-26

Almost inevitably, when you cite such Bible passages, Mormons will want to talk about good works. And just as predictably they will cite James chapter two especially verse 24. "Ye see then how that by works a man is justified, and not by faith only" (KJV). Many Christians are not familiar with this verse and subsequently are shocked by it. So that our witness doesn't come to a screeching halt when this passage is brought up, we need to understand it and be prepared to talk about it.

Before anything else, we need to see what constitutes a good work in the eyes of God. Contrary to what many think, it is more than doing something according to God's will. To please God, it also has to be done in faith. "Everything that does not come from faith is sin" (Romans 14: 23; see also Hebrew 11:6). In other words, only believers can do good works.

James, in chapter two, expands on that. There he shows that believers not only can do good works but they will do good works. He is writing to Jewish Christians who are in danger of giving nothing but lip service to Jesus. His intent, therefore, is to distinguish true faith from false faith. He addresses *what* saving faith is and how we can recognize it, not *how* it saves. He shows that true faith produces works, which then become visible evidences of faith's invisible presence.

That James is talking about how true faith reveals itself becomes apparent from verse 18. *"Show* me your faith without deeds, and I will *show* you my faith by what I do" (NIV, emphasis added). James then cites the example of how Abraham's willingness to sacrifice his son "made perfect" (NIV: "made complete") his faith.

That James is not saying Abraham's faith was not true faith until he was willing to sacrifice Isaac can be seen from the very next verse. There James quotes Genesis 15:6, which says Abraham's faith was credited to him as righteousness. But God spoke those words, before Isaac, Abraham's son, was even born! In other words, *before he did anything*, Abraham had saving faith. His willingness to sacrifice Isaac came after his faith. It was a *fruit* and not the *root* of his faith, thus serving as a visible evidence of his invisible faith. In that sense, his faith was made complete, "completed in the sense that an apple tree is completed when it produces what God intended and created it to produce, apples" (*Concordia Self-Study Commentary*, p. 253).

Verse 26 brings that thought out well. Good works are the "vital signs" indicating that faith is alive. Someone put it well by saying: "Faith alone saves, but faith is never alone." The important thing is to keep each in their proper place. Mormons place the cart of good works before the horse of faith.

When talking with Mormons, it is not essential, and probably not always wise, to go into all this detail. In the beginning at least, it is usually sufficient to show them that you are not intimidated by James 2, but rather that you not only understand it, but appreciate it. I have found it quite effective, when they bring up this chapter, to enter into a discussion of it with great eagerness. I often say something like this: "I'm glad you brought that up. It is one of my favorite chapters. I really like how it explains the relationship between faith and works. Let's look at the example of Abraham in verses 21-24." At times, I have even taken the initiative and introduced James 2 into the conversation. You can almost see the wind being taken out of their sails.

Especially in initial discussions, I feel that nipping their argument in the bud is a legitimate objective. Getting Mormons to understand the proper relationship between faith and works often is asking too much at first. But if we neutralize their interpretation of James 2, we can keep the discussion where we want it—on what Jesus has done for them.

Although it is extremely difficult for Mormons to grasp the biblical teaching concerning good works, one thing that I have found

208

beneficial to talk about is the tremendous difference in motivation that exists between Christians and Mormons. I illustrate that difference by telling them the story of "Little Orphan Andy."

Little Orphan Andy lived in an orphanage, desperately wanting to be adopted. That is all he could think about. Every night he fell asleep dreaming about what it would be like having a family.

One day a couple came to the orphanage and told Andy they thought they wanted to adopt him. But they wanted to make sure, so they had made arrangements to have Andy live for a month with them. After that, they would make their final decision.

Naturally Andy was ecstatic. But he was also quite fearful. That entire month he felt like he was walking on eggshells as he tried not to do anything to displease his potential parents. In fact, he was so careful that much of his shining personality didn't come out. It was one of the toughest months of his life.

That is one scenario. Suppose, however, that a second couple had come to the orphanage and told Andy that they had already adopted him. He was now their son; no ifs, ands, or buts about it. No trial period— it was already final. He was already part of their family.

How would Andy act? He would still be on his best behavior—but probably would do more because he would be liberated from his fear of being rejected.

Mormons are like Andy in the first scenario. Out of fear of rejection, they strive to please God. Christians are like Andy in the second example. Out of gratitude for being accepted, they are liberated to please God. Outwardly, the good works of Mormons and Christians might appear similar, but what a world of difference in motivation and joy!

Conclusion

What a wonderful message, what a powerful tool, God has given us in the gospel! Employing its rich diversity, may we share it clearly with our LDS friends. Trusting its awesome power, may we share it confidently. To God be all glory!

Discussion Questions

1. What is a good way to speak about heaven to a Mormon? Why?

2. How can you use Hebrews 10:10-18 to speak about a proper biblical understanding of perfection to a Mormon?

3. How is perfection to be understood as a completed action? Once again, how is this different from LDS thinking?

4. How can we emphasize the Bible's teaching of forgiveness to a Mormon?

5. When speaking about eternal life to a Mormon, what is to be our focus? How does John 6:47 explain this focus?

6. What strange fear do Mormons have when thinking about Satan?

7. How do Mormons use (misuse) James 2:24 to emphasize their position of "salvation by works"? What is the correct understanding of this verse? How is this demonstrated in the preceding verses of James 2?

CHAPTER TEN: REACH MORMONS WITH LOVE

The last two chapters spelled out various ways of speaking the truth of God's law and gospel to Mormons. Remember, however, we are to always speak the truth in love (Ephesians 4:15). That is easier said than done. We can easily become angered at their blasphemous beliefs. We can easily become irritated as they keep us at arm's length or unjustly accuse us of "Mormon bashing." We can easily become frustrated as they seemingly reject what we have to say, without even thinking about it.

It takes Christlike love to overcome such feelings. It takes a love that is rooted not in our emotions, but in our will. Our love is to be one of commitment. And that means we need to drink deeply of Christ's love for us. The more we experience his love, the more we can model it. Only because God first loved us, can we love our LDS friends.

This chapter presents a number of different ideas on how we can show love to our LDS friends. Such methods can prove helpful. But the essential thing is our motivation. Above all else, may we always say with St. Paul, "Christ's love compels us."

Love Mormons by "Becoming Like a Mormon"

We begin by seeing the importance of "becoming like a Mormon." Although this might sound startling, it is biblical. This was the mind-set of the greatest missionary of all time, St. Paul.

Though I am free and belong to no man, I make myself a

> slave to everyone, to win as many as possible. To the
> Jews I became like a Jew, to win the Jews. To those under
> the law I became like one under the law (though I myself
> am not under the law), so as to win those under the law.
> To those not having the law I became like one not having
> the law (though I am not free from God's law but am
> under Christ's law), so as to win those not having the law.
> To the weak I became weak, to win the weak. I have
> become all things to all men so that by all possible means
> I might save some. I do all this for the sake of the gospel,
> that I may share in its blessings. (1 Corinthians 9:19-23)

It is vital that we understand Paul correctly. Otherwise we might have him saying more than he does. Paul never gave ground when it came to biblical teaching. When the issue was doctrine, he stood firm. But in areas where God had not spoken, in areas of culture and methodology, Paul exhibited flexibility and bent over backwards for others.

In such areas he displayed amazing flexibility and commitment. He didn't just try to understand the people to whom he was witnessing, he acted on that understanding. No fewer than five times in the above paragraph he says he *became like* somebody. At the beginning of the paragraph, he puts it even stronger: "I make myself a *slave* to everyone." Again, we must not make Paul say more than what he said, but we must not make him say less either. Out of love for the people he was trying to win, he *changed* how he acted.

In that same spirit, we can become like Mormons to win Mormons. We can strive to bend over backwards for them. We can make every effort to avoid *unnecessary* obstacles as we reach out to them.

We can do that in various ways. One way is simply to know their culture and be sensitive to it. For example, it would not be very loving to invite your active LDS friend over for a cup of coffee on Monday night.

Other ways that we can bend over backwards for Mormons, however, are not as easy. As has become evident, one of the greatest obstacles in witnessing to Mormons is terminology differences. Therefore, we can make a concerted effort to learn "Mormonese" and speak it with them. (See the glossary for a dictionary of Mormonese.) This involves three basic principles.

First, as we have already seen, it means avoiding, as much as possible, terms and expressions (e.g., Christian, salvation, Scripture) that have different definitions in Mormonism than they do in Christianity. Some view this as a cop-out and a weakening of the biblical message. But the Bible encourages such an approach by presenting both the law and the gospel with much diversity. By using, instead of ignoring, this rich diversity, we can tailor our presentation to a particular audience and hit them more forcefully, rather than less.

Second, closely connected with avoiding certain terms, it means employing other terms that might not be familiar to us: terms like "agency," "exaltation," and "celestial kingdom."

Third, speaking Mormonese means making our witness personal or "bearing them our testimony." This is important since Mormons think non-Mormons have a very sterile relationship with God. Therefore, they often are taken aback, for example, when we tell them confidently that we know we have eternal life because of what Jesus has done for us. Saying "I know" to a Mormon is much more effective than saying "the Bible says." We can go on to explain that we know this because the Bible tells us. Still, we need to get across to them that our faith and our relationship with the Lord are on a personal level.

Another important thing to keep in mind when "bearing our testimony" is to turn the spotlight always on Christ and not on ourselves. As you bear your testimony, picture yourself as a speaker at a testimonial dinner. At such an affair the talk centers on the person being honored. Your talk, then, should center on Christ and what he did for us two thousand years ago. That was Paul's method:

> When I came to you, brothers, I did not come with eloquence or superior wisdom as I proclaimed to you the *testimony* about God. For I resolved to know nothing while I was with you except Jesus Christ and him crucified. (1 Corinthians 2:1,2 emphasis added)

Speaking Mormonese is one way we can become like a Mormon. Another way is to use the LDS edition of the Bible. This is nothing but the KJV with footnotes. Nevertheless, for the following reasons, it proves helpful to use their edition: (You can order one from Deseret Bookstore in Salt Lake City, 1-800-453-4532.)

1. Just because you have one often impresses Mormons and establishes your credibility with them. It shows that you have tried to understand them.

2. By using the same Bible, you can often save Mormons some embarrassment. Most of them aren't familiar with the Bible. Therefore, when you ask them to look up a passage, frequently they can't find it. And once people are embarrassed, their concentration is broken, and much of what you say makes little impression. But when you are using their edition of the Bible, you can give them the page numbers. For example, instead of asking them to look up Hebrews chapter ten, you could say: "Let's look at, p. 1531. I want to look especially at v. 14 on that page."

3. The LDS Bible contains portions of Joseph Smith's translation in the footnotes and the appendix. At times, it proves helpful to know what that translation says.

4. Often the first thing Mormons do when discussing a particular passage is to look to the footnotes for help. By having the footnotes in front of you, you can better anticipate how they will answer.

Another way of "becoming like a Mormon" is to be familiar with their scriptures, especially the Book of Mormon. One of the first things many will ask you is whether you have read it. If you aren't at least familiar with it, many will brush your witness off as uninformed. It is not important to know it very well since it doesn't teach much LDS teaching. But it is important to be able honestly to tell them that you are familiar with it and have read in it.

Finally, it also helps to be familiar with and use their current official writings. Fewer things have been more helpful to me than being able to quote directly from church manuals currently in use. To give you a stockpile of such references is one of the reasons why I have quoted so extensively in this book.

In summary, we can "become like a Mormon"

1. by being sensitive to their culture;
2. by speaking "Mormonese";
3. by using their edition of the Bible;
4. by being familiar with their scriptures;
5. by quoting current church manuals.

Love Mormons by Taking the Initiative in Establishing a Relationship with Them

One of the more frustrating aspects of witnessing to Mormons is the difficulty of getting into meaningful discussions with them, much less meaningful relationships. Mormons and non-Mormons don't mix easily for a number of reasons:

First, the cultural aspects of Mormonism tend to isolate them from non-Mormons. Our ways and language are just as unfamiliar to them as theirs are to us. They can be just as uncomfortable with us as we sometimes are with them. In addition, their lives are so wrapped up in the church that many times they don't have time to work on relationships with non-Mormons.

Second, Mormons are acutely conscious of the persecutions that the early Mormons experienced. This has caused many of them to have a persecution complex. In addition, since many non-Mormons still ridicule them, it is not surprising that they view any attempt to witness to them as nothing but "Mormon bashing."

Third, since Mormonism gives them "the fullness of the gospel," they frequently believe that they have nothing to learn from Christians.

Fourth, I have found some who were hesitant to talk for the opposite reason—because they were embarrassed by certain LDS teachings, or, at the very least, not sure of them. They didn't want to be put into the uncomfortable position of either defending these teachings or publicly denying them.

All these can be reasons it is difficult at times to establish a meaningful relationship with Mormons. In my opinion, however, the biggest factor is that they have no concept of true, sacrificial love. Mormonism teaches them, often quite blatantly, that it is every man for himself. This means that their motivation for helping others is the good it does them. Consider, for example, the following advice given to young men. Note especially the motivation employed:

> Our rules are the commandments of God. *You make points* when you serve your mission, draw close to the Lord, live the Word of Wisdom, stay morally clean, and live a life of service and Church activity. (Russell C. Taylor, *Ensign*, May 1989, p. 40, emphasis added)

Many times this self-centeredness is hidden quite well,

apparent neither to them nor to us. But how foreign a concept selfless love is to the LDS was driven home to me one night as I sat and talked with a member of the local stake presidency. He mentioned that his brother was presently inactive in the church. I replied by saying that must be a burden to him. He gave me a strange look and said: "Burden? It is a challenge!" The more we talked, the more I realized that he wasn't concerned about where his brother would end up eternally. His concern was whether he could "make points" by restoring him to active membership. Repeatedly, I have encountered such feelings.

As we look into the Bible, it shouldn't surprise us to discover such attitudes in Mormons. John wrote: "Everyone who loves has been born of God and knows God" (1 John 4:7). In other words, only Christians, because they alone have been born of God, can exhibit true sacrificial love.

Mormons, therefore, won't be able to identify with our motives for witnessing to them. Rather than believing that all we want to do is help them, they will be wondering what we are getting out of it. In my experience, that misreading of a Christian's motive serves as the greatest obstacle for Christians getting close to Mormons.

In spite of such obstacles, we need to take the initiative and attempt to establish meaningful relationships with Mormons. Jesus said go and make disciples, not wait until people come to us. As we go, however, we need to make sure that our concern remains genuine. It can easily wear thin as they keep us at arm's distance. Therefore, we must always keep in mind the great stakes involved, namely, that Mormons will spend their eternity in outer darkness if they continue believing that they have to earn eternal life.

When you remember that, it will be easier for you to go out on the limb and energetically work on your relationship with Mormons. You can discover a common interest and take the initiative to do it together. You can be alert to their needs and ready to offer a helping hand. You can find out their birthdays or anniversaries and remember them with a card. Above all, you can take the time to be friendly. You need to maintain regular contact. You need to take the initiative and try your hardest to make that relationship thrive.

Ask Them Meaningful Questions

One frequently overlooked aspect of witnessing is listening. Yet, listening is half of witnessing. The more we know about people, the

216

more effectively we can talk with them. One of the best ways of getting to know people is by asking them questions.

At times we hesitate to question people because we are afraid that our curiosity will turn them off. Most of them, however, are not repelled by questions, if we aren't continually pumping them for information. It helps to intersperse questions about them with comments about ourselves. Neither will they resist our questioning if they sense that we are genuinely interested in them. People detect our interest when we actively listen to them and ask follow-up questions that come to mind as they speak.

Following are some points that we will want to discover through tactful questioning:

1. *How much of Mormonism do they really know?* Even active Mormons often don't know many of the details of their religion. Therefore you could ask them questions about specific teachings. You could also ask about certain of their practices, especially when they make a passing reference to them. If asked in a non-threatening way, most are more than willing to answer. I have also found it quite effective to ask how they define certain words such as "repentance" or "forgiveness." Not only do such questions help you gauge their knowledge of Mormonism, but such questions can also begin to highlight for them the difference between Mormonism and Christianity. Remember: many Mormons think Christians believe much as they do.

2. *How active are they? If they are inactive, ask why.* Try to learn whether they feel guilty about being inactive or are apathetic about it. Don't assume they are inactive just because they aren't religious. Some are inactive because they are very religious. They be came inactive because they realized how impossible it is to live the Mormon religion. If they are active, ask what positions they hold or have held in the church. Find out if they are temple-worthy. Most will not view these as intimidating questions. Listen carefully to see if they describe

their activity positively or negatively. Many feel burned-out by all that the church requires of them.

3. *Are they lifelong church members or converts?*
If lifelong, how many generations does their membership go back? A badge of honor in Mormonism is being related to the early Mormons who settled Salt Lake City. If they are converts, you can often get into a fruitful discussion by asking what attracted them to the LDS Church.

4. *Are they experiencing stress in their lives?*
In what way? (See chapter six.) In the course of a normal conversation, they might make a passing comment about something that is bothering them. If we are actively listening, we can pick up on such a comment. Or else we can share with them some problem we struggle with, making sure to witness how our faith in Jesus helps us handle it. Such sharing might cause them to open up. In the course of such a discussion, we can find out how much help they feel Mormonism is giving them. One caution, however: Mormons are not conditioned to talk about their weaknesses. We often have to be patient before they open up to us.

Love Mormons by Entering a Spiritual Conversation with Them

It might seem as if this is a given, but it isn't. Often we spend a lot of time building a bridge of friendship to them and then fail to cross the bridge we built. Instead we continue to build the bridge. We come up with numerous reasons why now is not a good time to talk to our LDS friends about spiritual matters.

There comes a point, usually sooner than later, that the time is ripe to sit down and have a serious talk with them about their eternity. In chapter eight, I have suggested how to do that. Now, I am encouraging you to do it!

I have experienced, as have others, that many Mormons are open to such a discussion. If, however, they are reluctant, don't give up too quickly. Lovingly, but aggressively, "challenge" them to talk with you. Remind them that one of their main missions as members of the LDS church is "to proclaim the gospel." Be persistent. Always keep in mind the stakes involved: that they are on the road to hell and you have the only message that can change their direction.

Love Mormons by Sharing Your Spiritual Struggles and Joys

Although I mentioned this in the last section, I want to emphasize it. We can't expect our LDS friends to open up to us if we aren't open with them. Without becoming wearisome, share the problems and struggles you have because of sin. But always be sure to tell them of the strength and comfort you possess because of Christ. You don't always have to go into great detail. The idea is to pepper your normal conversation with such statements. In other words, model the gospel for them: it is not living a perfect life—it is being forgiven by a loving God.

Love Mormons by Discussing Spiritual Matters Repeatedly with Them

Don't expect too much too soon. Don't give up if it appears that you are not making any progress. Even if you have succeeded in getting your LDS friend thinking, he or she probably won't tell you that immediately. It took Nicodemus a couple of years to publicly identify with Jesus. It might take your LDS friend as long or even longer.

Don't try to do too much at one time. It is best to stick to one main point. Avoid marathon discussions. Attention spans are limited, and people need time to mull over what you have talked about.

In this connection, look upon questions that you can't immediately answer not as setbacks but as golden opportunities. They give you an opening to come back with the answer and continue the discussion at a later time. Don't be embarrassed by not knowing all the answers. Who does?

Persistently and regularly talk to them about spiritual matters. Plant the gospel seed in their hearts and then water it regularly and faithfully.

Love Mormons by Fervently Praying for Them

"The prayer of a righteous man is powerful and effective" (James 5:16). Praying makes a difference. Among other things you could pray

•that God fills your heart with love for Mormons and that
they see that love;

•that the Lord gives you opportunities to establish and
cement relationships with Mormons and then the
sacrificial love to make the most of those opportunities;

•that the Lord gives you the boldness to initiate spiritual
conversation with them;

•that he guides you as you witness so that you stick to the
essential topic of eternal life;

•that he gives you the persistence to witness to them
repeatedly;

•that he gives you the faith to believe that his Word is
powerful enough to convert Mormons;

•that he brings our LDS friends to saving faith in
Jesus Christ.

Conclusion

As this chapter demonstrates, witnessing to Mormons takes a
great deal of commitment on our part. We will usually have to take the
initiative in establishing a relationship and then work on cementing it.
We need to listen attentively to them, to plan carefully on how to
approach them, and to pray fervently for the Lord's blessing. In other
words, witnessing to the LDS (or to anyone!) is work and not play.

It is rewarding work, however. The Lord promises he will bring to
maturity some of the seed we plant. Therefore, we can be confident that
he will use our witness to bring some Mormons into his kingdom, and
nothing is more rewarding than seeing that happen.

Discussion Questions

1. How can I become "like a Mormon" to reach a Mormon based on 1
Corinthians 9:19-23?
2. How can I initiate a conversation and relationship with a Mormon in
order to share my faith with him or her?
3. Suggest some meaningful questions you might ask a Mormon.
4. How can a recounting of the joys and sorrows of my life serve as a
witness to Mormons?
5. Above all, what will help me pray regularly for them?

CHAPTER ELEVEN: REACH MORMONS WITH ATTENTION TO THEIR ARGUMENTS

A t all times, our aim is to speak the truth in love to our LDS acquaintances. Part of being a loving witness is to listen to their claims for Mormonism and, then, to address them. To ignore such claims, most of them quite easy to refute, is not loving or productive. Numerous books have dissected them and detail how to disprove them.

On some occasions, we will have to refute their arguments boldly and bluntly. But such occasions are fewer than what we might first think. It is not always the wisest thing to blow their arguments out of the water. Too often Mormons take this as blowing *them* out of the water. When that happens, we might end up winning the argument but losing the Mormon. Instead of making them stop and think, our rebuttal often makes them stop up their ears and cut off all further discussion with us. As we saw in chapter seven, "reasonable" arguments can't bring anybody into Christianity and have, in fact, turned numerous Mormons off to all religion.

I know of what I speak. I used to relish getting into discussions with Mormons, because it was so easy to demolish their arguments for Mormonism. That gave me momentary pleasure, but it didn't give me much opportunity to witness to them about Jesus. There had to be a better way.

There is. Instead of trying to win every argument, I have discovered that it is better to address their claims in such a way that keeps the attention on the vital subject of how they will live with Heavenly Father. Instead of debating various minor points of Mormonism with them, we need to find ways to use their own arguments to keep the focus on the "major" point, namely, the gospel.

This is extremely difficult to do. In the heat of discussions, it is easy to become sidetracked. We need always to keep in mind our objective, namely, not to win every point under discussion, but to win our LDS friend for Christ. To do so, we need to answer their arguments in a way that avoids the impression we are condoning any of their false teaching, while we also avoid turning the discussion into a debate about this or that point in Mormonism or even a debate about a specific scriptural teaching. Polygamy, the character of Joseph Smith, or a host of other points are all minor topics compared to the major subject of the Mormons' eternal happiness. *We need to beware of majoring in these minor points!* We need to stick to the critical message of Jesus being perfect for us. A positive presentation of Christianity, rather than a constant assault on Mormonism, is what the Holy Spirit uses to bring Mormons to faith.

In the remainder of this chapter, we will acquaint ourselves with some of the more popular claims made for Mormonism. Suggestions will be offered on how to address these arguments so that they do not become battlegrounds, but rather springboards propelling the discussion back to eternal life.

Joseph Smith: A True Prophet of God

Before anything else, Mormons want to discuss Joseph Smith. They will not only claim that he was a true prophet of God, but also offer many "proofs" of this. They likely will point to the various witnesses who "saw" the golden plates. They might ask how a young uneducated boy could write the Book of Mormon, if he wasn't sent from God. (Although he was 25 years old when it was published.) They like to speak of his success among hardships and talk about his "martyrdom." And they will surely mention his first vision.

None of this stands up under scrutiny. The Tanners and others have published devastating studies on almost every aspect of his life. The accounts of his first vision especially have been intensely investigated. There will come a point when troubled Mormons will need to wrestle with this evidence.

It is my conviction, however, that citing this evidence too soon is counter-productive. Instead of getting them to think, it usually puts them on the defensive. And people on the defensive don't think clearly. The discussion can easily turn into a heated debate about Joseph Smith rather than a loving witness of Jesus Christ.

Rather than debating the *history* or *character* of Joseph Smith, it is more effective to discuss his *teachings*. It is relatively easy to switch the conversation to that focus. After Mormons have broached the subject of Joseph Smith and his being a prophet of God, I proceed something like this: "Do you believe that everybody who claims to be a true prophet of God is a genuine prophet? How about Mohammed, the founder of Islam? He claimed to be a true prophet of God.

Listen to his own words:

"I was lying asleep when an angel came to me with a piece of material and said: "Read this!" I replied: "I cannot read!" Then he pressed the material against me so hard that I thought I would die. Then he let me go and said again: "Read!". . .
'I awoke from my sleep and it was as if these words were written in my heart. I came out of the cave and stood on the mountain-side. Then I heard a voice calling to me from heaven: "Muhammad, you are God's messenger and I am Gabriel."'" (quoted in *Eerdman's Handbook to The World's Religions*, p. 311)

"Not only did he claim to receive this vision but he also produced the Koran, the 'bible' of Islam. And today he has many millions of followers. Is that proof that he is a true prophet of God?" (The more one compares Mohammed and Joseph Smith and the claims made by them and about them, the more similarities between them surface.)

Or we could point them to Rev. Moon, the founder of the Unification Church, better known as the Moonies. He also claims to have received a vision in which God called him to be a prophet. In fact, his vision is similar to Joseph Smith's in that Jesus himself supposedly appeared to him when he was 16. We can ask our LDS friends if this proves that he too was a prophet of God.

223

These are just two of many people who have claimed to be prophets. We need to draw these parallels and then ask Mormons if they believe that all such people are true prophets of God.

At this point, they might say that they are not familiar with Mohammed or Rev. Moon. Don't let them off the hook. Make them take a stand. Ask them if everybody who claims to be a prophet is a prophet. If they remain true to LDS teachings they will have to respond negatively, because the LDS church teaches that no one can receive divine revelation outside the priesthood. However you get the point, get them to see that not everybody who claims to be a prophet can be a prophet. It they all were prophets, God would be contradicting himself constantly, seeing that all these "prophets" are giving contradictory prophecies

After establishing that point, ask them what the criteria are for being a true prophet, since it must be more than just claiming to be one. For most Mormons this question leads to uncharted waters. They have never thought this through, so that by now they are pretty befuddled. Therefore, you can usually lead them quite easily to the next point, namely, that it is not what a person *claims about himself,* but what he *teaches about God,* that shows he is from God. Now you can effectively cite Galatians 1:8,9:

> But even if we or an angel from heaven should preach a gospel other than the one we preached to you, let him be eternally condemned! As we have already said, so now I say again: If anybody is preaching to you a gospel other than what you accepted, let him be eternally condemned!

This passage serves as the hinge that turns the discussion away from Joseph Smith to the gospel. For example, you might continue by comparing his depressing "gospel" of forgiveness with the good news of biblical forgiveness. Or you might compare Ephesians 2:8,9 with 2 Nephi 25:23.

> Ephesians 2:8,9: For by grace are ye saved through faith; and that not of yourselves: it is the gift of God: not of works, lest any man should boast. (KJV)

> 2 Nephi 25:23: For we know that it is by grace we are saved, after all we can do.

The important thing is to move the discussion away from Joseph

Smith's character to a comparison of his "gospel" with the biblical gospel. The more you know about Joseph Smith, the greater the temptation will be to refute the LDS sanitized version of his history. Resist that temptation. Too often, when we attack Joseph Smith, we win the battle over his history but lose the war for the Mormons' souls.

The Need for a Living Prophet

One favorite LDS argument for the superiority of Mormonism is that they have a living prophet who can convey to them the latest word from God. In chapter four, we saw how important and how attractive this teaching is to Mormons. To support this claim they cite not only Amos 3:7, which was discussed in chapter four, but also Ephesians 2:20, where Paul talks about the church being "built on the foundation of the apostles and prophets." They maintain that this passage proves the church will always have apostles and prophets.

We can refute this argument in a number of ways. We can zero in on the word "foundation" in Ephesians 2:20 and talk about how foundations are laid only at the beginning of a building project. If you are building a skyscraper you don't lay another foundation every few floors. The church's foundation of the apostles and prophets was laid at the beginning. We are still building the church on it by basing our beliefs on their inspired words.

Or we can point Mormons to passages like Hebrews 1:1,2 and 2 Timothy 3:16,17 that talk about the all-sufficiency of the Bible. (See chapter 4) If the Bible is all-sufficient there is no need for more revelation.

Neither of those two approaches, however, deflects their argument back to the main topic of eternal life. They can prove extremely useful only if we don't spend too much time with them. The danger is always to engage in debate rather than in evangelizing. For that reason, I prefer handling this assertion the same way as the one about Joseph Smith. By using the approach given above, we can compare the "gospel" of the living prophet, which is nothing else than LDS teaching, with the genuine gospel of the Bible.

Pray about the Truthfulness of the Book of Mormon

It won't be long before your LDS acquaintance asks you if you have read and prayed about the Book of Mormon. Mormons lay great stress on Moroni 10:4,5:

> And when ye shall receive these things, I would exhort
> you that ye would ask God, the Eternal Father, in the
> name of Christ, if these things are not true; and if ye shall
> ask with a sincere heart, with real intent, having faith in
> Christ, he will manifest the truth of it unto you, by the
> power of the Holy Ghost. And by the power of the Holy
> Ghost ye may know the truth of all things.

   Mormons believe the Holy Ghost manifests the truthfulness of the
Book of Mormon by giving people a burning in the bosom. (See chapter 4.)
These subjective feelings, rather than any objective facts, make them
believe the Book of Mormon is true.
   Since this deals with Mormons' feelings, and sometimes quite
intense feelings, it is not the easiest subject to handle. The ideal is to use
a variation of the argument above and persuade them to compare the
Book of Mormon's message of eternal life with the biblical message.
(Ephesians 2:8,9 contrasted with 2 Nephi 25: 23 proves especially
helpful.) We might also refer to the Koran or numerous other "inspired"
books. Are they all genuine? What makes one true and another false?
   The problem is that, in examining the Book of Mormon's
message, the LDS usually will do nothing but rely on their feelings—on
the burning in their bosoms. Therefore, you probably will have to
discuss with them the fickleness of feelings. For example, you could ask
them if cocaine use is right when it feels right to the person using it. Or
is it right for a bully to terrorize a playground if it feels good to him.
Should we condone murder for those people who feel good doing it? Such
illustrations abound. But you might have to give Mormons a dozen or so
before they get the point, namely, feelings are feeble foundations.
   Or you might pose the question: if a Muslim asked them to pray
about the truthfulness of the Koran, would they do so? Most whom I
have asked that said they wouldn't because they already knew it couldn't
be true. You could then tell them that neither do you have to pray about
the Book of Mormon because God has already revealed to us that it isn't
true. If they say how has God revealed that, point to Galatians 1:8,9 and
get the discussion back on how to live eternally with Heavenly Father.
   One additional approach, at times, has proved useful. We can
refer to the claim made in the Doctrine and Covenants that the Book of
Mormon contains "the fulness of the gospel" (see D&C 20:9, 42:12,

135:3). On the basis of that, you can ask them what additional truth you should look for as you read it. This is a difficult question for many Mormons to answer for two reasons. First, the Book of Mormon doesn't contain many unique LDS teachings. Second, most Mormons aren't familiar with it.

If they do point to something, make sure that they prove it is in the Book of Mormon. Many Mormons think it contains a lot of their doctrine, and are surprised to find out it doesn't. About the only thing they can consistently point to is Jesus' supposed visit to the Americas recorded in 3 Nephi. Even there we don't see new *teachings*.

Two warnings need to be sounded. First, the urge is often strong to try to get our LDS friend to critically examine the Book of Mormon. This approach is attractive to us since the Book of Mormon has undergone thousands of changes over the years. In addition, among other things, there is substantial evidence of plagiarism on the part of Joseph Smith. But it has been my experience that very few Mormons are willing initially to look at this evidence. Only after they have wrestled with the possibility of their going to outer darkness have they been ready to examine the Book of Mormon critically. Let's first show them the deadliness of the LDS plan of salvation. After doubt is created, we can show them the many problems the Book of Mormon has.

Second, don't cite Revelation 22:18: "If any man shall add unto these things, God shall add unto him the plagues that are written in this book" (KJV). Many Christians have told Mormons that this rules out the possibility that the Book of Mormon is from God. When we say that, however, we paint ourselves into a corner. Many Mormons are eagerly waiting for us to use that passage. Almost before we are done speaking, they are pointing us to Deuteronomy 4:2 which says almost the same thing: "Ye shall not add unto the word which I command you" (KJV). They then ask if that means all the books in the Bible that follow Deuteronomy are not inspired. No matter how we answer we are trapped. Besides, technically, Revelation 22:18,19 applies only to the words of "this book," namely, the 66th book of the Bible, Revelation.

The Book of Mormon Proven True by Archaeology

Many Latter-day Saints will state that there is archaeological proof for the Book of Mormon. At times, they might even give you a copy of a magazine or newspaper article that supposedly details such proof.

Or else they might point to the ancient ruins in Mexico and Central America as confirmation of its truthfulness.

Such things need not intimidate us. No matter what "evidence" they present, be assured that the Book of Mormon has no archaeological proof. The Smithsonian Institute sends out a form letter categorically denying such proof. Numerous books have been written shredding their claims to bits. Many scholarly Mormons admit there is no proof.

It is especially noteworthy that such proof is conspicuous by its absence in their official manuals. We can be sure, if there were such documentation, it would be trumpeted loudly. But the subject is not addressed. That archaeology backs up the Book of Mormon is a myth widespread in grass-roots Mormonism, but not supported in their official writings. Such official silence is deafening.

One way to handle such assertions is to study up on the subject and refute them. However, besides wasting your time, you again risk getting sidetracked and arguing about the minor matter of archaeology. Much simpler, and frequently more effective, is to put the burden of proof on them. If they don't give you written proof, ask for some. In many cases, the discussion of archaeology ends right there. If, however, they do come up with something, it probably won't be from an official church source. In that case, you can turn one of their arguments back on them: namely, their argument that only official sources represent church teachings. Unless their proof comes from such a source, you can ignore it.

Once in a while, they might give you something from *Ensign* magazine or some similar source. Such material doesn't offer any hard proof. Rather, it is filled with assumptions and faulty logic. A careful reading of such an article will give you plenty of ammunition to refute it.

At the risk of tiresome repetition, the main thing to keep in mind is our goal. It is not to pulverize every one of their arguments; it is to win Mormons for the Lord. Therefore, the quicker we can move off the discussion of archaeology the better. Usually the quickest way is by demanding written proof.

The Bible Is Incomplete

The Book of Mormon claims that "many plain and precious truths" have been taken from the Bible (1 Nephi 13:28). But many ancient copies of the Bible exist which demonstrate that nothing was removed. There are numerous books which discuss these ancient copies and the proof they offer. One such book is *From God to Us: How We Got Our Bible* by Norman L. Geisler and William E. Nix.

Ask your friend to examine this proof. Often Mormons are not willing to do that. That need not disturb you. You can point out that until they are willing to look at such evidence, their refusal effectively puts that topic off limits for discussion. Then resume talking about perfection: LDS-style versus Christian-style.

Another effective strategy revolves around the topic of books which are mentioned in the Old Testament but are no longer in existence. For example, Joshua 10:13 mentions the book of Jasher. Mormons commonly cite such references as proof that books have been removed from the Bible.

When they make that claim, direct them to Luke 24:44. There we see the resurrected Lord referring to the "law of Moses, the prophets, and the psalms." That is significant because that is the title the Jews of Jesus' day used to refer to the Old Testament. But if the canon of Jesus' day was not accurate, if books were indeed missing as the LDS church claims, then Jesus had the moral obligation to point out that fact. But he didn't. Rather he put his stamp of approval on the accepted canon.

Ask if Jesus wasn't aware of the missing books. Or maybe he was aware of them, but didn't want to share that information. Either answer makes most Mormons uncomfortable and struggling to answer why Jesus didn't point out the existence of those missing books.

Jesus Didn't Attack Other Churches

Some Mormons, especially after we have talked to them about the errors of Mormonism, will claim that it is not Christ-like to attack other churches. They say Jesus concentrated on spreading his message and let the people decide who was right and wrong. They maintain that the LDS church follows his method.

It is tempting to react to such claims by citing chapter and verse illustrating how the LDS church attacks Christianity. But that usually creates more heat than light. Rather than reacting to their claim that the LDS church doesn't attack other churches, it has proven more beneficial to react to their premise that Jesus didn't attack other "churches." Not only did he come down hard on the Pharisees and Sadducees (e.g., Matthew 15:1-9; Matthew 23), he also warned his disciples about them (e.g., Matthew 16:5,6; Matthew 7:15-23). Warning people about false prophets is the Christ-like thing to do! It is not loving to stand by and let

229

people go to outer darkness without trying to stop it.

By pointing this out, you again get the conversation back to where you want it, namely, on the drastic difference between the LDS plan of salvation and the biblical plan of salvation. You can emphasize to them that the very reason you are pointing out the errors of Mormonism is that you know they are leading people into outer darkness and you don't want to see that happen.

Mormons Are Christians

Not much is gained by getting into a discussion with Mormons over whether they are Christians or not. (They base their claim of being Christian on the inclusion of Christ in their official church name.) Neither is it profitable to tell them that Mormonism is a cult. That is like waving a red flag in front of a bull. All it does is enrage them.

Sometimes, however, they will ask if we think they are Christian. When that happens, I tell them I don't like to discuss it because there are so many differing definitions of the word Christian. Usually they respond by asking what my definition is. The definition that I like to use is: someone who is already perfect in Heavenly Father's sight through Jesus' sacrificial death (Hebrews 10:14). By defining Christian in that way, it is usually quite easy getting the conversation back on the main track of how we can live eternally with Heavenly Father.

If they persist on asserting that they are Christians, you could refer to Acts 11:26, which states that the *disciples* were first called Christians in Antioch. Then, by referring to John 8:31, you can show that being a disciple, or a Christian, doesn't have anything to do with what you call yourself, but rather with what you believe. By doing that you have gotten the conversation back on track.

Seventeen Points of the True Church

A popular LDS tract offers the reader the "Seventeen Points of the True Church." Below I have reproduced these seventeen points. I have done so not only because this is a popular tract, but also because it demonstrates the almost unbelievable nature of LDS biblical interpretation.

1. Christ organized the Church. Eph. 4:11-16
2. The true church must bear the name of Jesus

Christ. Eph. 5:23

3. The true church must have a foundation of Apostles and Prophets. Eph. 2:19,20

4. The true church must have the same organization as Christ's Church. Eph. 4:11-14

5. The true church must claim divine authority. Heb. 5:4-10

6. The true church must have no paid ministry. Isa.45:13, 1 Peter 5:2

7. The true church must baptize by immersion. Matt. 3;13-16

8. The true church must bestow the gift of the Holy Ghost by the laying on of hands. Acts 8:14-17

9. The true church must practice divine healing. Mark 3:14,15

10. The true church must teach that God and Jesus Christ are separate and distinct individuals. John 17:11 and John 20:17

11. The true church must teach that God and Jesus Christ have bodies of flesh and bones. Luke 24:36-39 and Acts 1:9-11

12. The officers must be called by God. Heb. 5:4, Exodus 28:1, Exodus 40:13-16

13. The true church must claim revelation from God. Amos 3:7

14. The true church must be a missionary church. Matt. 28:19,20

15. The true church must be a restored church. Acts 3:19,20

16. The true church must practice baptism for the dead. 1 Cor.15:16,29

17. By their fruits you shall know them. Matt. 7:20

Rather than going into depth on all these points, I will limit myself to a few comments. Note, first, how none of these points deal with the critical topic of eternal life. Second, note how frequently the passage cited has nothing to do whatsoever with the point listed (e.g., #2). Third, note how they often take *descriptive* passages and make them *prescriptive.* In other words, they take passages that describe something and interpret them as binding commands (e.g., #8). Their misuse of the

Bible would be laughable if it weren't so damning.

There are a number of simple ways to counteract this tract. Often the simple question, "Who says that these are the 17 points of the true church?" stops them dead in their tracks. They have never questioned that or had anybody else question it. Or else you might ask how a particular passage proves the point it is cited under. Many Mormons have never taken the time to look up these scripture references and will be just as puzzled as you are by them. Or you might compile your own list of descriptive passages from the Bible and ask why these aren't characteristics of the true church (e.g., Acts 2:42-47). Again you risk getting sidetracked and majoring in these 17 minor points.

One additional comment is in place. Point six is the one many Mormons stress the most. They lay great stock in not having paid clergy. In 1 Corinthians 9:14 and 1 Timothy 5:18, however, we learn that church workers deserve to get paid. In addition, D&C 42:70ff., 43:12 and 70:12ff. describe how Joseph Smith himself received financial support.

Conclusion

These are just some of the typical arguments for Mormonism that will confront you when you start witnessing to a Mormon. Often it takes just a little thought or study to uncover their faulty logic or false facts. It takes a little more thought, however, to devise the means of refuting their arguments in ways that will not turn them off, but rather turn the discussion back to the all-important topic of their living with Heavenly Father. Out of love, take that extra time.

Discussion Questions

1. What is the best way to counter the LDS claim that Joseph Smith is a true prophet of God?

2. How can we help Mormons objectively compare the teachings of the Book of Mormon with the Bible?

3. How do we answer their claim that the Bible is incomplete?

4. What is the best way to define the word "Christian" for a Mormon?

5. How do we answer Mormonism's 17 points of a true church?

CHAPTER TWELVE: REACH MORMON MISSIONARIES

The most contact the majority of non-Mormons have with Mormons is when LDS missionaries come to their door. Some Christians, including many who specialize in witnessing to Mormons, advise not trying to witness to these missionaries. Their advice is to tell the missionaries politely that you aren't interested. They recommend this for two reasons: First, they think that it is nearly impossible to convert Mormons while they are serving on their mission. Second, they have seen thousands of people claiming to be Christian who convert to Mormonism each year. They therefore understandably feel that the less contact Christians have with LDS missionaries the better.

It is my opinion, however, that Mormon missionaries are excellent mission prospects. Before looking at the reasons on which I base that opinion, a little background is in order.

Background

By the end of 1996, the LDS church had close to 53,000 full-time missionaries. The majority of these were young men. Approximately one-third of all LDS young men serve a mission. Most begin their mission at the age of 19. They serve for two years.

An increasing number of missionaries are young women. They begin their mission at the age of 21 and go for eighteen months rather than two years. This trend of young women going on a mission is not one wholeheartedly endorsed by LDS leadership.

> I wish to say that the First Presidency and the Council of the Twelve are united in saying to our young sisters that they are not under obligation to go on missions. I hope I can say what I have to say in a way that will not be offensive to anyone. Young women should not feel that they have a duty comparable to that of young men. Some of them will very much wish to go. If so, they should counsel with their bishop as well as their parents. If the idea persists, the bishop will know what to do. (Gordon B. Hinckley, *Ensign*, Nov. 1997, p. 52)

The church is also encouraging more and more retirees to go on missions. The following statement by David B. Haight is frequently quoted:

> The goal of every physically able couple in the Church, just as it is for every 19-year-old young man in the Church, should be to serve a mission. (*Ensign*, May 1987, p. 61)

Many, but not all, missionaries are on the streets going door-to-door. Some of the young women and many of the older persons serve at visitor centers of family history centers.

Many Mormons boast that their missionaries support themselves financially. Although this is often the case, a significant percentage of them receive financial help from the church. According to the April 1991 *Ensign* (p. 55) more than 11,000 missionaries were receiving financial assistance. Furthermore, such assistance is nothing new. In that same article, Udell E. Poulsen, the manager of finance and personnel for the Church Missionary Dept., states:

> I have met many bishops, stake presidents, and other leaders from various countries who served as missionaries as a result of receiving money from the General Missionary Fund. They stand as living witnesses of the value derived from assisting these missionaries.

In addition, costs for serving a mission have recently been equalized. As of 1991, no matter what the actual monthly cost is, all missionaries called from the United States are to contribute $350 a month towards their mission. (Actual monthly costs run from $100 to $750 depending on where the missionary serves.) If the missionaries or their families can't contribute the whole amount, their local wards are to help them. All in all then, the claim that all LDS missionaries are self-supporting needs to be taken with a large grain of salt.

One more piece rounds out the picture of formal LDS mission efforts. In addition to these thousands of full-time missionaries, each stake calls stake missionaries from within its membership. Their main responsibilities are to unearth prospects for the full-time missionaries and to assimilate new members into the LDS church. They are to spend at least ten hours a week in these activities.

With these facts and figures in mind, we can now turn our attention to seeing why it is not a mission impossible to witness to LDS missionaries.

Reasons LDS Missionaries Are Ripe to Hear the Gospel

LDS missionaries, especially the young people, are ripe for hearing the gospel for various reasons:

1. Many are not committed to Mormonism or their mission.
2. Many undergo a great deal of stress during their mission.
3. They are coming to us. We don't have to go to them. We can make an appointment and then have time to prepare our witness. By studying their missionary discussions, we will have a good idea of what they will say, so that we can plan our witness to them.
4. Most important, the Word of God is powerful and can overcome all obstacles.

We now look at these reasons in depth.

Their Lack of Commitment to Mormonism

A revealing article was written by Barbara K. Christensen, the wife of a former head of the Missionary Training Center (MTC) in Provo, Utah. In that article she wrote:

> My husband and I often said that we had in Provo the mission with the greatest number of missionaries and fewest baptisms, but still many, many conversions . . . *How much it would mean if every young elder and sister came to the Missionary Training Center experience fully converted* and prepared to accept missionary discipline, needing only basic orientation before proceeding into the mission field. (*Ensign*, March 1989, p. 57, emphasis added)

The conversions she mentions are the conversions of the missionaries themselves, not of people they are converting! Persons familiar with young Mormons preparing to go on missions can verify that many of them go very reluctantly. One former missionary stated that his reason for going was that he thought it would help him get better leadership positions in the church. He also hoped that it would facilitate his chances of marrying a good LDS girl. Numerous others have cited pressure either from their families or peers as the reason for becoming missionaries. Not only are many not committed to their mission, but keeping in mind the words quoted above, many are not committed to Mormonism itself.

Furthermore, their stay at the Missionary Training Center is too brief to have much effect on them. Missionaries who remain stateside are there for only three weeks. During that time, they don't, and they couldn't, receive in-depth training in LDS doctrine. Rather, they receive their temple endowments, they are oriented to mission rules, and they become familiar with the six missionary discussions or lessons they will be using the next two years.

Those going to foreign lands stay for two months. But again the instruction does not center on the teachings of Mormonism. It consists mainly of language and cultural training.

Therefore, a substantial number of LDS missionaries don't know much about Mormonism. Many have never even read the Book of Mormon or the Bible. What Joseph Fielding Smith said in 1961 about the knowledge of LDS missionaries still holds true in many cases today:

"The missionary of the Church of Jesus Christ of Latter-day Saints is a modern miracle. In the world the idea prevails that a man must go to school, college, get an education, be trained and get a degree to qualify him to preach and to teach the gospel of Jesus Christ, as he understands it. We call our young men and women at the beginning, really of life . . . We send them out into the world untrained . . . They are unprepared, insofar as education and knowledge are concerned. Most of them have never read the Book of Mormon, a great part of them, if not the greater part, have never read the New Testament. They are not familiar with the revelations in the Doctrine and Covenants. I find this out when I interview them. But they have one thing that the world does not have, and cannot have, and that's a testimony." (quoted in Tanners' *Shadow and Reality*, p. 200)

Note how, as a good Mormon, he hangs everything on the testimony they have about the truthfulness of Mormonism. But do all LDS missionaries even have that? They themselves say no.

A number of years ago, in a meeting of returned mission presidents, we reviewed different ways to improve missionaries' spirituality. One person said: "We need to help all missionaries *experience* and recognize the 'burning of the bosom' taught in Doctrine and Covenants 9:7-9." (*Ensign*, April 1989, p. 21, emphasis added)

Occasionally there are other articles describing how a missionary didn't get a "sure testimony" about Mormonism until something happened on his or her mission. If more Christians testified to them about Jesus being perfect for them, more LDS missionaries would gain the sure testimony of eternal life through him.

Yet another body of evidence demonstrates that many missionaries lack commitment to Mormonism. That is the estimate that 50% become inactive in the church once they return from their mission. An article in the June 1991 *Ensign* addressed this problem. Note the following excerpts:

All missionaries accomplish good things during their service, but not all serve with full purpose of heart.

> Carefully note whether your missionary's testimony is superficial or strong. (p. 49)

> Too often, returned missionaries let their scripture study slacken, sleep in instead of saying their morning prayers, and turn their evening prayers into a few words voiced heavenward in the hope that this dutiful performance will salve guilty feelings. (p. 50)

> For some, post-mission life becomes a "me-oriented" time of life; my job, my car, my education, my dates. (p. 50)

Again, people familiar with returned missionaries (RM) can verify this. Numerous returned missionaries give the impression that, since they have put in their two-year stint, they don't have to do anything else.

All of this illustrates that a great percentage, if not the majority, of LDS missionaries have neither much knowledge of Mormonism nor commitment to it. For this reason alone, some will listen when Christians talk to them about the true Jesus. But there are other reasons as well why many Mormon missionaries are ripe for hearing the true gospel.

They Are Undergoing Many Stresses during Their Mission

Their very lack of commitment and knowledge causes stress in some missionaries. At the very least, many find it bothersome to speak convincingly of something they don't know well or are not convinced of themselves. Others find this more than bothersome. It troubles them deeply.

In addition, the following three factors in the missionary experience can cause them great stress:

1. *Their Isolation*

LDS missionaries are isolated from family and friends. Their contact with home is mainly through letters. Family members are not to call them. They can call home twice a year: on Christmas and Mother's Day (although I have heard of some mission presidents who don't even allow that). This restriction is strictly observed. In the article mentioned above, Barbara Christensen illustrates this in passing. She relates how a missionary at the Missionary Training Center stopped by with a personal request.

> "Would you call my dad and find out when my mother is going to have surgery? I really would like to know because when my youngest sister was born, my mother almost died." . . . I dialed his father's telephone number, then asked the elder if he would like to speak personally to his father.

> "No, because *I know it is against the mission policies.* Besides, I think, it would make me homesick if I heard my father's voice." (*Ensign,* March 1989, p. 61, emphasis added)

In the early 90's the Las Vegas mission experimented with a beeper system for missionaries. One reason cited was so missionaries wouldn't need a telephone in their apartment and thus be tempted to call home.

Even members of the same family serving missions in the same city are not to have contact with each other. I remember talking to one missionary in Salt Lake City. He mentioned that it was his sister's birthday that day. She was also on a mission in Salt Lake City. When I asked if they would be getting together later that day, he said they couldn't because it was against mission policy.

Increasing the stress of such isolation from family is the requirement that they be with their assigned companion 24 hours a day. Parents of one missionary told how they went to Salt Lake City to see their daughter off on her mission. They had not seen her for two months while she was at the Missionary Training Center. They arrived at the airport that morning and met her there. Since they had some time before her flight, her father asked if she wanted to get a bite to eat in the airport restaurant. She declined because she said she had to be in sight of her companion at all times.

Consider the following as related by a mission president. He had called the apartment of some missionaries wanting to talk to a certain one. His companion didn't know where he was.

> I said, "Lay down the phone and search the patio area."
> The missionary walked out to the patio and saw his

companion in an adjoining room. He was talking to a young woman about the same age. No one else was in the room. The missionary who had answered my telephone call approached his companion and said, "Elder, President Jensen is on the phone, He'd like to speak with you." When the elder came to the phone, I asked him where he had been. He replied, "Today two young ladies moved in next door, and one of them was having some serious problems. I was counseling her."

I strongly expressed my concern about where he had been, and he said that he was glad I called, that he hadn't realized what a precarious situation he had put himself into until his companion interrupted him. We decided that they should move to a new apartment the next day. (*Ensign*, April 1989, p. 24)

This is not an extreme case either. Consider the following excerpts of a letter from a mission president to his missionaries:

"Consider the following mission rules and live them! . . . *Never, ever, ever leave your companion*, even at church. *Always be together*—protect each other. *Never* be separated at a member's home. Always be in eye contact in the *same room*. . . .

"Keep your focus away from skimpily dressed females or suggestive pictures. You don't need that. In your apartment *protect each other* from succumbing to temptations of personal gratification. Leave bathroom doors ajar or carry on conversations. I feel 120 seconds (two minutes) is *maximum* time to be isolated. Keep showers short and conversation going—scripture questions—hymns—*help each other*. *Always be with your companion* in your apartment. The *Strengthening Missionary Conduct* instructions state 'we should arise and retire together.'" (quoted in *The Evangel*, May-June 1992)

Such isolation from normal social and family relations creates stress for many missionaries, especially if they are paired with companions they have difficulty getting along with.

In addition, they don't have much time to come to a working agreement with their companions. Every few months they change companions. If they weren't compatible, that is probably a welcome change. But if they were compatible, that can be depressing. Couple that with the need to change location frequently, and you have a situation where, by necessity, they have to depend almost totally on the church organization for support. Some prosper under such conditions; many more are suffering because of them.

2. *Their busyness*

Another thing that can add tension to their lives is the busy schedule they must keep. Typically they are on the go from early morning until late at night. Even on their day off, they are busy. On this 'Diversion Day' they do such chores as clean their apartments, do their laundry, and write home. During their entire mission they don't really relax, as the following excerpts illustrate:

> Your mission is a time of discipline and single-minded focus. You will be required to go without some things common to your current lifestyle: music, TV, videos, novels, even girls. (Dennis B. Neuenschwander, *Ensign*, Nov. 1991, p. 43)

> Their day in the mission field is demanding. It begins every morning at 6:30 A.M. with two hours of study, a dozen hours of hard and often discouraging work, continuing until bedtime-about 10:00 P.M. . . Excluded from their mission are dating, secular music, beaches, swimming, and many other activities considered normal for young men and women of this age. (Richard C. Edgley, *Ensign*, November 1996, p. 62)

> "One of the greatest secrets of missionary work is work. . . . There will be no homesickness, no worrying about families, for all time and talents and interests are centered on the work of the ministry. That's the secret— work, work, work. There is no satisfactory substitute,

especially in missionary work." (Ezra Taft Benson, quoted in *Missionary Guide*, p. 32)

Or listen to this advice to women:
We can also be careful not to infringe on the missionaries' time. When we invite them to our homes for meals, we can serve them promptly. Then we can encourage them to leave and continue their work. We should not expect or allow them to help with dishes. We should not invite them to watch television with us. We can learn mission rules and help the missionaries observe them.

Young women especially should refrain from taking the missionaries' time in frivolous activity. Young women should never be alone with a missionary or encourage a close relationship with him. Young women should not correspond with or telephone missionaries in their area. (*Latter-day Saint Woman A*, p. 144)

That advice reveals that even from fellow church members Mormon missionaries often don't receive much sympathy. As one LDS man told me: "Nobody made it easy for me when I went through it. I'm not going to make it easy for them." After hearing statements such as that, it is no wonder that some refer to the missionary experience as a rite of passage for Mormon young men.

3. *Their financial pressures*

The reason most LDS missionaries walk or ride bikes is strictly financial. No matter how well-off their family is, they live on a budget fixed by the church. This budget usually does not leave room for the luxury of a car. The sisters, however, as the women missionaries are called, often have use of a car.

More important, this fixed budget also means that many of their meals are quite simple. Even when they have the money for better meals, they might not have the skill. Simple meals and growing young men can be a formula for depression and frustration when joined with all the above.

The next time LDS missionaries come to your door, think about what they are going through. Remember that many are not fully committed to Mormonism. Realize that many are tired, hungry, stressed-out. Be assured that a friendly, caring Christian, witnessing the truth of God's Word to them, can have a major impact on them. Keep all these things in mind, and then see their coming to your door not as an irritating interruption, but as a golden opportunity to share with them the good news of Jesus' perfect life and sacrificial death for them.

We Can Plan Our Witness to Them

Another reason why we can view the arrival of Mormon missionaries at our door with eager anticipation rather than with dread is that we can have a good idea of what they will say. As anybody who has had any contact with Mormon missionaries soon realizes, they all follow the same script, namely the six printed missionary discussions or lessons. This is to be expected since many of them don't have much personal knowledge of Mormonism.

This is also what the LDS church encourages. As the following quote illustrates, they consider these memorized discussions as nothing less then an inspired approach:

> To those missionaries who may be asked to present memorized discussion, it may be well to say that the General Authorities have been inspired to present a basic knowledge of the gospel in this way. (*Sharing the Gospel Manual*, p. 114)

This gives us a great advantage. We can study the missionary discussions that they so religiously follow, and plan our witness accordingly. We are in the same position as a general who has the enemy's battle plans. It would be foolish for us not to take advantage of that.

Having these discussions is a must for anyone who is serious about witnessing to LDS missionaries. They are officially called the "Uniform System for Teaching the Gospel" and can be ordered from the LDS Distribution Center in Salt Lake City (1-800-537-5950). Before taking a brief look at the individual discussions, a few general words concerning their witnessing methods are in place.

One of the first things they will want to do, after entering your home, is to begin with prayer. It is essential that we take a stand here. The last thing we want to do is give them the impression, by praying with them, that we have anything in common with them. We can tell them that it is our belief that praying together is an exercise in Christian unity. Since such unity doesn't exist between them and ourselves, we would prefer not beginning with prayer.

Most missionaries respect our belief and refrain from praying. Taking this firm stand also often reaps the additional benefit of getting the conversation right to where we want it. They frequently wonder why we think we are not united with them. We can answer by saying we take Matthew 5:48 seriously and ask them if they have already fulfilled it. Such an approach almost always guarantees a thorough discussion of perfection.

A lot of fluff with not a whole lot of content probably best describes their witnessing technique. LDS missionaries use high quality materials and flattering words to impress people. They refer to people as "gods in embryo" rather than as sinners. They are experts at appearing to agree with you when, in reality, they don't. They are like a slippery running back in football, becoming very adept at avoiding painful and controversial subjects.

In the course of the six missionary discussions, they introduce many, but certainly not all, LDS teachings. But they don't explain any of them in depth. In addition, they try to give these discussions in rapid succession. Their goal is to teach a couple of them a week in the hopes that within two or three weeks the "investigator" (prospect) is baptized and joins the LDS church.

This obviously doesn't give investigators much time to examine the teachings of Mormonism. In fact, the LDS church does not encourage an objective examination of its positions. As one reads the instructions to missionaries, the thing that is constantly in the forefront is *feelings*. They are incessantly urged to find out how the investigator *feels* about this or that. They are continually encouraged to share with the investigator their *feelings* about Mormonism. Everything is focused on feelings. That is consistent with Mormonism. As we saw in chapter four, Mormonism is a religion based on feeling, not facts.

In line with that is an emphasis on the Book of Mormon. "A missionary's major task is to encourage people to find out if the Book of Mormon is true" (*Sharing the Gospel Manual*, p. 127). This fits the pattern of emphasizing feelings because the way, they believe, to discover its truthfulness is by receiving a "burning in the bosom." Not an objective comparison with the Bible, but this subjective feeling is what they encourage investigators to concentrate on.

244

Beside feelings, the other thing missionaries concentrate on is getting the investigators to make specific commitments. At the end of each discussion, they are urged to get the investigator to commit to some course of action. For example, already at the end of the second discussion, they are seeking a commitment from investigators to be baptized in the LDS church.

A Closer Look at the Missionary Discussions

If we are really serious about trying to speak the truth to Mormon missionaries, we can agree to take the six missionary discussions. The danger here is being dishonest. We don't want to give them the impression that we are interested in joining the LDS church. We can, however, tell them that although we don't want to join the church, we want to take the discussions so that our information about Mormonism is firsthand. Some missionaries won't want to waste their time with us, but many will, especially if we are friendly to them. For many, talking to us is better than knocking on doors.

If they agree to give us the lessons, they will set up an appointment when they can come back. Give yourself a couple of days to pray and prepare.

Once you begin meeting with them, the temptation will be great to argue every point with them. I have found it more effective, however, to be selective in the points that I discuss with them. Throughout their presentation, they will be asking for your reaction to this or that point. We can get them to move on to the points we want to discuss by saying that we need to hear more before we can react. By withholding our judgment in this way, we don't agree with them. Neither do we argue with them on minor points. In the beginning, everything is a minor point compared to the main topic of how to live eternally with Heavenly Father.

Rather than arguing every point with them, our goal is to find "entry points" in their presentation to a discussion of eternal life. The more familiar you become with these missionary discussions, the more such "entry points" you will find in them. The following are some suggestions.

Discussion One

"The main focus of this discussion should be the Book of Mormon and the Prophet Joseph Smith" (*Uniform System for Teaching the Gospel,*

p. 1-1). After telling you about Joseph Smith, the missionaries will ask how you feel about Joseph Smith. At that point, as was detailed in the last chapter, we can use Galatians 1:8,9 and change the subject from the character of Joseph Smith to his teachings.

Likewise, when they talk about the Book of Mormon being another testament to Jesus Christ, we can use the methods suggested in the last chapter.

Discussion Two

The focus of this second lesson is the responsibility of each person to be worthy. This purpose is hidden under some nice-sounding words about Jesus.

In this lesson, they introduce the word forgiveness. But they pass over it very lightly. It is printed on one of their flip charts, but often they don't even mention it. If they pass over it, ask them to go back to it because you want to discuss it more thoroughly. You can then ask them about their definition of forgiveness and use the method detailed in chapter nine.

In this discussion they will also introduce repentance among other topics. You can use their definition of repentance and bring God's law to bear on them as outlined in chapter eight.

Discussion Three

The main goal of this discussion is to convince the investigators that the LDS church is the only true church. Emphasis is put on the restoration of the priesthood and the presence of the living prophet.

Here again we can use Galatians 1:8,9 to good effect. It can serve as a good springboard propelling us into a discussion, not of the concept of a living prophet, but of the criteria for true prophets. The criteria are that they teach in accordance with the Bible.

Discussion Four

By now, if the missionaries are still willing to meet with you, they are more comfortable with you, even though they probably realize that you know quite a bit about Mormonism. This makes for easier, more frank discussion. Sometimes they might even come and ask what you want to discuss, as has happened with people who have used this technique. Don't hesitate to bring up some of the points you made in earlier lessons. For example, they might never want to talk about forgiveness again, but it is something that they need to wrestle with repeatedly.

The purpose of discussion four is briefly to introduce investigators to the LDS plan of salvation, with special emphasis on the eternal family. This is a good lesson in which to ask them a lot of questions in order to get them to elaborate on the teachings of Mormonism. Our purpose in doing this is not to argue every point with them, but to determine just how much of Mormonism they really know. The ever present danger is that we get sidetracked and major in such "minors" as whether God has a physical body.

One point to bring up in the course of this discussion is that the Bible talks about many people going to outer darkness. The parable of the marriage feast recorded in Matthew 22:1-14 serves the purpose well. In verse 13 we see the man without the wedding garment being thrown into outer darkness. Then immediately in verse 14, Jesus says, "For many are called, but *few* are chosen" (KJV). The context clearly shows that the few go to heaven and the rest end up in outer darkness. Incidentally, this parable also shows that people don't have to be "worthy" to be invited to heaven's marriage feast.

Discussion Five

The purpose of this lesson is to show that gaining eternal life requires great sacrifice. This gives you many opportunities to agree that eternal life was won by a great sacrifice—but Jesus', not ours. It has proven helpful to show them that the Bible talks about Jesus saving us by being our substitute, not by being our example. You can cite passages like Isaiah 53:3-6; 2 Corinthians 8:9; 1 Peter 3:18.

Discussion Six

This is the lesson that introduces the idea of exaltation—and perfection as the way to exaltation. Therefore, if you haven't yet done so, you could easily talk about Matthew 5:48 and Hebrews 10:10-18.

These are only a few ways that you can keep the discussion where you want it: on perfection and the way to obtain eternal life. The more you familiarize yourself with these discussions and the more you invite LDS missionaries into your house, the more "entry points" will become apparent to you.

Ways to Witness

As indicated above, I think the best way to witness to LDS missionaries is by agreeing to take the missionary discussions and meeting repeatedly with them. But you might not be ready to do that.

That doesn't mean, however, that you can't witness to them. If you have the time, invite them in and offer them a glass of water or lemonade. Tell them that you are curious as to how they view Matthew 5:48. Tell them that you take it seriously. In this way, you can move the conversation to a witness of Jesus rather than a debate about Mormonism.

Even if you don't have the time or the inclination to invite them in, give them a brief witness at the door. Witness to them not only about the certainty you have of living eternally with Heavenly Father because of Jesus' being perfect for you (Hebrews 10:14), but also of the joy that truth gives you right now. Bear them your testimony about what Jesus has done for you. Let the light that he has lit in your life shine out. The Holy Spirit can use your brief witness to plant the seed of faith in their hearts.

Conclusion

I hope that by now you are convinced that LDS missionaries are ripe mission prospects—so convinced that you won't wait for them to come to you, but you will take the initiative and stop them on the street to invite them over—so convinced that you will call the local Mormon ward and ask for some missionaries to come over. By the grace of God and the power of the Holy Spirit working through God's Word, some young LDS man or woman might thank you eternally for going out of your way and taking the time to witness to him or her.

Discussion Questions

1. Why might Mormon missionaries be "ripe" for hearing the gospel?

2. How might you respond to a Mormon missionary at your door without entering into an extended discussion?

3. If you are comfortable with allowing a pair of Mormon
missionaries to visit you in your home, how can you turn their
intent into a witnessing opportunity? What's the best way to
initiate this?

CHAPTER THIRTEEN: REACH MORMONS AND KEEP THEM

No matter what their background is, integrating new people into a Christian congregation takes time and effort. A conscious effort needs to be made to invite them to Bible classes and fellowship activities. Members need to go out of their way and introduce themselves to the newcomers. New members need to become acquainted with opportunities where they can use their time and talents in Christian service. Without such special efforts, many new people will end up on the fringes of the congregation rather than in the middle of things. Often they won't feel as if they belong.

When it comes to assimilating new Christians from an LDS background into our congregation, this applies all the more. Even though they are experiencing the great joy of knowing the true gospel, joining a Christian congregation is frequently difficult for them to do. In this final chapter, we will briefly explore some of the reasons for that and also ways we can help them make a smoother transition.

Fear of Leaving Mormonism

Few non-Mormons can understand the deep-seated fear many Mormons experience as they contemplate leaving the LDS church. At times, such fear makes them almost irrational. I remember one young man I was working with. It seemed as if he had not only seen the errors of Mormonism, but also the truth of Christianity. Then one week he didn't return my phone calls. Finally, the next week, he turned up at my doorstep extremely angry. He was so agitated that it was difficult to get any information from him. I did discover, however, that he had spent considerable time the week before talking with a member of the LDS stake presidency. That man convinced him not only that he would become apostate by leaving the LDS church, but that I was a tool of Satan himself. He couldn't leave my presence fast enough.

Or I think of the young lady who had left the LDS a church a few years previous. She had been very active, even going on a mission. She left Mormonism and became quite active in the Christian church. She came to one of my classes on Mormonism, and the topic of becoming apostate came up. I referred to some quotes stating that the church officially says many who left the church will go to outer darkness. She became visibly uneasy and, with a nervous laugh, said: "I always thought that if Mormonism might be true, I would still go to the terrestrial kingdom." She remained quite quiet the rest of the evening. I haven't seen her since.

These are not isolated examples. A book that helps us understand the problems ex-Mormons experience is *Ex-Mormons: Why We Left*. The people interviewed in it experienced the same thing.

> There is such a spirit of fear associated with leaving Mormonism. Many people face the prospect of losing their mates, their jobs, their friends, their families— that's the meaning of counting the cost. Add to that the fact that you have been taught that the only people who will be in hell are apostates—those who leave the Mormon church. (Sheila Garrigus, p. 119)

> It was very hard to put away my patriarchal blessing, to acknowledge that it was not Scripture. It was a frightening experience to take off my temple garments for the last time and wonder—just in the back of my mind— if all the stories about injury and death for those who did this were true. (Kevin Bond, p. 152)

As these quotes illustrate, it is not just the fear of being apostate that paralyzes many Mormons. In some ways, Mormons who become Christian face the same difficulties that new Christians in some other parts of our world encounter. Like them, ex-Mormons must rid themselves of superstitions. They, too, need to learn how to deal with rejection from family and friends. At times they, too, face serious social consequences.

As loving Christians, not only do we need to be aware of these difficulties, but also supportive in the midst of them. We need to give new Christians from an LDS background regular doses of the gospel, the only antidote to their fear of becoming apostate. We need to open our hearts and our homes to them, replacing with our warmth and friendship the warmth and friendship they sacrificed. We need to strive consciously both to reach Mormons and then to keep them.

Taking Them to the Cross of Christ

In the last paragraph, I mentioned the need for giving ex-Mormons regular doses of the gospel. That needs emphasis because it is something we too often take for granted. Because work-righteousness has been so ingrained in them, ex-Mormons regularly need to be taken to the cross of Christ for the assurance that the debt of their sins has already been paid. Without regular trips to Calvary, they can easily fall back into thinking that they must pay that debt.

One marvels to see how their view of Christ's cross changes. As Mormons, they were repulsed by it. But as they learn its true significance, that through Jesus' one sacrifice they are perfect (Hebrews 10:10-18), they cling to it tightly and defend it mightily. Reaching Mormons and keeping them is work—but it is heartwarming and rewarding work.

Coming to Grips with Mormonism Errors

As I said earlier in this book, there comes a time when ex-Mormons will have to wrestle with Mormonism's errors. Most will need to see especially the facts proving Joseph Smith was not a true prophet of God. Here is where a book like Jerald and Sandra Tanner's *Mormonism: Shadow or Reality* proves invaluable.

They react to this information in varying ways. Some become extremely angry at being duped. Others are shattered and find it difficult to trust anybody. "I believe them. How can I believe what you are telling me?" This is one reason why it is much better first to have the Holy Spirit, working through the gospel, convince them of the Bible's truthfulness, before confronting them with Mormonism's manifold errors. However they react, we need to be there helping them work through it. This too is part and parcel of keeping them.

Teaching Them about the One True God

Once Mormons have tasted the sweet gospel, and the Holy Spirit has worked powerfully in them, they usually don't have much difficulty believing the biblical teaching of the triune God. They see that the Bible not only says there is only one God but also identifies the Father, the Son, and the Holy Spirit each as God. They come to appreciate the God whose nature is totally different from theirs rather than a god who is nothing more than an exalted man. They marvel that God is intensely interested and active in their lives, which stands in striking contrast to the distant deity of Mormonism. Through the power of the Holy Spirit, they come to love the triune God.

Christian Liberty Can Be Frightening

Mormonism, as we have seen, is a tightly controlled society. Rules abound, and not just in the religious sphere. The ninth of Ezra Taft Benson's "Fourteen Fundamentals of Following the Prophet" states: "The prophet can receive revelation on any matter, temporal or spiritual" (*Teachings of the Living Prophets*, p. 16). Although the prophet rarely proclaims official revelations in any area, the church takes its cue from this and routinely sets policy in many areas of life.

In striking contrast to this is the biblical teaching of Christian liberty. In many areas of life, God gives us considerable liberty. Only in those areas where God has spoken directly to the New Testament Church, do we have specific direction. In all other areas, he has given us freedom. He expects us as mature Christians to use that liberty in Christian love and self control (Roman 14).

Sometimes in sinful selfishness, however, we are tempted to turn our liberty into license. Instead of practicing restraint and concern for others, we become self-indulgent. Ex-Mormons, recently liberated from the many constraints of Mormonism, sometimes fall into that trap. Sometimes they react like the stereotype college student living away from home for the first time.

In my experience, however, more of them have been frightened by the idea of Christian liberty. Some prefer having others make decisions for them. That might have been one of the things that attracted them to

Mormonism in the first place. Mormonism offered them a nice, warm cocoon. Leaving that cocoon can be an intimidating experience.

We don't help them if we try to replace the man-made rules of Mormonism with our own man-made rules. But we do help them if we deal patiently with them, if we thoroughly teach them the biblical doctrine of Christian liberty and the blessedness of that teaching, if we discuss the dangers of turning liberty into license, if we model for them mature Christian living.

Involvement

One thing the LDS church does extremely well is get its members involved. Therefore, when people leave Mormonism, they usually have a lot of time on their hands. This vacuum needs to be filled.

One way we can help them fill the vacuum is by joining them with a couple of members who will commit themselves to spending time with them. This serves a number of worthy goals. It helps establish meaningful friendships. It gives the ex-Mormon regular contact with somebody who is modeling mature Christian living. Most important, it affords abundant opportunities for them to study and discuss scriptural truths.

Another way we can help them fill this vacuum is by inviting them and encouraging them to do some task in the church. This not only takes time off their hands, but it also helps them feel that they are a meaningful part of the congregation.

Worship and Bible Study

By far the most important thing we can do to keep Mormons is to get them actively involved in worship and Bible study. In my experience most are more comfortable with Bible study than with worship. For many, worship is a foreign concept. They never really experienced it in the LDS church. There the emphasis was on what they had to do rather than what God did for them. Therefore, many ex-Mormons have to grow in their appreciation of worship.

We can help them do that by teaching them about worship. The more they understand, the more meaningful it becomes. Take, for example, the use of the Apostles' or Nicene Creed during a worship service. Because they were taught that all creeds were abominations, it is wise to explain thoroughly to them the history and the reason for the creeds. A little explanation often relieves a lot of uneasiness. Another area that will need thorough and repeated explanation is the Lord's Supper. There are numerous other examples. Being loving means not assuming anything, but explaining everything.

That is why getting them into Bible study is so important. It is through the Word that the Holy Spirit continues to work in their hearts and strengthen faith. Ex-Mormons need a forum where they can ask questions, a time when they can dig in and chew on God's Word. Biblical truth is so new to them that they need repeated contact with it. The more contact they have with the Bible, the more impact it will have on them. Therefore, above anything else, we need to get them into and keep them in Bible study.

Conclusion

Not only reaching Mormons, but also keeping them takes much understanding and time. The more we understand Mormons, the more effectively we can minister to them with the gospel. The more time we spend with them, the more impact we can have on them. Latayne C. Scott summed it up quite well:

> People who are leaving Mormonism have two acute needs: solid Bible teaching and warm (even sacrificial) fellowship. (*Ex-Mormons, Why We Left*, p. 160)

In love, let's give them that. In love, let's reach Mormons with the wonderful truth of what Jesus has done for them. In love, let's keep them with that same truth.

DICTIONARY OF
MORMONESE

One of the major difficulties in witnessing to Mormons is that they speak a unique language. Not only have they coined numerous words and expressions unique to Mormonism, but they have also given unique definitions to commonly used words and expressions. Some have called this language "Mormonese."

This dictionary is an attempt to help the non-Mormon understand Mormonese. On the one hand, I have tried to give as concise definition as possible. On the other hand, I have frequently elected to quote their authoritative writings. The reason for doing this is twofold: (1) to support the definition given; or (2) to illustrate how Mormons use a particular word.

In the case of numerous words, it was quite difficult to arrive at a single definition because Mormons themselves, and even their authoritative writings, differ on its definition. In such cases, I tried to give their most commonly used definition.

Occasionally, the biblical meaning of a word will be offered in contrast to the Mormon definition. These references to the biblical meaning are not meant to be thorough definitions.

Finally, it will be important to keep in mind that the definition given is not the biblical or Christian definition, but the *LDS definition.*

AARONIC PRIESTHOOD: Also known as the lesser priesthood. It serves as the entry point into the priesthood for boys twelve and older and adult male converts. Members of this priesthood supposedly experience "the ministering of angels." This priesthood is responsible for the church's temporal affairs.

ACCEPTING JESUS: (1) Believing that Jesus lives and is divine. Although Mormons say Jesus is divine, they view him as inferior to the Father. (See Son of God.) (2) Trusting in Jesus' *plan of salvation* (Mormonism). In reality, "accepting Jesus" is equivalent to accepting Mormonism.

ADAM: Equated with Michael, the archangel. Mormons believe he was one of Heavenly Father's finest spirit children. He was sent to earth to make man mortal, which he accomplished through his fall. Because of this, Mormons consider his fall good. See 2 Nephi 2:22-25; Moses 5:10,11 (also see fall of Adam).

ADAMIC LANGUAGE: The pure language, according to Joseph Smith, which God gave Adam. Smith claimed that God occasionally revealed to him a name or phrase from it. For an example, see Adam-ondi-Ahman.

ADAM-ONDI-AHMAN: A name supposedly from the "pure Adamic language." It means where Adam dwelt, in other words, the place where Adam lived after he was driven out of the Garden of Eden. Mormons believe this is in Davies County, Missouri (north of Independence, Missouri). They believe Adam will return there shortly before Christ's return. See D&C 116.

AGENCY: A person's free will and natural capacity to choose the right. The Bible, however, teaches that mankind, by nature, is spiritually dead (Ephesians 2:1) and thoroughly evil (Genesis 8:21). Agency is one of the most important underpinnings for Mormonism's works-righteousness. "No principle in time or eternity is so cherished as the right of agency, the right to consider alternatives and make choices without compulsion" (*Doctrines of the Gospel*, p. 30).

ANGELS: Not creatures of God distinct from humans as the Bible teaches. Mormons themselves seem to be confused about their exact description. Most common is the explanation that "an angel is a resurrected or translated body, with its spirit ministering to embodied spirits" (*D&C Student Manual*, p. 320). An example would be the angel Moroni who supposedly appeared to Joseph Smith. According to the Book of Mormon, Moroni was originally a Nephite leader who sometime after his death, was resurrected. But Mormons further state that this description does not apply to the angels who appeared before Jesus' resurrection. McConkie, in *Mormon Doctrine*, also includes preexistent spirits and the spirits of just men made perfect in his discussion of angels. Also see ministering spirits.

ANOINTING: Ordinance performed on the sick and injured by holders of the Melchizedek priesthood. Many priesthood holders carry small bottles of consecrated olive oil for use in emergencies. Stories of miraculous healings are regularly reported.

257

APOSTASY: (1) Most commonly used to describe the act of leaving the LDS church. (2) Mormons also talk about the Great Apostasy which they describe as the time between the death of the apostles and Joseph Smith's establishment of the LDS church. They teach that during this long period of time the true church was gone from the earth.

APOSTATES: (1) Most commonly used to refer to people who leave the Mormon church. (2) Sometimes used as a reference to Christians. "The term (Christian) also applies to the whole body of supposed Christian believers; as now constituted this body is properly termed apostate Christendom" (*Mormon Doctrine*, p. 131). Also see apostasy.

APOSTLES: (1) Sometimes a reference to the original twelve apostles. (2) More often a reference to the twelve current apostles of the Mormon church, who serve immediately under the First Presidency of the Church.

APOSTLES' CREED: Along with all historical Christian creeds, it is considered an abomination by the LDS Church. See the Pearl of Great Price, Joseph Smith—History 1:19.

APRIL 6th: (1) Date the LDS Church was organized. (2) Mormons also teach that this is the date of Christ's birth. See D&C 20:1.

AREA: Geographic regions of the church are divided into administrative "areas" that are supervised by area authorities.

AREA AUTHORITY: A new position established in 1995. "These will be high priests chosen from among past and present experienced Church leaders. They will continue with their current employment, reside in their own homes, and serve on a Church-service basis. The term of their call will be flexible, generally, for a period of approximately six years. They will be closely tied to the area presidencies." (Gordon B. Hinckley, *Ensign*, May 1995, p. 52) In 1997 these area authorities were grouped into the Third, Fourth, and Fifth Quorums of Seventies. "Though all Seventies have equal scriptural authority, members of the First and Second Quorums are designated General Authorities, while members of the Third, Fourth, and Fifth Quorums are designated Area Authorities." (Gordon B. Hinckley, *Ensign*, May 1997, p. 6)

ARTICLES OF FAITH: Thirteen brief statements of faith that are often given to interested individuals. They do not mention any of the distinctive Mormon doctrines and thus give a deceptive picture of Mormonism. Being part of the Pearl of Great Price, they are considered scripture.

ATONEMENT: (1) Used almost exclusively as a reference to Jesus' conquering *physical death* for all people. By conquering physical death, Jesus made it possible for them to enter again into the presence of Heavenly Father—if for no other reason then to be judged by him. In other words, they are again at-one with him, or atoned. (2) At times it includes the thought of Jesus' paying for their sins. But underlying all such references is the thought that they have to pay him back, For a good example of the LDS view of Jesus' atoning work, see *Gospel Principles*, pp. 75-77. This is in direct contradiction to Christianity which teaches that through his voluntary sacrifice. Jesus *made payment*, or atoned, for all sin. Therefore salvation is free and full in Jesus. No more payments can be made. See Hebrews 10:18.

AUTHORITY: Connected exclusively with the LDS priesthood. Thus the only valid voices in religious matters are LDS authorities; the only valid religious rites are those performed by members of the LDS priesthood.

AUXILIARY ORGANIZATIONS: The various organizations within the Church, "auxiliary" to the priesthood, such as the Relief Society, Primary, Young Men's and Young Women's associations.

BAPTISM: By immersion either at the age of eight or when converted to the church. Mormons consider valid only baptisms performed by a holder of their priesthood. Baptism signals people's acceptance of Mormonism as the truth. Even though they are baptized with water "in the name of the Father and of the Son and of the Holy Ghost" (D&C 20:73), it is not a valid Christian baptism since the LDS church is not a Christian church.

BAPTISM FOR THE DEAD: One of the three main missions of the LDS church is to redeem the dead by being baptized for them. Mormons believe that spirits who accept Mormonism in the spirit world cannot progress until they are baptized. Such spirits must receive baptism vicariously through a living person since they don't have a body that can be baptized. Such baptisms can be performed only in the temple.

BEAR A TESTIMONY: A popular expression for testifying about the truth of Mormonism. Also see testimony.

BEEHIVE: (1) A girl's organization. (2) The symbol of the state of Utah. (3) A popular LDS symbol emphasizing their work ethic.

BIBLE: One of four books Mormons consider scripture. They believe it to be the Word of God "as far as it is translated correctly" (Eighth Article of Faith). In addition, they believe many precious parts have been lost from it (1 Nephi 13:28). Consequently they consider it the least reliable of their scriptures. Most Mormons are not familiar with it.

BISHOP: The head of the local ward (congregation). Bishops have no formal theological training. Often the major criteria for becoming a bishop is success in the business or professional world. Bishops remain in their secular occupation during their term of office. Although there is no specified length of service, most of them serve approximately five years. Bishops are highly respected in the LDS community.

BISHOPRIC: Each bishop has two counselors. These three men comprise the bishopric of each ward. Also see counselors.

BLESSINGS: There are various blessings in Mormonism. These include, but are not limited to, the naming and blessing of children, confirming of new members, dedicating of homes and graves, and blessings administered by fathers on the members of their families. Melchizedek Priesthood Study Guide #3, *Come unto the Father in the Name of Jesus*, gives the proper wording and procedure for each blessing. See pp. 135-141.

BLOOD ATONEMENT: A concept not discussed much in modern Mormonism. Historically Mormonism taught that the only way murderers could atone for their crime was through the shedding of their own blood. A remnant of this teaching can be seen today in that Utah still offers the option of being executed by firing squad.

BODY: Having a physical body is essential for the attaining of godhood. "No other people on earth understand the sacred nature and purpose of our physical bodies as do Latter-day Saints. . . .We knew that by gaining physical bodies to house our spirits, we would have the opportunity to become more like our Father" (*Come Unto Me*, p. 143). Also see mortal.

BOOK OF ABRAHAM: A section of the Pearl of Great Price, and thus a part of LDS scripture. It talks about gods creating the world and about Kolob, the star closest to God's throne. Joseph Smith claimed to have translated it from Egyptian papyri he obtained. This was disproved in 1967 when these papyri were found in the Metropolitan Museum in New York and it was ascertained that they contained a description of Egyptian burial rites.

BOOK OF MORMON: Subtitled "Another Testament of Jesus Christ," it is one of four books Mormons consider scripture. It contains the story of the supposed migration of groups of Jews to the Americas and their subsequent history in the Americas. It does not contain much LDS teaching. Mormons highly respect it, but many have never read it. Certain of its stories are commonly known, being taught to them since childhood.

BOOK OF MOSES: A section of the Pearl of Great Price and thus considered part of Mormon scripture. It contains teachings on the plurality of gods, Adam's "good" fall, and Satan's rebellion and fall.

BOOK OF REMEMBRANCE: See personal history.

BORN AGAIN: An expression not commonly used in Mormonism. Following are a couple of examples of LDS usage. "Your key to becoming perfect in Christ is found through faith and obedience, which leads to being 'born again.' Then comes the 'mighty change in us, or in our hearts, *that we have no more disposition to do evil, but to do good continually*' (Mosiah 5:2)" (*Life and Teachings of Jesus & His Apostles*, p. 393, emphasis added). "The phrase, 'born again,' has a deeper significance than many people attach to it. This *changed feeling* may be indescribable, but it is real" (*To Make Thee a Minister and a Witness*, p. 19)

BRANCH: A congregation too small to qualify as a ward.

BRETHREN: The General Authorities.

BRIGHAM YOUNG: The second president of the LDS church. After Joseph Smith's death, he led the Mormons to Utah where they prospered under his leadership.

BROTHER: Male church members are commonly addressed as brothers.

BURNING IN THE BOSOM: (1) A feeling of peace and assurance that the Holy Ghost supposedly gives a person to confirm the truthfulness of the Book of Mormon. (2) Also used to describe the feeling the Holy Ghost supposedly gives to confirm an individual's action. Also see feeling.

BYU: Brigham Young University, located in Provo, Utah, with an enrollment of approximately 27,000. Very few non-Mormons attend.

CAFFEINE: See cola drinks.

CALLING: A common expression for a specific task members have been called to within the Church. They might hold the calling, for example, of primary teacher or priesthood quorum president.

Most active members serve in a specific calling. No one receives a lifelong calling except for the President of the Church, the Twelve Apostles, and members of the First Quorum of Seventy. Also see magnify a calling.

CANONIZED SCRIPTURE: Another term for the four standard works. At times, Mormons use this term to distinguish these books from the words of the living prophet which are also considered scripture. This does not mean, however, that these books are more important than his words, since Mormonism also teaches that his words can supersede these scriptures. Also see president of the church.

CELESTIAL KINGDOM: The highest of the three kingdoms of LDS heaven. There people will live with Heavenly Father and Jesus. There are three levels within the celestial kingdom: the top level equals exaltation, the purpose of the second level has not been revealed, and the third level is for faithful Mormons who were not married in the temple. These individuals become ministering servants.

CELESTIAL MARRIAGE: Being married in the temple for time and *eternity*, which is essential for exaltation. It is also called eternal marriage. This can also be performed vicariously for the dead. "Everything required of us by God is associated with the law, but the major crowning point of the law which man must obey is eternal marriage. Therein lie the keys of eternal life, or, as the Doctrine and Covenants puts it, "eternal lives.' In other words, an eternal increase of posterity" (*Achieving A Celestial Marriage*, p. 4)

CELESTIALIZED: The process of entering the celestial kingdom or entering celestial glory.

CHOICE SPIRIT: A common LDS expression roughly equivalent to being a good person. It is rooted in their teaching of preexistence.

CHOOSE THE RIGHT: A common slogan in Mormonism. LDS youth often wear rings engraved with the initials CTR.

CHRISTIAN: (1) Mormons are increasingly applying this term to themselves. They claim that Mormonism is true Christianity. They base their claim to being Christian on the fact that they have Christ in their church name and because they honor him highly. "Mormonism is Christianity; Christianity is Mormonism; they are one and the same, and they are not to be distinguished from each other in the minutest detail" (*Mormon Doctrine*, p. 513).

(2) Christians. But they believe that Christians do not have the "fullness of the gospel."

CHURCH: The Church of Jesus Christ of Latter-day Saints.

CIVIL WAR PROPHECY: D&C Section 87. Mormons often cite this as proof that Joseph Smith was a true prophet. Such "prophecies," however, were not uncommon in that period of history. Also parts of it did not come true. They also fail to mention, or don't even realize, that Smith made many other prophecies—none of which came true. For example, see D&C 84.

CLERK: The member in the ward who keeps track of church attendance and other data. During sacrament meetings he sits up front taking attendance and recording statistics.

COFFEE: The drinking of hot drinks is condemned in the Word of Wisdom. Hot drinks have been officially interpreted as coffee and tea. Drinking coffee disqualifies Mormons from entering the temple and is one of the worst sins they can commit.

COLA DRINKS: Many Mormons believe that it is a violation of the Word of Wisdom to drink caffeinated drinks even though it does not specifically forbid them. "The First Presidency has declared: 'With reference to cola drinks, the Church has never officially taken a position on this matter, but the leaders of the Church have advised, and we do specifically advise, against the use of *any drink containing harmful habit-forming drugs under circumstances that would result in acquiring the habit.* Any beverage that contains ingredients harmful to the body should be avoided.' [italics added]" (*Remember Me*, p. 226).

CONFIRMATION: An ordinance performed immediately after baptism. Mormons believe it confers the gift of the Holy Ghost, which means that he becomes their constant companion and will give them revelation through their feelings. Also see gift of the Holy Ghost.

CONSECRATION: To devote everything to the church. "The formal law of consecration, however, has been established only at certain times on the earth. It is an organized way in which individuals can dedicate all of their time, talents, and material resources to building up the kingdom of God on earth" (*Learn of Me*, p. 40). For a brief period of time, Joseph Smith tried to put this into practice through a system called the United Order.

CONSTITUTION OF THE UNITED STATES: On the basis of D&C 101:80 Mormons believe that it was inspired by God.

CONTINUATION OF THE SEEDS: The ability to bear spirit children, which is the essence of being a god. Thus only those who attain godhood will be able to have a continuation of the seeds. See D&C 132:19,20.

CONVERSION: Acceptance of Mormonism, which is evidenced by a change of lifestyle. "What does it mean to be converted? President Harold B. Lee said: One who is converted 'strive(s) continually to improve inward weakness and not merely the outward appearances.'" (*Ensign*, May 1996, p. 74-75). This contrasts with biblical conversion, which is a turning away from trust in one's own work to trust in Jesus' saving work. LDS conversion is rooted in feelings. "They will be converted when they feel the Spirit and act on the promptings they receive." (*Missionary Guide*, p. 1)

COUNSELORS: Every organization of the church, at every level of the church, is run by a presidency that consists of a president and two counselors. The counselors aid the president and act on his or her behalf.

COVENANT: A popular Mormon word. LDS covenants are always bilateral and conditioned on the obedience of man (unlike God's covenant of grace, which is unilateral and unconditional). Almost everything in Mormonism is considered a covenant. "Each ordinance and requirement to man for the purpose of bringing to pass his salvation and exaltation is a covenant" (*Achieving A Celestial Marriage*, p. 197).

CREATE: To organize eternal matter, in contrast to the biblical description of God creating the universe out of nothing. Mormons believe Jesus, under Heavenly Father's direction, "created" the earth, being aided by persons such as Moses, Abraham, James, John, Peter, and Joseph Smith in their preexistent forms.

CREEDS: Mormonism teaches that all historical Christian creeds are abominations. See Joseph Smith—History 1:19 in Pearl of Great Price. Mormons feel the early church's theology quickly became corrupted. Stephen E. Robinson is representative of this view. "I would point out, however, that disagreeing with the Councils of Nicaea and Chalcedon is not the same as disagreeing with the New Testament. (*How Wide the Divide*, p. 60)

CROSS: Mormons are repulsed by symbols of Christ's cross. They do not exhibit crosses in their meetinghouses or homes. Nor do they wear them as jewelry. They view the cross as a symbol of death and think that Christians have made it their idol.

CULT: Labeling Mormonism a cult is highly offensive to Mormons. They define a cult as a group that isolates its members from their families and thus cannot understand how anybody could consider Mormonism a cult.

CUMORAH: The hill, in western New York State, where the gold plates containing the Book of Mormon were supposedly hidden and subsequently found by Joseph Smith.

DAMN: Refers to the stoppage of a person's progression to godhood, not to suffering eternal punishment in hell. The LDS concept of damnation is similar to the idea of damming a stream. All who do not gain godhood experience damnation to some extent.

DEACON: The first office of the Aaronic priesthood. Worthy boys enter it at the age of 12. Deacons help distribute the sacrament.

DEMONIC POSSESSION: The way demons attempt to gain a physical body. See body.

DEMONS: The spirit children who joined Satan in his rebellion. They were immediately consigned to outer darkness, thus depriving them of any chance of continuing their progression to godhood. Also see Satan, outer darkness.

DESERET: The Book of Mormon name for honeybee (Ether 2:3). Frequently used in names of LDS businesses because it implies industry.

DESERET INDUSTRIES: Similar to Goodwill Industries. This church-run organization employs handicapped and impaired persons who recondition and repair donated items that are then sold in outlet stores.

DISCIPLINARY COUNCILS: Church "courts" held on the ward or stake level to decide appropriate "punishments" for serious sins. " A council can reach one of four decisions: (1) no action, (2) formal probation, (3) disfellowshipment, or (4) excommunication" (M. Russell Ballard, *Ensign*, Sept. 1990, pp. 15,16). In the recent past, members desiring to leave the church had to go before such a council. That no longer holds true.

DISFELLOWSHIP: This is a judgment arrived at by a disciplinary council for serious sin. It is one step removed from excommunication. "Disfellowship is usually temporary, though not necessarily brief. Disfellowshipped persons retain membership in the Church. They are encouraged to attend public Church meetings, but are not entitled to offer public prayers or to give talks. They may not hold a Church position, take the sacrament, vote in the sustaining of Church officers, hold a temple recommended, or exercise the priesthood. They may, however, pay tithes and offerings and continue to wear temple garments if endowed" (M. Russell Ballard, *Ensign*, Sept. 1990, p. 16).

DISPENSATION: "A dispensation of the gospel is a period of time in which the Lord has at least one authorized servant on the earth who bears the holy priesthood and the keys, and who has a divine commission to dispense the gospel to the inhabitants of the earth" (*LDS Bible Dictionary*, p. 657). Mormons believe the last dispensation was inaugurated at the time of Joseph Smith.

DOCTRINE AND COVENANTS: One of Mormonism's four scriptures. It consists of 140 "divine revelations and inspired declarations" received mostly by Joseph Smith. It teaches more Mormon doctrine that the other three LDS scriptures combined.

ELDERS: All holders of the Melchizedek priesthood.

ELIAS: The KJV translation of the name Elijah in the New Testament. Mormons, however, don't equate Elias with Elijah. Instead they surround this name with a confusing set of teachings. At times they speak of Elias as a separate individual, other times as a title for a forerunner, and still other times they identify him with Noah. The following quote illustrates this confusion: "The term *Elias* means forerunner. Noah, Elijah, John the Baptist and John the Revelator have been referred to as *Elias* in scripture, though the references to Elijah by this name are mistranslated. Summarizing the facts—Joseph Smith revealed that Gabriel was Noah; Luke declared that it was the angel Gabriel who appeared to Zacharias and Mary; and the Lord has declared that Elias appeared to Zacharias and Joseph Smith. Therefore, Elias is Noah" (*Old Testament Manual I*, p. 54).

ELIJAH: Holder of the sealing power of the Melchizedek priesthood. Mormons believe he appeared to Joseph Smith and Oliver Cowdery in the Kirtland Temple in fulfillment of Malachi 4:5,6. Mormons claim he conferred on them the keys to this sealing power, which especially includes the power to perform ordinances for the dead (D&C 110: 13-16).

ELOHIM: The Hebrew word for God. Mormons identify it exclusively with Heavenly Father. They say Jesus was Jehovah (translated LORD in English), although the Bible often uses both names in reference to the same person. For example see Genesis 2:4. Also see Jehovah.

ENDOWMENT: The initiatory temple rite that consists of being ceremonially washed, receiving a new name, receiving sacred garments, viewing the LDS version of creation and the fall, and learning various handshakes that are essential for exaltation. These rituals "are called endowments, because in and through them the recipients are endowed with power from on high" (*Mormon Doctrine*, pp. 226f.). Endowments are also performed vicariously for the dead.

ENSIGN: (1) The name of the official monthly magazine of the LDS church. According to the title pages it is "pronounced N'sign not ensun." The May and November issues contain the transcripts of all speeches given at the latest general conference. These issues are called conference editions and are considered scripture. "If you want to know what the Lord would have the Saints know and to have his guidance and direction for the next six months, get a copy of the proceedings of this conference, and you will have the latest word of the Lord as far as the Saints are concerned" (Harold B. Lee, quoted in *D&C Student Manual*, p. 42). (2) "This ensign is the new and everlasting covenant, the gospel of salvation [D&C 49:9]; it is the great latter-day Zion [D&C 64:41-43]; it is the Church of Jesus Christ of Latter-day Saints" (Bruce R. McConkie, quoted in *Come unto the Father in the Name of Jesus Christ*, p. 31)

EPHRAIMITES: Mormons believe that converts to Mormonism literally become Israelites (see Israel). Up to this point in history they believe that "the great majority of those who have come into the Church are Ephraimites" (*D&C Student Manual*, p. 138).

ETERNAL DEATH: To Mormons, this is not a description of hell. Rather, it refers to the inability to procreate spirit children because of the failure to obtain godhood. Mormonism pictures this inability to produce offspring for all eternity as one of the worst fates that can befall people.

ETERNAL FAMILY: A favorite LDS expression. There are two aspects to an eternal family: (1) the earthly family unit will remain a family unit for all eternity; (2) the family will increase through the procreation of spirit children for all eternity. Only those who attain godhood will be able to have eternal families. "Our earthly families will remain permanently ours. And we can also continue to increase, adding spirit children to our posterity" (*The Latter-day Saint Woman A*, p. 69).

ETERNAL INCREASE: Another term for spirit children. See spirit children.

ETERNAL LIFE: (1) Officially, this is distinct from immortality. It doesn't describe living eternally with God but living eternally as God. Thus it is another name for godhood and synonymous with exaltation. "Exaltation means the same thing as eternal life" (*Learn of Me*, p. 72). (2) Unofficially, many Mormons equate it with immortality.

ETERNAL LIVES: Another name for spirit children. See spirit children.

ETERNAL MARRIAGE: See celestial marriage.

ETERNAL PROGRESSION: The LDS belief that a person can continue to progress throughout eternity, eventually obtaining godhood. This teaching is the heart and core of Mormonism.

ETERNAL PUNISHMENT: Not punishment that lasts for all eternity, but punishment inflicted by an eternal god (cf. D&C 19:6-12). Mormonism's eternal punishment lasts a relatively short time. Also see hell.

ETERNITIES: Mormons often talk about "the eternities" although they never explain what they mean by this plural form.

EVANGELIST: See Patriarch.

EVERLASTING BURNINGS: A reference to where God dwells, not a reference to hell. "You have got to learn how to be Gods yourselves . . . until you . . . are able to dwell in everlasting burnings, and to sit in glory, as do those who sit enthroned in everlasting power" (Joseph Smith, quoted in *The Life and Teachings of Jesus & His Apostles*, p. 24).

EXALTATION: The highest level of the celestial kingdom, godhood. One of Mormonism's more popular "theological" terms.

EXCOMMUNICATION: "Excommunication is the most severe judgment a Church disciplinary council can take. Excommunicated persons are no longer members of the Church" (M. Russell Ballard, *Ensign*, Sept. 1990, p. 16). With a great degree of effort an excommunicated person can be restored to church membership.

EXEMPLAR: A popular LDS title for Jesus. It reveals the Mormons' belief that Jesus saved them by being their example, not by becoming their substitute who has done everything for them.

EXTRACTION: The process of extracting names from centuries-old records (e.g., census rolls, church records). This work is vital since it supplies the raw data for the genealogical work. There are two extraction programs: the family home extraction program allowing members to work at home and the stake extraction program where members work at a centralized location. The LDS church claims to have already extracted over two billion names.

EYE BEING SINGLE: An expression for single-mindedness. An example of its use: "My eyes would be single to the Lord's purpose in Brazil" (*Ensign*, June 1991, p. 45).

FAITH: A word commonly used in Mormonism but quite difficult to define. (1) The belief that God exists and has given a good plan of salvation (Mormonism). "If we have faith, we trust in Jesus Christ to help us find ways to live his commandments" (*The Latter-day Saint Woman, Part A*, p. 7). (2) Often described as the power God gives people to resist sin and become perfect. The more righteous a person is, the more power (faith) God will give him. "To those who have not begun the quest of comprehension, the word faith appears to be only a synonym for a kind of belief or conviction . . . It is a principle of power" (*Sharing the Gospel Manual*, p. 82). In contrast, biblical faith receives its value from its object, namely, Jesus and his death for our sins. Biblical faith involves more than knowledge. It is *trusting* only in Jesus' works, and not in one's own works, to get to heaven.

FAITH-PROMOTING: A popular expression used to describe approved types of literature, activity, etc.

FALL OF ADAM: Mormons believe it gave mankind the ability to have children; thus they regard it as good (2 Nephi 2: 22-25). "Adam voluntarily, and with full knowledge of the consequences, partook of the fruit of the tree of knowledge of good and evil, that men might be. . . . For his service we owe Adam an immeasurable debt of gratitude" (Marion G. Romney, quoted in *Doctrines of the Gospel*, p. 20).

FAMILY HISTORY: Genealogy. "We have worked earnestly to simplify genealogical research. The name was changed from genealogy to family history as a part of that effort." (*Learn of Me*, p. 81)

FAMILY HISTORY CENTERS: See genealogical library.

FAMILY HOME EVENING: Every Monday evening families are to spend time together studying and playing. No church activities are scheduled for Monday night.

FAREWELL: Shortly before people go on their missions, their local ward devotes one of their Sunday meetings to giving them a farewell. Family members and friends give speeches, making these farewells often quite emotional.

FAST AND TESTIMONY MEETING: Held on the first Sunday of every month. Instead of having assigned speakers, any member can come forward and give his or her testimony. Since the members have been fasting, these are usually quite emotional meetings. Also see fasting.

FASTING: Members are urged to fast for two meals or 24 hours the first weekend of the month. "The law to the Latter-day Saints, as understood by the authorities of the church, is that food and drink are not to be partaken of for twenty-four hours, 'from even to even,' and that the Saints are to refrain from all bodily gratification and indulgences" (Joseph F. Smith, quoted in *To Make Thee a Minister and a Witness*, p. 116). Many Mormons, however, do not follow this strictly. The money that would have been used for food is donated as their fast offering to help the poor.

FEELINGS: Subjective feelings, rather than objective facts, are the most important thing to Mormons. They believe that revelation, knowledge, guidance, and the answers to prayer all come through the medium of a person's feelings. "The Holy Ghost also helps us remember things we once learned but have forgotten . . . Other ways the Holy Ghost helps us solve problems are by revealing answers to us directly in a still, small voice . . . [If we receive the answer to our prayers from someone else, the Holy Ghost will give us the feeling that it is correct.] . . . Such promptings may simply be a feeling that we ought to spend more time with someone in our family or do something special for him . . . He tells us that if the decision we make is right, we will receive a feeling of peace in our hearts and in our minds" (*Duties and Blessings of the Priesthood B*, p. 106).

FELLOWSHIPPING: Many Christians use this term to describe socializing with their fellow Christians. Mormons, however, use it to describe the act of being friendly with nonmembers or new members as a way of doing mission work. An example of its usage: "Fellowshipping investigators (investigators = mission prospects) also has an effect on the quality of teaching." (*Ensign*, June 1991, p. 14)

FIRESIDE: A talk, often transmitted over satellite, given by a church leader, usually to one specific church organization. An example would be a fireside for the priests' quorum.

FIRSTBORN: "Jesus Christ is the Firstborn, then, in two senses of the word - he is the first spirit child born to God the Father in the premortal world, and he was the first one on this earth to be resurrected, or born from the grave." (Larry E. Dahl, *Ensign*, April 1997, p. 15). Also see only begotten.

FIRST ESTATE: See preexistence.

FIRST ORDINANCES: Baptism by immersion and the laying on of hands for the gift of the Holy Ghost.

FIRST PRESIDENCY: The President of the Church and his two counselors.

FIRST PRINCIPLES: Faith and repentance.

FIRST QUORUM OF SEVENTY: Title for, not the number of, a group of General Authorities. (In November, 1997, there were 44 members in the First Quorum of Seventy.) Members of this body supervise a particular area or activity of the church's work. These men serve until the age of 70.

FIRST VISION: The vision Joseph Smith supposedly received in 1820 when Heavenly Father told him not to join any church since they were all corrupt. Mormons believe that it proves that Joseph Smith was a true prophet of God. "The key to a testimony of the gospel is Joseph Smith's first vision. All that we believe hinges on this account. . . .The greatest event that has ever occurred in the world since the resurrection of the Son of God from the tomb and his ascension on high, was the coming of the Father and of the Son to that boy Joseph Smith, to prepare the way for the laying of the foundation of His kingdom" (*Sharing the Gospel Manual*, pp. 33,34).

FLESH AND BLOOD: A description of mortality. "Blood did not flow in Adam's veins (before the Fall), for he was not yet mortal, and blood is an element that pertains exclusively to mortality" (*Mormon Doctrine*, p. 268). Also see flesh and bones.

FLESH AND BONES: A description of immortality. "After the resurrection from the dead our bodies will be spiritual bodies, but they will be bodies that are tangible, bodies that have been purified, but they will nevertheless be bodies of flesh and bones, but they will not be blood bodies, they will no longer be quickened by blood but by the spirit which is eternal and they shall become immortal and shall never die" (Joseph Fielding Smith, quoted in

Book of Mormon Student Manual, p. 76). Also see flesh and blood.

FORGIVENESS: Mormonism teaches that a person must earn God's forgiveness. "Peace comes only through forgiveness. But forgiveness has a high price. President Kimball tells us: 'To every forgiveness there is a condition . . . The *fasting, the prayers, the humility must be equal to or greater than the sin.* There must be a broken heart and a contrite spirit. . . . There must be tears and genuine change of heart. There must be conviction of the sin, abandonment of the evil, confession of the error to properly constituted authorities of the Lord'" (*Gospel Principles*, p. 252 emphasis added). Contrast this to the biblical view that God forgives us freely because Jesus has already paid the entire debt of our sin. See Hebrews 10: 17-18.

FOUR GENERATION PROGRAM: The program in which Mormons are to trace their family history back a minimum of four generations in order to make sure the temple work has been done for all their ancestors.

FREE SALVATION: An expression not commonly used in Mormonism. The LDS church defines it as the salvation that is *freely and fully available* to all people, but not free in the sense that they don't have to earn it. "Though salvation is free (fully available and not withheld from anyone because of time, location, or lineage), we must reconcile ourselves to God" (*Ensign*, July 1989, p. 60). In fact, Mormons label the Christian teaching of free salvation as satanic. "One of the most fallacious doctrines originated by Satan and propounded by man is that man is saved alone by the grace of God; that belief in Jesus Christ alone is all that is needed for salvation" (Spencer W. Kimball, quoted in *Book of Mormon Student Manual*, p. 36).

FRIENDSHIPPING: See Fellowshipping.

FULLNESS OF THE GOSPEL: Mormonism. Mormons believe that Christian churches, at best, have only a part of the truth.

GABRIEL: "By modern revelation we know that Gabriel was known on earth as Noah, that he stands next in authority to Adam in the priesthood" (*Ensign*, Dec. 1990, p. 7). But also see Elias.

GARDEN OF GETHSEMANE: The place of Jesus' greatest suffering. "Where and under what circumstances was the atoning sacrifice of the Son of God made? Was it on the Cross of Calvary or in the Garden of Gethsemane . . . In reality, the pain and suffering, the triumph and grandeur, of the atonement took place primarily in

Gethsemane." (*The Life and Teachings of Jesus & His Apostles*, p. 172) Mormons base this on the fact that many people were crucified but only Jesus sweat drops of blood.

GATHERING OF ISRAEL: An important concept within Mormonism. (1) Mormons believe Israel is now being gathered spiritually by people joining the LDS Church (see Israel). (2) In addition, they believe Israel will be gathered literally at Christ's Second Coming with the ten tribes gathering at Independence, Missouri and Judah gathering at Jerusalem.

GENEALOGICAL LIBRARY: One or more rooms, often attached to a stake house, equipped for genealogical research. These libraries have extensive microfilm and computer resources. Non-Mormons can, and many do, make use of these facilities. The name has recently been changed to "Family History Centers." See family history.

GENEALOGICAL RESEARCH: Before ordinances can be performed for the dead, they must be accurately identified. Hence the importance of genealogical research. Doing this research, especially in regard to their own families, is an important duty for every Mormon. Also see four generation programs.

GENERAL AUTHORITY: The title for a church leader whose authority is not limited to one geographical area but is general. The General Authorities consist of the First Presidency of the Church, the Quorum of the Twelve Apostles, the First and Second Quorums of Seventy, and the Presiding Bishopric.

GENERAL CONFERENCE: Held twice a year (April and October) in Salt Lake City. The General Authorities give speeches, which are then considered scripture. Also see *Ensign.*

GENTILES: Non-Mormons. "Some Latter-day Saints have referred to those who are not members of the Church as Gentiles, even though the nonmembers might be Jews!" (*Ensign*, Jan. 1991)

GIFT: Rarely, if ever, used to describe an undeserved blessing. "By the grace of God — following devotion, faith and obedience on man's part — certain special spiritual blessings called gifts of the Spirit are bestowed upon men. Their receipt is always predicated upon obedience to law, but because they are freely available to all the obedient, they are called gifts" (*Mormon Doctrine*, p. 314).

GIFT OF THE HOLY GHOST: The Holy Ghost becomes a person's constant companion and thus they become eligible to receive revelation. "The gift of the Holy Ghost is the privilege given to a baptized person, after he has been confirmed a member of the Church, to receive guidance and inspiration from the Holy Ghost. . . . A person may be temporarily guided by the Holy Ghost without receiving the gift of the Holy Ghost. . . . Today many nonmembers of the Church learn, by the power of the Holy Ghost, that the Book of Mormon is true. But that flash of testimony leaves them if they do not receive the gift of the Holy Ghost" (Gospel Principles, p. 138)

GOD: Mormons believe that Heavenly Father was once a man who subsequently obtained godhood. A popular couplet states: "As man now is, God once was; As God now is, man may be." They call him an exalted man and believe he has a physical body. "'I say, if you were to see him today, you would see him like a man in form' [Teachings of the Prophet Joseph Smith, p. 345]. God is a glorified and perfected man, a personage of flesh and bones" (Gospel Principles, p. 9). Believing that God has a physical body is one of the most important tenets of Mormonism.

GODHEAD: Mormons don't believe in the Trinity, but they do talk about the godhead of Father, Son, and Holy Ghost. They believe it is structured similar to the first presidency of the church. Also see trinity.

GODHOOD: A Mormon's goal is to attain godhood; to become a god.

GODS: Although Mormons don't often talk about gods with non-Mormons, it is not uncommon to run across such references in their literature. They believe there are many who have progressed to become god and many more who will progress to godhood.

GOING TO HEAVEN: Since Mormons believe that nearly everyone will go to one of three kingdoms in heaven, it is often unproductive to talk to Mormons about "going to heaven." It is better to speak to them about living with Heavenly Father.

GOLDEN CONTACTS: Persons who are good prospects for joining the church.

GOLDEN PLATES: The plates on which the Book of Mormon supposedly was written. Mormons believe that the angel Moroni led Joseph Smith to the place on the hill Cumorah where they were allegedly buried.

GOSPEL: A common term for Mormonism or its intricate plan of salvation. "Mormonism so-called—which actually is the gospel of Christ, restored anew in this day" (Sharing the Gospel Manual,

p. 176). It has nothing in common with the gospel contained in the Bible. That gospel is the *good news* of free and full salvation won for mankind by Jesus Christ.

GOSPEL DOCTRINE CLASSES: Adult Sunday School classes.

GOSPEL PRINCIPLES: (1) The laws of Mormonism. (2) The title of a manual for new members. It summarizes the teachings of Mormonism better than any other of their manuals.

GRACE: Not the unconditional, undeserved, unfathomable love on God's part that moved him to save us. Rather it is the power God gives people to save themselves, which he grants *only* after they have done everything they can do. "This grace is an enabling power that allows men and women to lay hold on eternal life and exaltation after they have expended their own best efforts" (*LDS Bible Dictionary*, p. 697). "We know that it is by grace that we are saved, after all we can do" (2 Nephi 25:23). Also see free salvation.

GRACER: Slang term some Mormons use for Christians.

HEAVEN: Consists of three kingdoms: celestial, terrestrial, telestial.

HEAVENLY FATHER: The most popular LDS term for God. Its popularity is rooted in their belief that they were spiritually procreated by him in the preexistence.

HELL: (1) Not a place of eternal punishment but the temporary state of suffering wicked spirits experience in spirit prison before Judgment Day. "That part of the spirit world inhabited by wicked spirits who are awaiting the eventual day of their resurrection is called hell. . . . Hell will have an end" (*D&C Student Manual*, p. 165). (2) The regret the inhabitants of the lower kingdoms of heaven will experience as they see the glories of the celestial kingdom. "Of course, those who enter the telestial kingdom, and those who enter the terrestrial kingdom will have the eternal punishment which will come to them in knowing that they might, if they had kept the commandments of the Lord, have returned to his presence as his sons and his daughters. This will be a torment to them, and in that sense it will be hell" (*Life and Teachings of Jesus & His Apostles*, p. 66).

HIGH COUNCIL: A council of twelve men on the stake level assisting the stake presidency.

HIGH PRIEST: An office of the Melchizedek priesthood. "General Authorities, stake presidencies, bishoprics, and patriarchs, are ordained as high priests" (*D&C Student Manual*, p. 436).

HOLY GHOST: In Mormonism, unlike in Christianity, the Holy Ghost and the Holy Spirit are two distinct entities. The Holy Ghost is a member of the godhead but not equal to the Heavenly Father. "The Holy Ghost is the third person in the Godhead. As such he possesses the power of Deity. However, he is not fully like the Father and the Son in that he does not have a body of flesh and bones, He is a personage of Spirit" (*Sharing the Gospel Manual*, p. 104). "He is a spirit that has the form and likeness of a man (see D&C 130:22). He can be in only one place at a time, but his influence can be everywhere at the same time" (*Gospel Principles*, p. 37).

HOLY SPIRIT: A very confusing concept in Mormonism and therefore an expression Mormons don't employ much. It is not synonymous with the Holy Ghost but with the Spirit of the Lord, the Light of Christ, and the Spirit of Christ. "This other spirit is impersonal and has no size, nor dimensions; it proceeds forth from the presence of the Father and Son and is in all things. We should speak of the Holy Ghost as a personage as 'he' and this other Spirit as 'it,' although when we speak of the power or gift of the Holy Ghost we may properly say 'it'" (*Ensign*, June, 1991, p. 26).

HOME TEACHER: "It is the practice of the Church to send priesthood brethren out as home teachers to visit the homes of all church members each month. These brethren go out two-by-two, frequently one holding the lesser priesthood going with a possessor of the Melchizedek Priesthood" (*Mormon Doctrine*, p. 363). They are to teach a brief lesson but their main purpose is to encourage and check up on their fellow members. These visits also serve as good training for future missionaries. "Home teachers should be charged more clearly to describe their mission to watch over, to strengthen, to see that members do their duty. . . . They think of themselves as teachers of the gospel message only. . . . We must do something to change the emphasis from teaching to guardians watching over the Church kind of concept. Until we get that into their minds, we are not going to do the kind of home teaching that is going to get results" (Harold B. Lee, quoted in *To Make Thee a Minister and a Witness*, p. 111).

IF: One of the biggest words in Mormonism. Every promise of God is conditional on the obedience of man. "All blessings are conditional. I know of none that are not" (Spencer W. Kimball, quoted in *Remember Me*, p. 23). Also see D&C 130:21

IMMORTALITY: See flesh and bones.

INDEPENDENCE, MISSOURI: (1) An important site to Mormons, sometimes referred to as Zion. They believe Jesus will return there and rule both from there and Jerusalem during the Millennium (see D&C 133). Before that happens, however, they believe a temple needs to be built on the spot indicated by Joseph Smith. (2) The site of the Garden of Eden.

INSPIRED VERSION: Another name for the Joseph Smith Translation of the Bible. LDS edition of the Bible contain excerpts of it in footnotes and an appendix. It is not widely used since the church claims that he never completed it.

INSTITUTE: College level courses on Mormonism. Near many college campuses, the LDS church has built institute buildings, which serve as the center of college life for many LDS students.

INTELLIGENCES: The part of mankind that Mormons say is eternal. They believe Heavenly Father (pro)created spiritual bodies for these intelligences to inhabit. "The word when preceded by the article *an*, or used in the plural as *intelligences*, means a person, or persons, usually in the spiritual estate. Just as we speak of a person or persons, we speak of an *intelligence*, or *intelligences*" (*D&C Student Manual*, p. 220).

INVESTIGATORS: Prospects; non-Mormons who are interested in (investigating) the church.

ISRAEL: Mormons. They believe that most people who join the church have at least some of Abraham's blood. If they don't, Mormonism teaches that their blood will literally be changed. ". . . the effect of the Holy Ghost upon a Gentile is to purge out the old blood, and make him actually the seed of Abraham. That man that has none of the blood of Abraham [naturally] must have a new creation by the Holy Ghost" (Joseph Smith, quoted in *Doctrines of the Gospel*, p. 57).

JACK MORMON: A slang expression for a non-active Mormon.

JAREDITES: According to the Book of Mormon, they were people whose language was preserved by faith at the time of the Tower of Babel. According to it, they subsequently came to America.

JEHOVAH: Jesus. "Jesus is Jehovah. He was God of the Old Testament" (*The Life and Teachings of Jesus & His Apostles*, p. 21). Also see Elohim.

JESUS: Mormons regard him in the following ways: (1) As the first spirit child of Heavenly Father. (2) As Jehovah. (3) As the only begotten

Son. They believe he is the only child Heavenly Father *physically begat on this earth*. Also see only begotten. (4) As the Savior. Not a Savior who did everything for mankind but rather one (a) who conquered physical death for mankind, (b) who paid our debt and is patient with us as *we pay him back in full*, (c) who served as our example, showing us what we have to do to save ourselves.

JOHN THE BAPTIST: The last legal administrator of the Aaronic priesthood. Mormons believe he appeared to Joseph Smith and Oliver Cowdery on May 15, 1829 and bestowed upon them the Aaronic priesthood.

JOSEPH SMITH: The founder of the Mormon religion. Mormons often refer to him simply as the Prophet. They believe that he participated in the creation of the world, that his coming was prophesied in the Book of Mormon, and that all who enter the celestial kingdom will have to be approved by him. "Joseph Smith, the Prophet and Seer of the Lord, has done more, save Jesus only, for the salvation of men in this world, than any other man that ever lived in it" (D&C 135:3). Also see first vision.

JOURNAL: A personal record to be written in daily or weekly that will serve as a testimony to a person's descendants. Keeping a journal is an important responsibility. "I urge all of the people of this church to give serious attention to their family histories, to encourage their parents and grandparents to write their journals, and let no family go into eternity without having left their memoirs for their children, their grandchildren, and their posterity. This is a duty and a responsibility, and I urge every person to start the children out writing a personal history and journal" (Spencer W. Kimball, quoted in *Latter-day Saint Woman B*, p. 161).

JST: Joseph Smith Translation of the Bible. See Inspired Version.

JUSTIFICATION: A term unfamiliar to most Mormons. In contrast to the biblical concept of justification (God's declaring us not guilty on the basis of Christ's atoning work), Mormonism describes it as God's strict confirmation of the merits or demerits of man's own actions. In other words, LDS justification is God's act of rewarding the right and punishing the wrong.

KEYS: Common LDS term denoting the power and authority of the priesthood. "Two different usages of the term *keys* are found in the revelations. One has reference to the directive powers whereby the Church or kingdom and all its organizations are governed. . . . The other usage refers to the means provided whereby something is revealed, discovered, or made manifest. . . . President Joseph F. Smith said: 'What is a key? It is the right or privilege which belongs to and comes with the priesthood to have communication with God'" (*Mormon Doctrine*, p. 410).

KINGDOM OF GOD: The Church of Jesus Christ of Latter-day Saints. "Let us understand that The Church of Jesus Christ of Latter-day Saints is the literal kingdom of God in the earth" (Marion G. Romney, quoted in *Book of Mormon Student Manual*, p. 108).

KING FOLLETT SERMON: The funeral sermon Joseph Smith preached in 1844 for a man named King Follet. Many Mormons consider this the greatest sermon ever preached. In it Smith outlined his thoughts on the nature of God and how man can become a god.

KINGDOMS OF GLORY: The three kingdoms of Mormon heaven: celestial, terrestrial, telestial.

KOLOB: The star nearest the throne of God (Book of Abraham 3:3-9). One of their hymns (284) is entitled: "If You Could Hie to Kolob." Also see everlasting burnings.

LAMANITES: (1) According to the Book of Mormon, the branch of Lehi's descendants that became unfaithful. (Lehi, according to the Book of Mormon, was a Jew who traveled to the Americas around 600 B.C.) Mormons believe they became the ancestors of the American Indians. (2) Most commonly used today as a term for the American Indians.

LAMBDA DELTA SIGMA: The church-sponsored sorority for college women. "Lambda Delta Sigma is open to any single college woman under the age of thirty, regardless of religious affiliation, provided she is willing to live by Latter-day Saints standards." (*Relief Society Handbook*, p. 32)

LAW: In Mormonism most things are described as a law. Some examples are: the law of the gospel, the law of forgiveness, the law of justice, the law of the sacrament. "Law provided the way for the Saints to grow, progress, and obtain happiness" (*D&C Student Manual*, p. 393).

LDS: Abbreviation for Latter-day Saints. This abbreviation is used not just in connection with Mormon doctrine, but also Mormon people. Commonly Mormons describe themselves as LDS.

LEHI: An important figure in the Book of Mormon. He, with his family, supposedly traveled from Judah to America in 600 B.C. His descendants became the Lamanites and Nephites. LDS children learn about him and his voyage across the ocean.

LIGHT OF CHRIST: "All men are enlightened by the Spirit of God, or Light of Christ sometimes called conscience." (James E. Faust, *Ensign*, April 1996, p. 2).

LINE OF AUTHORITY: "Every priesthood holder should be able to trace his 'line of authority' back to Jesus Christ. This means he should know who ordained him and who ordained the person who ordained him, and so on back to Joseph Smith, who was ordained by Peter, James, and John, who were ordained by Jesus Christ. This is called the 'priesthood line of authority'" (*The Latter-day Saint Woman A*, p. 77). Members of the priesthood carry cards, called "line of authority cards," that contain this information.

LINE UPON LINE, PRECEPT UPON PRECEPT: A common LDS expression roughly equivalent to progressing "one step at a time."

LIGHT OF CHRIST: See Holy Spirit.

LIVING PROPHET: See the President of the Church.

LORD'S SUPPER: See sacrament.

MAGNIFY A CALLING: A common Mormon expression equivalent in meaning to performing your assigned tasks as faithfully as you can.

MAKE YOUR CALLING AND ELECTION SURE: "Means that the Lord seals their exaltation upon them while they are yet in this life" (*D&C Student Manual*, p. 326). Mormons believe this happens to only a select few.

MANKIND: (1) Existed in premortality as Heavenly Father's spirit children. (2) Are "gods in embryo" with the potential to obtain godhood. "Having within him the seeds of godhood and thus being a god in embryo, man has unlimited potential for progress and attainment" (*The Miracle of Forgiveness*, p. 3).

MANUALS: The LDS church provides manuals for every church organization and activity. These manuals are excellent sources for discovering what is being *officially* taught in the church.

MARTYRDOM: A reference to Joseph Smith's death on June 27, 1844 in the Carthage, Illinois jail.

MEETINGHOUSES: Mormon church buildings. Also commonly referred to as "stake houses" or chapels.

MELCHIZEDEK PRIESTHOOD: The higher priesthood that worthy young men enter at the age of 18 or 19. Mormons believe Peter,

James, and John bestowed it on Joseph Smith and Oliver Cowdery in 1829. The offices of the Melchizedek priesthood are elder, seventy, high priest, and patriarch.

MIA: Abbreviation for Mutual Improvement Associations, the name of their youth organizations.

MILLENNIUM: Mormons believe Jesus will return and rule for a thousand years on earth. They say that he will rule both from Jerusalem and Independence, Missouri. During this time, the temple work will be completed. To be ready for his coming is the driving force behind their food storage program and their political activism.

MINISTERING OF ANGELS: The belief that holders of the Aaronic priesthood can receive help from angels.

MINISTERING OF SERVANTS: The people who will inhabit the lowest level of the celestial kingdom. These are faithful Mormons who were not married eternally and thus cannot reach exaltation.

MINISTERING OF SPIRITS: "Joseph Smith explained the difference between an angel and a ministering spirit: an angel is 'a resurrected or translated body, with its spirit ministering to embodied spirits,' and a ministering spirit is 'a disembodied spirit, visiting and ministering to disembodied spirits'" (D&C Student Manual, p. 320). One example of ministering spirits are the spirits in paradise who go on missions to the spirits in spirit prison. Also see angels.

MISSION OF THE CHURCH: The LDS Church has a threefold mission: (1) to perfect the saints; (2) to proclaim the gospel; (3) to redeem the dead.

MISSION PRESIDENT: The head of a mission district. There were over 275 mission districts in June of 1992.

MISSIONARY: Many young LDS men, at the age of 19, go on a two year mission. Some young women go on eighteen-month missions at the age of 21. Increasingly, retired persons are also serving on missions. Ideally, all who go on missions are to support themselves, although many also receive support from the church. Missionaries who remain in the United States receive only two weeks of training, while those going to a foreign country receive two months of language and culture training.

MISSIONARY DISCUSSIONS: The six lessons missionaries give to investigators. Their official title is Uniform System for Teaching the Gospel. "To those missionaries who may be asked to present memorized discussion, it may be well to say that the General Authorities have been inspired to present a basic knowledge of the gospel in this way" (*Sharing the Gospel Manual*, p. 114).

MORMON: Popular name for members of The Church of Jesus Christ of Latter-day Saints. It is derived from the name of a prophet in the Book of Mormon. Although some Christians claim that using this name is derogatory to LDS people, it is one they themselves often use (e.g., Mormon Tabernacle Choir).

MORONI: The angel who supposedly appeared to Joseph Smith. His statue adorns the top spire of LDS temples. See angel.

MORTAL: Included in the Mormon definition of mortality is the ability to have children. They claim that Adam and Eve's fall was a blessing since it made mankind mortal (able to have children). "When Adam and Eve were placed in the Garden of Eden they were not yet mortal. They were not able to have children. . . . Their physical condition changed as a result of their eating the forbidden fruit. As God had promised, they became mortal. They were able to have children" (*Gospel Principles*, pp. 32f).

MOTHER IN HEAVEN: Although not often mentioned, Mormonism teaches that there is an exalted mother in heaven, the spouse of Heavenly Father. "For as we have a Father in heaven, so also we have a Mother there, a glorified, exalted, ennobled Mother" (*Achieving A Celestial Marriage*, p. 129).

MTC: Abbreviation for the Missionary Training Center. The main one is in Provo, Utah. There are twelve such centers worldwide.

MURDER: On the basis of 1 John 3:15 and D&C 42:79 Mormons believe that murderers will never obtain exaltation but will still inherit the telestial kingdom.

MUTUAL: See MIA.

NEPHITES: According to the Book of Mormon, both they and the Lamanites descended from Lehi, a Jew who came to America in 600 B.C. The Nephites were his faithful descendants, who became corrupt, and were finally destroyed by the Lamanites. Much of the Book of Mormon is a description of the wars between these two groups.

NEW CREATION: See Israel

OBEY: A very important word in Mormonism. "Obedience is the first law of heaven, the cornerstone upon which all righteousness and progression rest. . . . The whole system of creation and existence is thus centered around the eternal principle of obedience to law"

(*Mormon Doctrine*, pp. 539f.). Also see if.

OFFERINGS: These are contributions given over and above their tithes (e.g., fast offerings and offerings to missionary fund or building fund).

ONLY BEGOTTEN SON: Mormons use this expression, not as Christians do to express Christ's divinity, but to refer to their belief that Jesus is the only person Heavenly Father physically begat on earth. "God was the Father of his fleshly tabernacle, and Mary— a mortal woman and a virgin—was His mother. He is, therefore, the only person born who rightfully deserves the title 'the Only Begotten Son of God'" (Ezra Taft Benson, *Ensign*, April 1991, p. 2). "We believe that he came into the world, born of Mary, literally and actually, as we are born of our mothers: that he came into the world, born of God the Eternal Father, the Almighty Elohim, literally and actually, as we are born of our earthly fathers" (Bruce R. McConkie, quoted in *Sharing the Gospel Manual*, p. 74).

ORDINANCES: rites administered by the priesthood (e.g., first ordinances, temple ordinances, blessings of children, dedicated of graves).

OUTER DARKNESS: The closest Mormonism comes to the biblical concept of hell. (Mormons define hell differently. See hell.) Outer darkness is the abode of Satan, demons, and the sons of perdition. Many Mormons believe that only a handful of people will qualify as sons of perdition and thus go to outer darkness. Also see son of perdition.

PARADISE: The section of the spirit world for the spirits of deceased Mormons. There they can continue their progression towards godhood; from there they can go on missions to spirit prison in order to convert non-Mormon spirits to Mormonism. It is obvious, however, that Paradise is a biblical term for heaven itself. Compare Revelation 22:2 and its reference to the tree of life with Revelation 2:7. From this it becomes obvious that Jesus, in Luke 23:43, was telling the thief on the cross that he would be with him in heaven.

PATRIARCHAL BLESSING: A one-time blessing, given by a patriarch, that supposedly reveals a person's lineage and his or her future potential. The blessing, however, is conditioned on a person's faithfulness. These blessings are typed out and are highly valued. "In 1957 the First Presidency of the Church explained that a patriarchal blessing contains an inspired declaration of lineage . . . which tells us through which tribe of Israel we receive our blessings . . . Because a patriarchal blessing is personal and sacred . . . its content should only be shared with those who are close to us and as we are directed by the Spirit" (*Duties and Blessings of the Priesthood A*, p. 74).

PATRIARCH: A man who is called to give patriarchal blessings. There is a patriarch for the whole church and one in most stakes. "In the organization of the Church in Jesus' time, patriarchs were called evangelists. . . .Most stakes of the church have at least one worthy Melchizedek Priesthood bearer who is called and ordained by a member of the Quorum of the Twelve to be the stake patriarch" (*Duties and Blessings of the Priesthood A,* pp. 70, 71).

PEARL OF GREAT PRICE: One of the four Mormon written scriptures. It contains a collection of five brief items: the Book of Moses, the Book of Abraham, Joseph Smith—Matthew, Joseph Smith—History, and the Articles of Faith. Because it is short, it is usually printed with the Doctrine and Covenants in one volume. Most Mormons have never read it.

PEEP STONES: Magical stones that were said to have been buried with the golden plates. Joseph Smith supposedly used them to translate the Book of Mormon from the golden plates. He said he put these stones in his hat and the translation would miraculously appear on them. Also called the Urim and Thummim.

PERFECTION: The major emphasis of Mormonism. Becoming perfect is the key to becoming exalted. This emphasis places great stress on many Mormons. "Perhaps no idea creates more emotional stress for some of us than the idea that we need to be perfect right now—or soon! . . . And when we fail to achieve perfection in some area, we criticize ourselves harshly, even to the point of despair" (*Ensign*, Sept. 1990, p. 50).

PERSONAL GOD: The expression Mormons use to refer to their belief that God has a physical body. They ridicule the biblical concept of God. "Soon pagan beliefs dominated the thinking of those called 'Christians.' . . . Members of this church believed that God was a being without form or substance" (*Gospel Principles*, p. 105).

PERSONAL HISTORY: "A personal history is much shorter than a journal. A journal may be used as a basis for writing a personal history" (*Remember Me*, p. 131).

PLAN OF SALVATION: All the laws and ordinances of Mormonism. Following the plan of salvation is the key to being exalted. But the biblical plan of salvation centers on the work of God for us. It tells us how God, in his grace, sent Jesus to do everything to save us.

PLURALITY OF GODS: Mormons prefer this term to polytheism. They claim they are not polytheists, although they believe in a plurality of gods, because they worship only one god: Heavenly Father. Polytheism "is not to be confused with the gospel truth that there are "gods many, and lords many. But to us there is but one God, the Father . . . and one Lord Jesus Christ' [1 Cor. 8: 4-7]. The saints are not polytheists" (*Mormon Doctrine*, p. 579).

PLURAL MARRIAGE: Mormons use this term instead of polygamy. In 1843 this doctrine became part of LDS scripture (D&C 132). Plural marriage had been practiced by Joseph Smith and selected others previous to this and continued to be practiced openly until 1890. At that time, the living prophet, Wilford Woodruff, supposedly received a revelation which forbade this practice (cf. D&C Declaration 1).

POLYGAMY: See plural marriage.

POLYTHEISM: See plurality of gods.

PRAYER: Answers to prayer come through feelings. A good feeling constitutes a positive reply while a bad feeling signifies a negative reply. Most Mormons do not fold their hands when they pray; instead they fold their arms.

PREACHING: Not a common word in Mormonism. Their Sunday service centers on testimonies and talks given by different members each week rather than a sermon given by the bishop.

PREEXISTENCE: Also called premortality or our first estate. Mormons believe we existed before our earth-life as spirit children of Heavenly Father. Also see spirit children.

PRESIDENCY: Each organization of the church is run by a presidency that consists of a president and his two counselors.

PRESIDENT: The head of a church organization (e.g., stakes president, quorum president).

PRESIDENT OF THE CHURCH: Also called the "Prophet, Revelator, and Seer" or the living prophet. They believe that he, and he alone, receives direct revelations for the entire church. These revelations take precedence even over their written scriptures.

This is a lifetime position. The apostle with the longest tenure becomes the church president at the death of the current church president.

PRESIDING BISHOPRIC: The three General Authorities who supervise the Church's financial affairs.

PRIESTHOOD: Entered into by all worthy male members. Defined as both the *authority* and *power* God gives to act on His behalf. "The priesthood is the greatest power on earth" (*Duties and Blessings of the Priesthood B,* p. 19) Only those rites and ordinances performed by holders of the priesthood are valid in Mormon eyes. They also believe that it gives them the power to receive divine revelations. There are two types of priesthood: the Aaronic and the Melchizedek.

PRIMARY: A Sunday school-like organization for children ages three to eleven.

PROBATION: "*Formal probation* is a temporary state of discipline, imposed as a means to help the member fully repent. The presiding officer of the council specifies the conditions under which the probation can be terminated. During the probation, the bishop or stake president keeps in close contact to help the individual progress" (M. Russell Ballard, *Ensign,* Sept. 1990, p. 16).

PROPHET, THE: Joseph Smith.

PROPHETS: The President of the Church and the twelve apostles.

PROSELYTING: Evangelizing; doing mission work. Unlike in Christianity, it doesn't have a negative connotation. In Mormonism it is used in a positive sense.

QUORUMS: "A specified group of men, holding the same office in the Priesthood, organized for the more efficient advancement of the work for which the Priesthood in the Church is responsible" (*D&C Student Manual,* p. 435). The various priesthood quorums on the ward level meet every Sunday.

RAISING RIGHT HAND TO THE SQUARE: When Mormons sustain their leaders they raise their right hands in such a way that a right angle is formed at the elbow. Also see sustaining.

RECOMMEND: (1) Often used in reference to a temple recommend. See temple recommend. (2) Persons also receive a recommend from their bishop when they transfer from one ward to another. (3) Members of the priesthood receive recommends to perform certain ordinances.

REDEEM: Mormons use this synonymously with atonement. Their view, like their view of atonement, differs drastically from the biblical view of redemption. In the Bible, redemption is another beautiful word describing how Jesus, with his voluntary sacrifice, *bought us back* from the curse of sin.

REDEEM THE DEAD: One of the three main missions of the LDS church. See baptism for the dead.

REFORMED EGYPTIAN: According to Mormon 9:32, the language in which the Book of Mormon was supposedly written.

RELEASED: The vast majority of church positions are not lifelong callings. After a varying period of time, persons are released from their calling. Often they will be called to a new position.

RELIEF SOCIETY: The main LDS women's organization. Its emphasis is more on practical matters (e.g., being good homemakers, self-improvement) than on theological matters. It meets every Sunday while the men meet in their various priesthood quorums.

REPENTANCE: Abandoning the sin. Mormon repentance follows faith rather than preceding it. "If we sincerely repent, we turn away from our sins and do them no more. We no longer have any desire to commit the sins" (*Uniform System for Teaching the Gospel*, p. 2-14). "There is one crucial test of repentance. This is abandonment of the sin. . . . The saving power does not extend to him who merely wants to change his life. . . .Nor is repentance complete when one merely tries to abandon sin. To try is weak" (Spencer W. Kimball, quoted in *Sharing the Gospel Manual*, p. 94). Biblical repentance, however, describes the *change of mind* when people turn away from trust in themselves and their works to trust in Jesus and his work for them.

RESTORATION: The period of history ushered in by Joseph Smith. Mormons assert that after the apostles died the true church left the earth (the great apostasy) until it was restored by Joseph Smith.

REVELATION: Their own feelings, even more than their written scriptures, are the vehicle through which Mormons receive revelation (e.g., "burning in the bosom"). "Feeling is a big part of the process of revelation. . . the assurance comes through feeling" (*Lay Hold Upon the Word of God*, p. 56).

RLDS: Abbreviation for The Church of Jesus Christ of Reorganized Latter-day Saints, based in Independence, Missouri. It is not connected with the Salt Lake church and is much smaller. After

Joseph Smith's death, a group of Mormons recognized Smith's son rather than Brigham Young as their leader and founded the RLDS church. Until very recently it was led by a direct descendant of Joseph Smith.

RM: Abbreviation for returned missionary.

SABBATH: Sunday. On Sunday they are not to work (even around the house), shop, go to the movies, or engage in sports. They are to attend church meetings, rest, visit with family or sick, read inspirational literature.

SACRAMENT: Used exclusively as a reference to the Lord's Supper. Mormons partake of the sacrament every Sunday. It consists of bread and water, and all members, including toddlers, receive it. Its purpose is to remind then of their obligation to obey God. "To keep his saints in constant remembrance of their obligation to accept and obey him—or in other words, to eat his flesh and drink his blood—the Lord has given them the sacramental ordinance" (*Life and Teachings of Jesus & His Apostles*, p. 93).

SACRAMENT MEETING: The Mormon Sunday church service.

SACRED GROVE: The place where Heavenly Father supposedly appeared to the boy Joseph Smith and told him not to join any church because they were all corrupt.

SAINT: The term Mormons use to describe themselves. "A saint is not necessarily a person who is perfect, but he is a person who strives for perfection . . ." (*The Life and Teachings of Jesus & His Apostles*, p. 361).

SALVATION: (1) For most Mormons this is equivalent to resurrection, which is the only free gift in Mormonism. This is why many can say they believe that they are saved by Jesus alone. They mean that they believe they don't have to do anything to gain resurrection. (2) Sometimes used as a synonym for exaltation.

SANCTIFICATION: A term not commonly used in Mormonism. They use it to refer to a state of saintliness which is obtained as people purify themselves by overcoming sin. The Bible uses this term in two ways: (1) to describe the Holy Spirit's work of bringing people to the faith; (2) to describe the good works believers do by the power of the Holy Spirit.

SATAN: Heavenly Father's spirit child who proposed an alternate plan of salvation. After Heavenly Father rejected it, Satan rebelled. Heavenly Father sent him, along with his followers (demons), to outer darkness. This meant that they lost forever their chance to obtain physical bodies and to continue their progression to godhood. For many Mormons, Satan is the spiritual being of whose presence they are most aware.

SAVIOR: Mormons often refer to Jesus as their Savior. They believe he paid their debt to Heavenly Father and also conquered death for them. But they also believe that they have to pay him back in full (For a good example of this, see *Gospel Principles*, pp. 75-77). In other words, they believe he saved them by assuming their loan, refinancing it, and spreading out the payments. They do not believe that he saved them fully and freely by paying for their sins and then canceling the debt. Also see free salvation, Jesus.

SCRIPTURE: The Book of Mormon, Doctrine and Covenants, the Pearl of Great Price, and the Bible. Mormons also refer to the messages of the living prophet and the talks given at general conferences as scripture. Also see *Ensign.*

SEALINGS: Being united for eternity. This can be done only in the temple. (1) Spouses are sealed to each other by being married in the temple. (2) Children are sealed to their parents in another temple ceremony. Both of these ceremonies can also be performed vicariously for the dead.

SECOND QUORUM OF SEVENTY: A title, not a number, for a group of General Authorities. (In November 1997 there were 23 members in this quorum.) They help supervise the worldwide operation of the church. Unlike members in the First Quorum of Seventy, these men do not receive a lifetime calling. Also see seventy.

SECTS: Christian churches. "Division and dissension, contention, confusion and discord—these are among the prevailing characteristics of the *sects* of Christendom. These various sects or *denominations* . . ." (*Mormon Doctrine*, p. 699).

SEER: The President of the Church is often referred to as "the Prophet, Seer, and Revelator."

SEMINARY: Not a theological school but the daily set of instructions on Mormonism offered to high school students. Often the LDS church will build a building close to a high school in which they conduct these classes. These seminary buildings become the social center for many LDS students.

SETTING APART: "Through a priesthood blessing, we are set apart from the world to focus our time and talents on a specific labor for the Lord . . . As a priesthood ordinance, the action of setting an individual apart involves divine power, promise, and holiness. . .

When we are set apart, we also receive the right to obtain knowledge and revelation to accomplish our assigned tasks" (Ronald D. Maines, *Ensign*, Feb 1992, p. 51).

SEVENTY: A title, not a number, of an office in the Melchizedek priesthood devoted to mission work. The name is taken from the account of Jesus sending out the seventy to witness. This office does not exist on the local level. In 1997 there were five Quorums of Seventies. The first two were comprised of General Authorities, the last three consisted of Area Authorities.

SIN: A word not commonly used by Mormons since Mormonism has a weak view of sin. Instead of talking about sin, they use words such as bad habits, infractions, mistakes, and poor judgments.

SISTER: Female members are commonly addressed as sister.

SKINS: A slang term some Mormons use to refer to their temple garments.

SON OF GOD: That Jesus is the Son of God is part and parcel of every Mormon's testimony. In saying that, however, they are not saying that they believe Jesus is equal with God the Father. "Jesus is greater than the Holy Spirit, which is subject unto him, but his father is greater than he!" (*Book of Mormon Student Manual*, p. 74).

SON OF PERDITION: A person who goes to outer darkness. Some Mormons believe that hardly any, if any, will qualify as sons of perdition, while others use this mainly in reference to apostates. In referring to sons of perdition Joseph Smith said, "This is the case with many apostates of the Church of Jesus Christ of Latter-day Saints" (*Doctrine of the Gospels*, p. 93).

SOUL: "It is peculiar to the theology of the Latter-day Saints that we regard the body as an essential part of the soul. . . . You will find that nowhere, outside of the Church of Jesus Christ, is the solemn and eternal truth taught that the soul of man is the body and spirit combined" (James E. Talmage, quoted in *D&C Student Manual*, p. 198).

SPIRIT BODIES: The "bodies" of spirit children. "What are we like as spirits? (We do not have bodies of flesh and bones, but our spirit bodies are in the same form as the physical bodies we will have on earth.) . . . As spirits, what can we do? (As spirits, we are able to move about, talk, listen, think, learn, make choices, and prepare for earth life.)" (*Walk In His Way A*, p. 22).

SPIRIT CHILDREN: Mormons teach that in preexistence everyone lived as a spirit child of Heavenly Father and mother. They claim that spirit children can develop characteristics and begin their progression to godhood through the wise use of their agency. Also see spirit bodies and intelligences.

SPIRIT OF CHRIST: A term confusing to many Mormons, sometimes equated with conscience. "If a man who has never heard the gospel will hearken to the teachings and manifestations of the Spirit of Christ, or the Light of Truth, which come to him, often spoken as conscience . . ." (Joseph Fielding Smith, quoted in *Book of Mormon Student Manual*, p. 146). See also Holy Spirit.

SPIRIT PRISON: The section of the spirit world where non-Mormon spirits go. LDS spirits from paradise can convert the inhabitants of the spirit prison to Mormonism.

SPIRIT WORLD: (1) The place where all spirits go after death. It consists of two parts: paradise and spirit prison. (2) Sometimes used as a reference to the preexistent world.

SPIRITUAL DEATH: Except for the sons of perdition this is a temporary condition since everybody else attains some level of heaven. "Spiritual death is to be cast out of the presence of the Lord, to die as to the things of righteousness . . . Spiritual death ceases for those spirits who come up out of hell to receive an inheritance in the telestial world" (*Mormon Doctrine*, pp. 756, 758).

STAKE: Similar to a diocese in Catholicism. It is an organizational unit consisting of a number of wards. The term is derived from the picture of stakes holding down a tent, which, in this case, would be Zion or Mormonism.

STAKE HOUSE: The meetinghouses that house the office of the stake president.

STAKE MISSIONARY: A person who is called to do part-time missionary work. "Your highest priority in planning your work is to provide enough people from this list so that each pair of full-time missionaries can teach twenty to thirty discussions each week" (*Stake Mission Handbook*, p. 2).

STAKE PRESIDENT: The head of a stake. He has no theological training. He, along with his two counselors, wields great power and authority. He is not a full-time church worker, but continues to work in his secular occupation while serving as a stake president. Usually, successful business or professional men are chosen for this position. There is no set term of office, but most stake presidents serve for five to ten years.

STANDARD WORKS: Synonymous with canonized scripture. Refers to the Book of Mormon, Doctrine and Covenants, Pearl of Great Price, and the Bible.

STEWARDSHIP: A favorite LDS term for responsibility.

STICK OF EPHRAIM: The Book of Mormon. This identification is based on a misinterpretation of Ezekiel 37:15-19. Mormons identify the stick of Ephraim with the Book of Mormon because it supposedly is the history of Ephraim in the new world (see D&C 27:5). This Ezekiel passage, and the LDS interpretation of it, is one of the first things Mormons learn.

STOREHOUSES: Regional bishop's storehouses are maintained as part of the church's welfare plan. The goods from these storehouses can be distributed among the poor at the discretion of the bishops. During the early 1980s, the LDS Church downplayed their welfare program and closed many of these storehouses.

SUNDAY SCHOOL: "Sunday School is for all Church members and interested nonmembers twelve years of age and older. . . . All Sunday School classes must follow the course of study and use the manuals approved by the First Presidency and the Quorum of the Twelve for the current curriculum year" (*Sunday School Handbook*, p. IV). Also see primary.

SUSTAINING: A procedure where the entire church body ratifies the calling of persons to various church positions. They do this by having members raise their right hands. Sustainings are a formality, being almost always unanimous, since they believe the person was called to that position by direct revelation. "When we sustain officers, we are given the opportunity of sustaining those whom the Lord has already called by revelation . . .To sustain is to make the action binding on ourselves to support those people whom we have sustained" (*D&C Student Manual*, p. 54).

TEA: The Word of Wisdom (D&C 89) forbids the drinking of hot drinks. This has been officially interpreted as coffee and tea. There is some debate over whether this forbids the drinking of iced tea. Also see Word of Wisdom.

TELESTIAL KINGDOM: The lowest kingdom or heaven. It is not visited by Heavenly Father or Jesus but only by the Holy Ghost. This will be the final destination of carnal and wicked people. Although it is the lowest kingdom, its glory, which is symbolized as the glory of stars, is described as surpassing all mortal understanding. Some Mormons refer to it as the "slums of heaven."

TEMPLE: A place not of joint worship but of individual sacred work. (Mormons would say that participating in the sacred work is worship.) Only temple-worthy Mormons can enter. There are three main temple rituals: (1) baptisms for the dead, (2) endowments both for the living and the dead, (3) celestial marriage (sealings) both for the living and the dead. Participating in these rituals is essential for exaltation. Mormons are encouraged to have a picture of the temple hanging in their houses. In many ways, the temple holds the same place of reverence in a Mormon's life as Christ's cross does in a Christian's life.

TEMPLE GARMENTS: (1) The special garments worn only in the temple; (2) The sacred undergarments worn at all times which many feel gives them supernatural protection. Only temple-worthy Mormons can wear either of these garments.

TEMPLE MARRIAGE: See celestial marriage.

TEMPLE MORMON: A Mormon who is worthy to enter the temple. Only about 25% of Mormons qualify. See temple-worthy.

TEMPLE RECOMMEND: The small card that allows temple-worthy Mormons to enter the temple. Each time they go, it is checked at a security gate. It is issued by their bishop and a member of their stake presidency. It is good for one year, after which it needs to be renewed. Also see temple-worthy.

TEMPLE WORK: A favorite expression in Mormonism to describe participation in the various temple ordinances.

TEMPLE WORTHY: Mormons who are worthy to enter the temple. To be worthy they must keep the Word of Wisdom, tithe, be morally upright, and be supportive of the church leaders. This is determined in yearly interviews with their bishop and a member of the stake presidency.

TERRESTRIAL KINGDOM: The middle kingdom of heaven where people will be visited by Jesus but not by Heavenly Father. This will be the final destination of honorable people and non-valiant Mormons. (Jack Mormons).

TESTIMONY: The one thing Mormons believe assures them of the truthfulness of Mormonism. It is the most important thing a Mormon can possess. Nearly every testimony contains the following four parts: (1) Jesus is the true Son of God. (2) Joseph Smith was a true prophet of God. (3) The Book of Mormon is the true word of God. (4) The Church of Jesus Christ of Latter-day

Saints is the true church of God. They believe they receive their testimony, *not through facts*, but through *feelings*. "If the sole source of one's knowledge or assurance of the truth of the Lord's work comes from reason, or logic, or persuasive argument that cannot be controverted, it is not a testimony of the gospel. In its nature a testimony consists of knowledge that comes by revelation" (*Mormon Doctrine*, p. 785). They are encouraged to "bear their testimony" as often as possible. By "bearing their testimony" they also "build their testimony." Also see revelation.

THE CHURCH OF JESUS CHRIST OF LATTER-DAY SAINTS: The church's official name. They prefer it to the name Mormon.

THREE WITNESSES: Oliver Cowdery, David Whitmer, and Martin Harris testified that they saw the golden plates that contained the Book of Mormon. Their testimony is printed in the front of every copy of the Book of Mormon. Mormons state that their testimony is proof that Joseph Smith was telling the truth about the Book of Mormon.

TITHING: Giving 10% of your income to the church. It is an important requirement for remaining in good standing in the church. It is essential for becoming temple-worthy. "Accordingly, tithing becomes one of the great tests of the personal righteousness of church members. By this principle,' President Joseph F. Smith says, 'the loyalty of the people of this Church shall be put to the test. By this principle it shall be known who is for the kingdom of God and who is against it. . . . There is a great deal of importance connected with this principle, for by it shall be known whether we are faithful or unfaithful'" (Bruce R. McConkie, quoted in *Temple Preparation Seminar Discussions*, p. 62).

TITHING SETTLEMENT: A yearly meeting members have with their bishop to make sure that they have paid their tithes.

TOBACCO: Forbidden in the Word of Wisdom (D&C Section 89).

TRACTING: An expression LDS missionaries use to describe handing out tracts door-to-door.

TRANSLATED BEINGS: Persons who are taken to heaven without dying. "During the first 2200 or so years of the earth's history . . . it was a not uncommon occurrence for faithful members of the Church to be translated and taken into the heavenly realms without tasting death. Since that time there have been occasional special instances of translation, instances in which a special work of the ministry required it" (*Mormon Doctrine*, p. 804).

TRANSLATION: Not often used as a term to describe the process of rendering something from the original language into another language. Rather used to refer to (1) the transmission of the original text over the centuries, (2) the interpretation of the text, and (3) the revision of the text. "By translation is meant a revision of the Bible by inspiration or revelation" (*D&C Student Manual*, p. 136).

TRINITY: Mormons do not believe in the Trinity. "And virtually all the millions of apostate Christendom have abased themselves before the mythical throne of a mythical Christ whom they vainly suppose to be a spirit essence who is incorporeal, uncreated, immaterial, and three-in-one with the Father and the Holy Spirit" (Mormon Doctrine, p. 269).

TRIPLE COMBINATION: One volume that contains the Book of Mormon, Doctrine and Covenants, and Pearl of Great Price.

UNIFORM SYSTEM FOR TEACHING THE GOSPEL: See missionary discussion.

UNITED ORDER: See consecration.

UNRIGHTEOUS DOMINION: A common LDS expression describing the abuse of power and authority of a priesthood holder. Often used to describe the actions of an overbearing husband or father. (See D&C 121:39).

URIM AND THUMMIM: See peep stones.

VALIANT: Common LDS Term for being faithful.

VEIL: (1) Most commonly used as a term for death. Dying is passing behind the veil. (2) Sometimes used as a term for ignorance.

VEIL WORKER: A temple worker who represents Heavenly Father in the endowment ceremony.

VICARIOUS WORK: A common Mormon expression describing temple work for the dead. It is most often used to describe being baptized for the dead.

VISITING TEACHERS: In contrast to home teachers, who are always male, these are women from the Relief Society. Like home teachers they are to visit their assigned women on a monthly basis.

WARD: The name for a local LDS congregation. Usually more than one ward meets in the same meetinghouse. (e.g., one meets from 9-12 on Sundays; the other from 1-4.) Wards vary in size from 400 to 800 members. When a ward reaches 800 members, it is divided. Wards are set up on a geographical basis, with the result that church members do not have a choice of what ward they can attend.

WELFARE PROGRAM: A highly publicized relief or assistance program of the LDS Church. In recent years it has come under intense scrutiny by non-Mormons. It appears that it is not very effective, and recently the Mormon church has downplayed it.

WORD OF WISDOM: Section 89 of the Doctrine and Covenants. It rules out the use of liquor, tobacco, and "hot drinks" (which have been officially interpreted as tea and coffee). In a survey of LDS youth the #1 sin cited was breaking the Word of Wisdom; sexual immorality came in #5 (see *Miracle of Forgiveness*, pp. 64,65). A Mormon must keep the Word of Wisdom to be temple-worthy.

WORKS: To some Mormons this is a confusing term. Some equate it almost exclusively with trying to overcome a sin.

WORSHIP: Mormons have a weak view of worship, equating it most often with service. "We worship God as did our Master, by serving our fellowmen and by growing line upon line to the point at which we are prepared and fit to dwell with the Father of lights" (*By Grace Are We Saved*, p. 41).

WORTHY: A common word in Mormonism. Whatever Mormons do or whatever responsibilities are assigned them, they need to be worthy.

ZION: A commonly used LDS term that has a variety of meanings. Zion is where God dwells. Therefore it can refer to (1) The Church of Jesus Christ of Latter-day Saints, (2) Utah, (3) Independence, Missouri (since they believe that is where Jesus will return and from where he will rule), or (4) a condition of the heart.

SELECTED

BIBLIOGRAPHY

The LDS church publishes a wealth of material. Its official material bears either the copyright of the "Corporation of the President of the Church of Jesus Christ of Latter-day Saints" or "The Church of Jesus Christ of Latter-day Saints". That material alone runs into thousands of pages. Those are the books that served as the primary sources for this book. The first three categories of sources have those official copyrights and are published by the Church of Jesus Christ of Latter-day Saints, Salt Lake City. They can be obtained through the LDS Distribution Center (1-800-537-5950).

Since there is so much material, in a few cases, I have indicated some pages that I think would be quite helpful for a Christian to read. Another reason for doing this is to help you find pertinent quotes on specific subjects. Fewer things aid us in reaching Mormons more than quoting directly from official LDS sources.

LDS Scriptures

The Book of Mormon. 1981 edition.

1 Nephi sets the stage for the rest of the book by describing Lehi's family and their supposed journey to the Americas.

Much of 2 Nephi is taken directly from Isaiah. Chapters 2-5 detail how "Adam fell that man might be"; a prophecy of Joseph Smith; and the curse of black skin on the Lamanites.

3 Nephi records events involving Christ that supposedly happened in America. Chapter 1 describes events surrounding his birth; chapter 8 events surrounding his crucifixion; and chapters 11-26 events surrounding his supposed appearance to the Nephites. Chapters 12-14 parallel his Sermon on the Mount.

Mormon gives information about the supposed origin of the Book of Mormon. Chapter 6 describes the defeat of the Nephites at Cumorah.

Moroni chapters 1-6 give regulations for baptism, ordination,

Lord's Supper, and other observances. Chapter 10 contains the often cited "promise" that the Holy Ghost will prove the Book of Mormon true.

Doctrine and Covenants/Pearl of Great Price. 1982 edition.

<u>Important verses in Doctrine and Covenants</u>
20:77ff.: Sacramental prayers
42:18,79: No forgiveness for murderers
42:70ff.: Reimbursed clergy (also 43:12; 70:12ff.)
Section 76: Three kingdoms in heaven
76:31ff.: Sons of perdition
Section 87: Civil war prophecy
Section 89: Word of Wisdom
101:80: The U.S. Constitution: divinely instituted
124:29ff.: Baptism for the dead
124:58: "in thee (Joseph Smith) and thy seed shall all the earth
 be blessed"
Section 127: Baptism for the dead
130:22: God has flesh and bones
Section 131: Celestial marriage
Section 132: Plural marriages/eternal marriages
132:19f.: Exaltation
135:3: "Joseph Smith has done more, save Jesus,
 for salvation of world"
138: Explanation of 1 Peter 3:18ff. as a basis for mission work in
 the spirit world
Official Declaration #1: Renouncing of plural marriage
Official Declaration #2: Allowing blacks into the priesthood

<u>Important verses in Pearl of Great Price</u>
Moses 4:1-4: Satan's rebellion in heaven
Moses 5:10,11: Adam and Eve praise God for their fall
Abraham 3:1-4: Mention of Kolob
Abraham 4: The account of how the gods created the world
Joseph Smith—History 1-20: Account of the first vision
Joseph Smith—History 66-75: Smith receives the Aaronic
 priesthood

The Holy Bible. 1987 LDS edition.
The Bible translation employed is the King James Version. This edition, however, contains extensive references to an appended topical

298

guide. In addition, it contains excerpts from the Joseph Smith Translation of the Bible. It also has a Bible Dictionary that, at times, gives insights into some of the unique teachings of Mormonism.

LDS Church Manuals

Achieving A Celestial Marriage. 1976.
    Pages 129-132 contain some good quotations on (1) the teaching of how the Heavenly Father was a man who became a god; (2) the concept of a glorified Mother; (3) the concept of men as gods in embryo; (4) the teaching that celestial marriage is essential to the attainment of exaltation; (5) the possibility of having spirit children.

Book of Mormon Student Manual (Religion 324 and 325). 1981.
    This contains section-by-section commentary on the Book of Mormon. It does not detail LDS doctrine as clearly as some other manuals. It does say that the LDS church is the only true church while condemning especially the doctrine of salvation by grace alone. See pages 14, 23, 36, 37, 108.
Doctrine and Covenants Student Manual (Religion 324 and 325). 1981.
    This provides section-by-section commentary on the *Doctrine and Covenants*. It is one of the best resources on LDS teaching. This is the manual I would recommend studying after *Gospel Principles*. Because of its length, I have supplied the following "index."
    <u>Helpful pages</u>
    p. 2: The importance of Doctrine and Covenants
    pp. 4, 45: Danger of questioning church leaders
    pp. 7,8,276,277,316-319: Redeeming the dead
    pp. 20,21: Burning of the bosom
    p. 41: Explanation of "one god"; explanation of sanctification
    p. 54: Description of sustaining
    p. 88: Joseph Smith received financial support
    p. 106: Marriage is a must
    p. 122: Repentance is forsaking the sin
    p. 127: The law of the fast
    pp. 138, 292-294: The importance of tithing
    p. 144: The words of the living prophet are scripture
    p. 161: Apostates become sons of perdition
    p. 164,165: No second chance for LDS to gain exaltation; hell is temporary

p. 166: The tremendous glory of the lowest kingdom,
the telestial kingdom

p. 181: "Explanation" of why the Independence,
Missouri temple was not built as Smith had prophesied

p. 198: Importance of the body

pp. 206-211: Explanation of the Word of Wisdom

p. 218: LDS definition of grace

p. 224: LDS concept of forgiveness

pp. 231,232: United States Constitution—
a divinely inspired document

p. 259: Temple endowment gives protection and knowledge
of signs to enter celestial kingdom

p. 298: Continuous revelation

p. 324: Requirements for perfection

p. 325: Exaltation consists of procreation of spirit children

pp. 327-334: Importance of temple marriage for exaltation

pp. 340,341: Christ's Second Coming

p. 349: the greatness of Joseph Smith

pp. 351,352: Brigham Young a modern Moses

pp. 355,356: Exaltation for small children

pp. 358,359: Many can become gods; many can have
spiritual children

p. 359: Missionary work in the spirit world

pp. 361-363: Discontinuation of plural marriage

pp. 375-380: Receiving personal revelation

pp. 380-385: Jesus' person and work

pp. 389-392: The importance of the living prophet

pp. 393-397: The importance of the law

pp. 406-411: The role of bishops

pp. 430-438: The priesthood

pp. 445-449: Redemption of the dead

Doctrines of the Gospel (Religion 231 and 232). 1986.
Summarizes LDS teaching. It is not as beneficial as some other manuals.

Duties and Blessings of the Priesthood (Part A). 1980.
Contains detailed information concerning the priesthood. Pages 58-62 explain the duties and powers of bishops.

Duties and Blessings of the Priesthood (Part B). 1980.
     This is a companion volume to the above. Pages 111-121 contain instructions concerning family homelife in the evening. Pages 247-252 contain instructions concerning the observance of the Sabbath.

Endowed From On High, 1995.
     This teacher's manual reveals how they prepare members for their first visit to the temple.

From You to Your Ancestors. 1980.
     This explains LDS's genealogical work. It contains samples of many of the forms used for this work.

Gospel Principles. 1995.
     This is the *basic manual* of the LDS church. It is the manual that all members are encouraged to continue to use as the following quote illustrates. "The standard works of the Church and the Gospel Principles manual should be the basic books or tapes in our library" (*Duties and Blessings of the*

Priesthood A, p. 109).
     It presents the basic teachings of Mormonism better than any other single source. I strongly encourage any person who is serious about witnessing to Mormons to become familiar with it, index it, and refer to it often as you witness to your LDS friends.

Latter-day Saint Woman, The (Basic Manual for Women, Part A). 1988.
     This and the following manual give insights into what the LDS church expects of its women.
Latter-day Saint Woman, The (Basic Manual for Women, Part B). 1979.

Life and Teachings of Jesus & His Apostles, The (Religion 211 and 212). 1979.
     This serves as their commentary on the New Testament. It illustrates the way the LDS church twists Bible passages to serve its own purposes. Throughout, it stresses the idea of perfection.

Melchizedek Priesthood Leadership Handbook. 1990.
     This brief handbook is an excellent resource on the "nuts and bolts" of the Melchizedek priesthood. It outlines the duties of the home

301

teacher, bishops, and stake presidents.
Melchizedek Priesthood Personal Study Guides

These are the manuals used in their priesthood meetings. Each manual contains a year's curriculum. They stress LDS living more than doctrine. They also lay out the procedures for many of the priesthood ordinances.

A. *Lay Hold upon the Word of God.* 1988.
B. *To Make Thee a Minister and a Witness.* 1990.
C. *Come unto the Father in the Name of Jesus.* 1990.
D. *Strengthen Your Brethem.* 1991.

Missionary Guide (Training for Missionaries). 1988.
Missionaries are to study this with their companions while they are on their mission. It instructs them in the techniques they are to use in their witnessing endeavors. It illustrates the way the LDS church emphasizes feelings over facts.

Old Testament: Genesis—2 Samuel (Religion 301). 1981.
This contains section-by-section commentary on the first half of the Old Testament. It illustrates how Mormonism glorifies the law. For example, pages 127-135 talk about the Ten Commandments, which "are an integral part of the restored gospel of the Lord Jesus Christ and are essential to our becoming perfect."

Old Testament: 1Kings-Malachi (Religion 302) 1982.
This contains section-by-section commentary on the second half of the Old Testament. It illustrates how the Mormon church refers to many Old Testament passages as "prophecies" concerning either Joseph Smith, the Book of Mormon, or the LDS church.

Relief Society Handbook.
This brief handbook gives guidelines for administering the Relief Society and outlines the various duties assigned it.
Relief Society Personal Study Guides
These study guides parallel the Melchizedek Priesthood Personal Guides and are used as the course of study for Relief Society meetings. They illustrate the great demands placed on LDS women and thus demonstrate why so many LDS women experience considerable stress.

A. *Remember Me.* 1989.
B. *Learn of Me.* 1990.

C. *Come unto Me.* 1991.
D. *Follow Me.* 1992.

Scouting Handbook. 1985.
　　This brief handbook discusses the mechanics of administering the Scout program in the LDS church. It illustrates how Mormons use the scouting program to instill the principles of Mormonism in young men.

Sharing the Gospel (Religion 130). 1976.
　　This manual encourages each member to be a missionary. It summarizes LDS teachings quite well.

Stake Mission Handbook. 1988.
　　This brief handbook describes the purpose and work of stake missionaries and their relationship to full-time missionaries.

Sunday School Handbook. 1990.
　　This brief handbook gives instructions on the mechanics of running an Sunday School. It illustrates the regimentation of the LDS church.

Teachings of the Living Prophets (Religion 333). 1982.
　　This is an excellent resource on the supremacy of the Living Prophet. Pages 10-22 especially contain numerous enlightening quotations.

Temple Preparation Seminar Discussions. 1978.
　　This manual does not focus on the temple ordinances but rather on how people become worthy to enter the temple by keeping the laws of Mormonism. It deals mainly with the basics of Mormonism.

Walk in His Ways (Part A). 1987.
　　This is a teacher's manual for primary teachers. It illustrates how keeping the laws of Mormonism as the way to exaltation is instilled in LDS children.

Walk in His Ways (Part B). 1987.
　　This is a companion volume to the above manual.

Other Official LDS Sources

Come unto Christ through Temple Ordinances and Covenants. 1987.
    This booklet contains brief descriptions of the temple ordinances. It also gives examples of some of the forms required for some of the temple work.

Discussion for New Members. 1987.
    This is a set of six brief discussions that the stake missionaries are to work through with new members. They follow the same format as the initial missionary discussions. They stress earning exaltation by fulfilling the threefold mission of the LDS church.

Ensign.
    The official magazine of the LDS church. The May and November issues always contain the general conference addresses, which are considered scripture. Most other issues contain very little LDS teaching, but they are good resources for becoming acquainted with the "flavor" of how the LDS church "encourages" its members.
Hinckley, Gordon B. *Truth Restored.* 1979.
    The official popular history of the LDS church.

Hymns of the Church of Jesus Christ of Latter-day Saints. 1985.
    By using many hymns common to Christianity, the LDS church portrays itself as Christian.

My Kingdom Shall Roll Forth. 1980.
    This book is subtitled "Readings in Church History." It contains excerpts from the writings of each church president.
Talmage, James E. *The Articles of Faith.* 1982.
    Originally written in 1899, it has been repeatedly copyrighted and reprinted by the LDS church. It gives a thorough explanation of LDS teaching and is still widely quoted in their current manuals.

Temples of the Church of Jesus Christ of Latter-day Saints. 1988.
    This is the best single *official* resource on the importance of the temple and its various ordinances. Even at that, it does not give many details.

Uniform System for Teaching the Gospel. 1986.
    These are the six initial missionary discussions. They are

essential to have for anyone wanting to give an in-depth witness to Mormon missionaries.

Nonofficial LDS Sources

Deseret News 1991-1992 Church Almanac.
> Excellent source for statistical information.

Kimball, Spencer W. *The Miracle of Forgiveness.* Salt Lake City: Bookcraft, 1969.
> Kimball, one of their church presidents, talks about sin and the difficulty of obtaining forgiveness more clearly than most LDS books. His descriptions of repentance and forgiveness illustrate the stress the LDS church places its members under. And it is recommended reading. "Encourage quorum members to read *The Miracle of Forgiveness*" (*Lay Hold upon the Word of God,* p. 108).

Maughan, Joyce Bowen. *Talk for Tots.* Salt Lake City: Deseret, 1985.
> Illustrates how Mormonism is instilled in children at a young age.

McConkie, Bruce R. *Mormon Doctrine.* Salt Lake City: Bookcraft. 1979.
> The book most quoted by Mormons and non-Mormons alike. McConkie was an LDS apostle. It is similar to a dictionary of theology in that it addresses doctrinal issues in alphabetical order. Although widely quoted, many Mormons discount it when non-Mormons refer to it because it is not an official source.

Millet, Robert L. *By Grace Are We Saved.* Salt Lake City: Bookcraft, 1989.
> Abundantly illustrates the way Mormons explain away the biblical teaching of salvation by grace alone.

Morris, Carroll Hofeling. *If the Gospel Is True, Why Do I Hurt So Much.* Salt Lake City: Deseret, 1991.
> Illustrates not only the stress many Mormons feel but also how they try to overcome that stress through faithfulness to Mormonism.

Nelson, Zane. *Sanity Strategies for Everyday Mormons.* Covenant Communications, 1991.
> Nelson is a psychologist who mixes psychological methods with Mormonism in an attempt to relieve the stress many LDS people feel.

Richards, LeGrand. *A Marvelous Work and a Wonder.* Salt Lake City: Deseret, 1976.
> Richards was an LDS apostle. This book is considered a classic by Mormons.

Scharffs, Gilbert W. *The Truth About "The Godmakers."* Salt Lake City: Publishers Press, 1986.
> A page-by-page response by an LDS professor to the popular non-Mormon book, *The Godmakers.*

Smith, Joseph Fielding. *The Way to Perfection.* Salt Lake City: Deseret, no copyright date, 19th printing—1985.
> A classic written by one of their church presidents.

Talmage, James E. *Jesus the Christ.* Salt Lake City: Deseret, 1979.
> Originally written in 1915, it is considered a classic.

Turpin, John C. *The New Stress Reduction for Mormons.* Covenant Communications Inc., 1991.
> Turpin is a popular LDS author and lecturer.

Non-Mormon Sources

Ball, John M. *Saints of Another God.* Milwaukee: Northwestern Publishing House, 1989. Ball summarizes LDS history in a readable way.

Becker, Siegbert W. *The Foolishness of God.* Milwaukee: Northwestern Publishing House, 1982.
> This book is subtitled, "The Place of Reason in the Theology of Martin Luther." Through extensive references to Luther, Becker convincingly demonstrates how God's Word and human reason are diametrically opposed.

Brodie, Fawn M. *No Man Knows My History.* New York: Alfred A. Knopf, 1971.
> This is considered the classic on the life of Joseph Smith and deservedly so. Anyone who wants to understand the origins of Mormonism needs to read this book.

Decker, Ed and Dave Hunt. *The Godmakers.* Eugene, OR: Harvest House, 1984.

Heinerman, John and Anson Shupe. *The Mormon Corporate Empire.* Boston: Beacon Press, 1985.
> A well-researched book on the business endeavors of the LDS church.

Kaiser, Edgar P. *How to Respond to . . . The Latter-day Saints.*

St. Louis: Concordia, 1977.

Shupe, Anson. *The Darker Side of Virtue.*
Buffalo: Prometheus Books, 1991.
Contains some interesting glimpses into LDS culture and business dealings.

Scott, Latayne C. *Ex-Mormons Why We Left.* Grand Rapids: Baker, 1990.
Helpful for understanding the obstacles faced by Mormons who want to leave the LDS church and the ways Christians can help them.

Smith, John L. *Witnessing Effectively to Mormons.* Marlow, OK: Utah Missions, Inc., 1975.
Details his method of using the Book of Mormon in an attempt to reach Mormons.

Spencer, James R. *Beyond Mormonism.* Grand Rapids: Chosen Books, 1984.

----------. *Have You Witnessed to a Mormon Lately.* Old Tappen, NJ: Chosen Books, 1986.
Illustrates the "nature of God" approach to witnessing to Mormons.

Tanner, Jerald, and Sandra Tanner. *Mormonism—Shadow or Reality.* Salt Lake City: Utah Lighthouse Ministry, 1982.
In this book the Tanners have done an excellent job of detailing numerous contradictions in LDS history and historical documents. This is an essential resource for any serious student of Mormonism.

Index

146, 157, 162, 170, 193, 198, 203-205, 210, 217, 224, 246, 247

Garden of Eden, 51, 65, 154
Garden of Gethsemane, 77, 78
Genealogical, 118, 154, 160
Genealogy, 55, 137, 144, 196
General Conference, 14, 89, 123, 124, 130, 148, 168
Gift of the Holy Ghost, 39, 40, 231
God, 13-19, 21-23, 25, 26, 28, 29, 30, 31, 32, 33, 34, 36, 37, 41, 47, 52, 54, 58, 61-63, 66, 68, 70, 72, 74-78, 83-86, 88-91, 93-96, 98, 100-102, 105, 108-111, 114-116, 118, 120-122, 124-127, 129-131, 134, 138, 144-147, 149, 150, 154, 157-160, 162, 164, 166, 169, 172, 176-183, 185, 186, 189, 191, 194, 198-201, 202, 203, 205-209, 211-213, 215, 216, 219, 220, 222, 223, 225, 227, 229, 231, 232, 235, 247, 248, 252-254
Goddesses, 16
Godhead, 87
Godhood, 13, 14, 16-21, 24-26, 31, 33, 34, 36, 37, 38, 44, 51, 52, 54, 60, 64, 86, 107, 159, 160
Gods: human, 13-15, 16, 18-21, 27, 31-33, 36, 77, 107, 110, 159
Gods, 177, 193, 244
Gospel, 14, 15, 17, 20, 27, 29, 32-34, 39, 41, 43, 44, 47, 51, 52, 54, 55, 56, 58, 59, 61-63, 68, 74, 75, 78-80, 83, 86, 88, 92, 93, 95-99, 107, 112, 113, 115, 120, 131, 132, 138, 139, 141, 145, 146, 148, 149, 151, 154, 161-163, 167-170, 176-184, 186, 188, 190, 191, 195, 197, 199-201, 203-205, 209, 211-213, 215, 219, 222, 224, 226, 235, 237, 238, 243-245, 248, 250, 252, 253, 255
Grace, 19, 27, 28, 41, 65, 73, 77, 78, 89-91, 96-100, 200, 224, 248

Heavenly mother, 20
Hebrews 10:10-18, 190, 201, 202, 210, 230, 247, 248, 252
Hebrews 10:14, 190, 202, 230, 248
Hell, 51, 55, 58, 62, 64, 73, 159, 178, 187, 188, 197, 219, 251
Holy Ghost, 39, 40, 73, 87, 116, 122, 127-132, 154, 226, 231
Holy Spirit, 87, 128, 131, 187, 203, 205, 222, 248, 252, 253, 255
Home Teacher, 112
Human reason, 160, 180, 182, 197

Incarnation, 87, 100
Institute, 137, 228
Investigators, 129
investigators, 244-247
Israel, 70, 105, 113, 120, 152-154, 169

James 2:10, 185, 191
James 2:14-26, 207
Jaredites, 106
Jehovah, 85
Jesus, 14, 16-19, 23, 27, 28, 29, 32, 34, 36, 38-40, 42, 43, 49, 51-53, 55-58, 60, 61, 63, 65, 69-73, 76, 77, 79, 83-88, 90, 91, 93, 95, 96, 98-100, 103-106, 113-115, 119, 120, 124, 125, 129, 130-132, 146, 148-151, 153, 154, 156-158, 161, 165, 166, 176-178, 182, 183, 190-192, 193-195, 198-203, 206-208, 213, 216, 218-223, 227, 229-231, 236-238, 243, 246, 247, 248, 252, 255
John the Baptist, 114
Joseph Smith, 15, 19, 21, 25, 38, 46, 47, 58, 83, 85, 103, 104, 107, 109, 111, 114, 121, 122, 127, 129, 131, 134, 135, 139, 149-154, 155, 157, 176, 190, 194, 201, 222-224, 225, 227, 232, 245, 246, 252
Joseph Smith Translation, 104, 134, 190, 201
JST, 104, 201